A Lake District Grand Tour

by

Mike Carden

"This is one hell of a way to see the National Park!
A great description of the grandest of Lake District tours.
Get pedalling!"
Richard Leafe
Chief Executive of the Lake District National Park

"A book to inspire both the armchair adventurer and the
hardened cyclist. Discover the Lakes through the humorous
and insightful account of Mike Carden's Grand Tour.
Whether from your armchair at home or reading it as a
companion to your own journey, you will learn all kinds of
interesting trivia as Carden's keen observations and propensity
for chatting to strangers brings many Lakeland tales to life. "
Hannah Reynolds
Fitness Editor, Cycling Weekly

"An affectionate Grand Tour of the ups and downs
of cycling the Lake District."
Lord Inglewood
President of the Friends of the Lake District

Published by
Bike Ride Books
Rannerdale, 39 Market Place, Cockermouth,
Cumbria, CA13 9NF, Great Britain

www.bikeridebooks.co.uk

ISBN: 978-0-9556602-2-1

Printed in Britain by
Martins the Printers, Berwick-upon-Tweed

For maps of the ride, links to other websites,
what to see, where to go, and photography:

www.lakedistrictgrandtour.co.uk

A
Lake District
Grand Tour

Pedalling through Lakeland:
The Challenge, The History, The Wildlife,
The Scones.

Mike Carden

*"No doubt God could have made
a lovelier country than the Lake District,
but I cannot believe he ever did."*

Woodrow Wilson
28th President of the United States of America,
on a cycle tour of the Lake District.

*"I think that sign for a hill says 30%.
Does that say 30%?
I can't believe that.
THIRTY PER CENT."*

Me.

Beginning

I had my plan.

"Richard," I said to my son, "how do you fancy cycling from Brockhole to Bowness as a sort of a Lake District tour?

Brockhole was the Lake District National Park's Visitor Centre, while Bowness-on-Windermere was probably the busiest tourist spot in Lakeland. From one to the other was about three miles.

I was going to take a detour, of course. I just hadn't mentioned that yet.

Our journey would be via every lake in the Lake District and over every mountain pass: Ullswater and the Kirkstone Pass; Derwentwater and Honister Pass; Wastwater and Hardknott Pass - and a good few more.

We would visit the towns of Lakeland - Ambleside, Windermere and Keswick, plus the 'gateways' to the Lake District - Kendal, Penrith and Cockermouth.

There would be Grasmere for poets; Beatrix Potter's Hill Top and Arthur Ransome's Wild Cat Island for the young in us; Langdale and Wasdale for climbers; Hardknott Roman Fort and Cartmel Priory for historians; pubs, tea shops and Cumberland Sausage for, well, me.

We would cycle to the farthest North, South, East and West of the National Park, well beyond the tourist trail.

We would hunt for red deer and red squirrels, golden eagles and wild ponies, ospreys and ravens, and there was an excellent chance we'd miss every single one of them. (Nature has a bit of a way of eluding me - unless you count Cumberland Sausage and Coniston

5

Bluebird Bitter as Nature. I can usually find them.)

It would be a cycling challenge, a chance to learn about Lakeland, and an excuse to visit one of the most beautiful places in the world.

"Brockhole to Bowness? Is that it? That's about quarter of an hour on a bike."

"Well, maybe a little more. I thought we'd go the long way round."

"Sounds good."

"OK. When do you have nine days free?"

My plan was to cycle very roughly anti-clockwise. With the lakes laid out on a map like the spokes of a wheel, there would be some riding out to the periphery and then in again. That was the only way we could ride past every lake, and cycle over every mountain pass that had a road on it.

I planned to break myself in relatively easily in the south. Gentler hills, I hoped. And we would go in search of the sea at Grange-over-Sands.

Then we would head east. Past Kendal and up the eastern border of the National Park via Shap to Haweswater and Penrith. Back via the Kirkstone Pass into Ambleside, and then north towards the Skiddaw fells and Caldbeck.

Next, round the north-western lakes via Cockermouth and Keswick, including Derwentwater and Buttermere, and then down the harsher western rim to Ennerdale Water and Wastwater. I had lived in Cockermouth for approaching thirty years, so this was the area I knew best. I had to admit that there were many parts of the Lake District that I knew only fleetingly, if at all.

We would complete the circuit via the sea at Ravenglass and the far south west, and then head back north for the final challenge: Hardknott Pass and Wrynose Pass, before a ferry ride carried us over Lake Windermere to Bowness.

I guessed it would be 350 to 400 miles, depending on how often I got us lost.

The ride would be quite a challenge for me.

I had done two long bike rides before. I had cycled the length of Scotland and the length of England, and those rides had included parts of the Cairngorms and the Pennines. But not one of the hills on those rides featured in a book that Richard has: '100 Greatest Cycling Climbs'.

This ride would have six of them.

The climbs might not be too much for Richard. He was twenty years old, for heaven's sake, and had spent the previous summer cycling in France, riding over the cols of the Pyrenees and the Alps used in the Tour de France.

At fifty three, I was not young in body (though I would cheerfully admit to needing some growing up in the head), and I was only moderately fit. It was going to be a major challenge to see if I could cycle up some of those passes. Richard might just have to wait at the top for me.

Kirkstone Pass would be the first climb featured in '100 Greatest Cycling Climbs'. It scored 7 out of 10 but, after a few days of rolling hills, maybe I would be ready for that. Round on the west side of the Lakes, I would have a big day: Honister Pass (9/10) and Newlands Pass (8/10) on the same day. Crikey.

Whinlatter Pass would be a mere 5/10.

But the really hard bit would be on the final day: Hardknott Pass at 10/10, and then Wrynose Pass marked as 10/10 for east to west, though, admittedly, I would be going west to east. Even so, that seemed like a challenge. By my ninth day of cycling through the Lake District, would I be able to cycle up "the king of climbs and arguably the hardest road in the land" with "brutal switchbacks" and hills that have you "straining every sinew"?

To be honest, it seemed a bit unlikely.

I had been over them with Richard the year before. He had carried weights (yes, real dumbbells) in his panniers, when he was training for his France ride, but there had been no way I could get over them on two wheels.

I had pushed.

So as well as The Journey - the Grand Tour of the Lake District, with its nature, its history and its beauty - there was The Challenge: could I, at the end of that journey, cycle over the hardest two Lake District passes in a single day?

Well, we'd find out.

See www.lakedistrictgrandtour.co.uk
for a full set of maps

9

THE PLAN

DAY ONE – YAN

WOODS AND WATER
Brockhole Visitor Centre – Wray Castle
Esthwaite Water – Hill Top, Near Sawry
Grizedale Forest – Hawkshead – Tarn Hows – Coniston

DAY TWO – TAN

CARTMEL AND KENDAL
Coniston – Brantwood – Haverthwaite – Cartmel
Grange-over-Sands – Sizergh Castle – Kendal – Staveley

DAY THREE – TETHERA

GOLDEN EAGLES AND YELLOW EARLS
Staveley – Shap – Bampton Grange – Haweswater
Bampton – Askham – Lowther Castle – Penrith
Greystoke – Motherby

DAY FOUR – METHERA

POETRY CORNER
Motherby – Dacre – Pooley Bridge – Aira Force
Glenridding – Patterdale – Kirkstone Pass
Ambleside – Chapel Stile – Great Langdale
Grasmere – Rydal – Grasmere

DAY FIVE – PIMP

AROUND SKIDDAW
Grasmere – Thirlmere – Castlerigg – Mungrisdale
Hesket Newmarket – Caldbeck – Bassenthwaite
Braithwaite – Whinlatter Pass – Cockermouth

DAY SIX – SETHERA

BUTTERMERE AND BORROWDALE
Cockermouth – Buttermere – Honister Pass – Seatoller
Rosthwaite – Grange – Ashness Bridge – Keswick
Newlands Pass – Buttermere – Cockermouth

DAY SEVEN – LETHERA

THE RUGGED WEST
Cockermouth – Lorton – Loweswater – Fangs Brow
Ennerdale Water – Ennerdale Bridge – Gosforth
Wastwater – Wasdale Head – Wasdale YHA

DAY EIGHT – HOVERA

SEA AND SAUSAGES
Wasdale YHA – Ravenglass – Waberthwaite
Silecroft – Millom – Broughton-in-Furness
Ulpha – Eskdale Green – Boot – Eskdale YHA

DAY NINE – DOVERA

THE HARD BIT IN THE MIDDLE
Eskdale YHA – Hardknott Pass – Wrynose Pass
Hawkshead – Near Sawry – Far Sawry
Windermere – Bowness-on-Windermere

DAY ONE – YAN

WOODS AND WATER

Brockhole Visitor Centre – Wray Castle
Esthwaite Water – Hill Top, Near Sawry
Grizedale Forest – Hawkshead
Tarn Hows – Coniston

30 miles

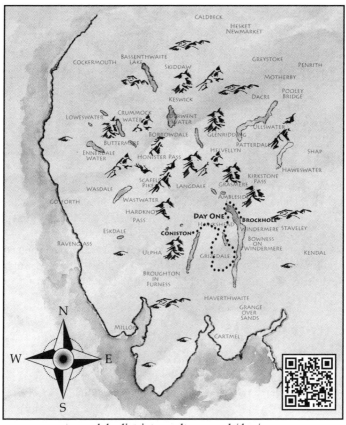

www.lakedistrictgrandtour.co.uk/day/one

The Lake District National Park Visitor Centre, Brockhole.

"I think we should start as we mean to go on," I said. "I'll have a scone and a cappuccino."

We had arrived late morning by car in heavy rain, and I knew that up the steps through the trees was the visitor centre café, where it would be dry.

"Think of it as carbohydrate-loading. Scones will fortify us for the day."

Half day, anyway. We were cycling to Coniston but, in the spirit of a Grand Tour around the Lake District, we were going the long way round.

From the back seat of the car, Richard was looking out at the rain. Probably thinking that carbohydrate-loading sounded like a good idea.

We found seats in the café with a view down through the woods to Windermere's lakeshore.

Half an hour later, fortified, we returned to the car under drying skies to find our bikes dripping with water, while around the car park, tall trees were continuing with the downpour.

We lifted panniers on to bike racks and mounted up. The panniers were pretty well loaded - enough for a few days' ride. We would feel the weight in them going over the hills. I would, anyway.

"Ready?"

"Ready."

Feet into toe clips.

And pushed off.

Bowness-on-Windermere was about three miles south. We turned north.

It was nearly twelve o'clock now, but today had always been intended to be a half day's cycling, and a relatively easy half day in the soft centre of the Lake District. There would be no major passes. In fact, no major hills at all – so long as we didn't get lost. This afternoon would ease us into our tour. Even so, it was still thirty miles for the afternoon, which was five miles more than the longest of my training rides so far. And there was always the issue of 'not getting lost'.

There was also the issue that my cycle tours don't just involve cycling. I like to stop off and see things along the way. So today I had three planned stop-offs: Wray Castle, Hill Top and Grizedale Visitor Centre, before finishing in Coniston, where there was a possibility of a pint of ale in the pub where it was brewed. There was a lot to fit in.

Pedalling up the hill out of the car park, we came out on to the main road. Fortunately there was a combined footpath and cycleway, because the traffic was busy.

The cycle lane took us at easy gradients up and down through woods. Tall trees overhung the road, a small reminder that at one time, the whole of the Lake District would have been carpeted in trees up to around 2,000 feet. After the retreat of the Ice Age, the valleys of Lakeland would have been filled with pine and birch. As the climate warmed, these worked their way up the sides of the fells, while oak and ash and elm took over the valley floors. Above 2,000 feet, the summits would have stood proud as stony islands in a sea of dark green during the summer. In autumn, the deciduous woodland would have turned golden brown and russet red, like the pictures we see of New England in the Fall. Winter would have brought a bare landscape of grey branches encompassing frozen lakes below the misty heights, before green shoots brought life back to the valleys in springtime.

The woodland around Richard and me was not as untamed as that. Large Victorian houses - like Brockhole – stood back from the road, many now hotels.

It was noisy on the cycleway with all the cars and coaches rushing past on their way north towards Ambleside, and a bit unpleasant. Then the cycleway ran out and we were on the road itself, and that was definitely unpleasant. Fortunately, it wasn't for long.

We came out of the woodland and pulled over in a gateway to look down to the lake. At the bottom of a grassy field, a smattering of wind-blown trees lined the water's edge. The sun was prickling through the clouds and sparkling off wavelets dancing on to the grassy shore. A handful of boats plied across the lake, their small white sails held taut in the wind. The lake, stretching away into the distance, was framed on either side by woods, with white houses

15

and hotels punctuating the greenery. Fabulous.

We cycled on to Waterhead, the terminus for the launches linking Ambleside with Bowness. Boats were pulled up on the beach, and there were families eating ice creams by the water, kiosks for tickets, and ducks.

Smart hotels sat back from the lakeshore, wide windows giving them glorious views down the lake. We wouldn't be having quite that standard of accommodation on this ride.

"Rich, let's pull over. I'm overheating."

We took our jackets off, our second stop in just a few miles.

"This is probably not going to be the fastest ever ride," I said.

"It's not far to Coniston."

"We're going the long way round though."

Richard had really only glanced at the route I had planned for us. He was getting ready for a harder ride later in the summer through Europe, and to him this was 'good training'.

"Rich, when we get to Coniston, we need to watch out for ring ouzels."

"Ring ouzels? What's a ring ouzel?"

"It's a bird."

"You've made that up."

"I haven't."

"Well, I've never heard of an ouzel. It sounds like something from Winnie the Pooh."

"It's ring ouzel. And if you haven't heard of it, then clearly I didn't give you a sound-enough education."

"How do you know about ring ouzels?"

"I looked up 'birds of the Lake District' on the internet."

"Go on then. What's a ring ouzel?"

"Bit like a blackbird, but with a white flash on its chest. Spends the winter in the Mediterranean and the summer in the mountains in this country."

"I reckon I could do that."

"Anyway, I found the website for the Ring Ouzel Study Group. Apparently they are - and I think I quote here - 'a group of enthusiastic ornithologists with a particular interest in ring ouzels'."

"I'm sure you're making this up."

"No, really. Anyway, a couple of people had reported on the

website that they had seen ring ouzels near Coniston. And they're getting rarer. Endangered even."

"And your chance of spotting one?"

"Huh."

On balance, it's probably good that Richard and I share a sense of humour. Well, I think we do. On the other hand, maybe he just has high tolerance levels.

We were stopped just by Ambleside's Roman fort, over in the field towards the lakeshore.

When the Romans invaded Britain, they moved north and found here a still untamed area of mountains and forest.

Early incomers would have made little mark on the forest. Neolithic man quarried for flint on the fell tops, including the slopes of Scafell Pike. They and their bronze-using successors cleared enough ground to build cairns and stone circles, like Castlerigg Stone Circle near Keswick. But there was no overall clearing of the forest, not even with the arrival of the Celts in Lakeland with their iron tools and weapons in the second and third centuries BC. They built hill forts on fell tops, as at Carrock Fell, and would have lived in the valleys, but a squirrel would have been able to climb from tree to tree across most of the Lake District.

So when the Romans came, Lakeland was not a welcome farming country like much of the south. Theirs was a military occupation, with roads crossing north-south and east-west guarded by forts, as here at Ambleside, where there are low walls and raised ridges in the ground, showing where five hundred troops were stationed.

The forts in and around Lakeland were probably not a favoured posting. After all, a stone has been found at Ambleside's fort inscribed, 'To the good gods of the underworld, Flavius Romanus, Record Clerk, lived for 35 years, killed in the fort by the enemy.'

The Celts, it seems, were still living in the fells and valleys, and when Rome withdrew from their province of Britannia, there was precious little lasting effect from their occupation of Lakeland, the fort at Ambleside abandoned, their language forgotten. Lakeland became once again a land of the Celts.

We pedalled on, the lake on our left, then turning off in the

17

direction of Coniston. Another turn took us off into little Clappersgate on the Hawkshead road, crossing the River Brathay, gushing and gurgling underneath. It was very, very pretty.

We turned left and were on to the quietest of country lanes, hedges alternating with dry-stone walls along either side, each with wild flowers at their bases. We pedalled up and down mostly gentle hills in sunshine. At the top of each small hill we could look across green fields speckled with lone trees and small copses to the fells beyond, rounded and green, with shadows of clouds chasing across their faces. It was all so different to just a few miles back. This was why we were cycling around the Lake District.

"This is wonderful riding," I said.

"Fantastic."

A hill, and Richard rode on ahead of me. Change gear, down, down again, feet rhythmically pressing the pedals, and pull to the top, where Richard is waiting. This might become a common pattern.

A sign pointed to Wray Castle. I'd heard of it as the holiday destination for the family of a young Beatrix Potter, and I knew the National Trust were opening it up. I'd also seen a photo of an imposing castle-like building. It seemed well worth a short stop, even though we really hadn't been very far.

Down a short lane through trees, and we were in front of a castle. There were stone turrets and arrow slits for windows. There were battlements and a wide entrance.

"Just what the average Victorian tycoon would want from a home."

"It's not a real castle then?"

"No, it was a way for a rich industrialist from Lancashire to spend his money."

We took a moment to take in the view down to Windermere and across to the east side, with Brockhole almost opposite. It was quite a view from a front door.

We went inside. The grand hall rose past balconies on the first floor level to a high vaulted oak ceiling. Arched doorways led through to high rooms with arched windows.

"I can think of worse ways of spending your money," Richard

said. "I could build myself a castle."

We poked our heads into different rooms. There was virtually no furniture, and the rooms were mostly in need of a lick of paint. Restoration had begun – one room had a beautifully painted ceiling of blue, red and cream – but there was a great deal still to do. It was as if it had been a guest house, and suddenly the owners had moved out and all they had left was the children's games. A giant Connect 4. A giant chess set. Colouring books and crayons.

A couple were clearly as bemused as we were.

"Do you understand what's going on here?" I asked.

"The National Trust had rented it out to a company," the lady said. "But the company have moved out, and they're opening it up to the public."

Maybe they had opened it to the public before it was really ready and, by the time you read this, restoration will be complete. Still, Wray Castle and its surroundings had been one of the places that had influenced the young Beatrix Potter in her love of nature and of the Lake District in particular.

Beatrix used memories and sketches from family holidays in Lakeland and Scotland to create her early books from her bedroom in London: The Tale of Peter Rabbit, The Tale of Squirrel Nutkin, The Tailor of Gloucester, and so on.

At Wray Castle she also first met the local vicar, Hardwicke Rawnsley. He was later to become the driving force in the creation of the National Trust, and Beatrix herself was heavily involved. From here, though, the story goes on to Hill Top.

Back outside we walked around the side of the building, past the conservatory (also with its own turret) and a little way down the path that leads around the quiet western lakeshore – far enough to see exquisite views out over the lake. Between the trees, a yacht turned into the wind, its white sail leaning towards the water before the boat righted itself.

Behind us, Wray Castle dominated the hill, and even its turrets had their own turrets.

The road climbed beyond Wray Castle, and we pedalled up through the little village of High Wray, with its neat cottages and bungalows. Above us was the viewpoint of Latterbarrow, National

Trust-owned like much of the land around here, fulfilling the National Trust's original principle of preserving the best of Britain's countryside from development. 'For ever, for everyone,' is their motto, and long may that be their aim.

We dropped down through woods on a single-track lane.

"Lovely, quiet road," I said, just as a car coming round a corner saw us and braked to a sudden halt. At the same time, there was a squealing of brakes behind us, and a white van going far too fast for this road almost skidded into us. There was a drive-way on our left, so we pulled over to allow both to manoeuvre around each other. The white van roared forward, only to have to come to a breathless stop as another car came the other way. He reversed fast towards us, and we got hastily out of the way as he swung into the drive to make space for the car, then again put his foot down to get away.

"Lovely," Richard said.

At the bottom of the hill we found our second lake of the day, Esthwaite Water. We were on the eastern shore, just a fence and short, sloping field away from the water, now grey and dark as black clouds rolled in.

Esthwaite Water is renowned amongst fisherman. Rainbow trout, brown trout, pike, roach, rudd, tench, gudgeon. You name it, they're here. Or so I am led to believe. The lake has a range of deep basins and shallows, plus a rich mix of nutrients and minerals, that make the water particularly enamoured by fish. And therefore by anglers.

Today, there was just the one small boat braving the threatening clouds above, rods poking over the water.

The road gripped the lakeshore for about a mile, and at the far end, there was a climb, and then a sign for Hill Top. We pulled into a full car park.

A lady in a fluorescent waistcoat approached and directed us, smiling, to a bike park.

In the shop to buy our tickets we were behind a young Japanese couple, and in front of another young Japanese couple.

"The tickets are timed," the lady behind the counter told us, "but we're not busy. By the time you are at the entrance, you'll be able to go in."

We walked around by the road towards Hill Top itself, past a whitewashed cottage with a cottage-garden of lupins, geraniums and pansies. Peter Rabbit was poking out of a watering can, and on a bench sat a papier-mâché Mr McGregor with a waistcoat and a tweed hat. There was a sign inviting you to take a photo of your-self on the bench and to make a contribution to charity.

"You've got to, Rich," I said.

"Do I?"

"Oh, yes."

So he did.

From the road, a path led us up through what looked like Mr McGregor's garden from The Tale of Peter Rabbit (even though the book's main inspiration was probably from Beatrix's Scottish holidays rather than just here: the clue is the gardener's name).

We arrived at the front of Hill Top, not a pretty-pretty house at all, but grey-clad, with climbing plants growing up the walls. It would not stand out in most Lake District villages but that was not why the National Trust owned it.

The 'Miss Potter' film with Renée Zellweger showed the romantic side to her life. How she was brought up in a strict, wealthy family, coming on holiday each summer to either the Lake District or Scotland. How she poured out her creative talents in her art, both scientific drawings and sketches of her pets, such as her rabbit, Peter. How, against her family's wishes, she published her first story, The Tale of Peter Rabbit, and went on to huge success with a succession of children's stories, allowing her to buy Hill Top farm. How her first love died before they could be married, and she eventually moved to Near Sawry, marrying a local solicitor and becoming Mrs Heelis. Good film, of course.

The less Hollywood side was that Beatrix, after becoming Mrs Heelis, threw herself into Lake District life.

The taming of this corner of the Lake District had started in earnest with the arrival of the railways, allowing the factory owners of Lancashire to build their mock-castles and mansions away from the smoke and noise of the industrial revolution.

Mrs Heelis used her wealth to buy land locally which would

otherwise have been developed by incoming money, driving out and changing forever the farming community

Alongside the Reverend Rawnsley, she was also one of the founders of the National Trust, whose original intention was the prevention of more development in Lakeland and around the country, rather than the ownership of mansions and stately homes. With Mrs Heelis's bequests in her will and subsequent purchases and gifts, the National Trust today owns about a quarter of the land in the Lake District.

Inside the front door, a girl was checking the tickets. Another smiley face.

"Can you tell me," I asked quietly, "why there are so many Japanese here?"

"They use Beatrix Potter books to learn English at school. The sentence structure is really accurate, and of course the furry animals fit with Japanese culture. Mind you, they never spend very long in the house. I think they don't really know what they are looking at."

We didn't spend too long looking round either. It was a dark, oak-lined farmhouse, with paintings by members of the Potter family, and occasional books and pictures showing where Beatrix's stories were set within the house. I felt sorry for a mum doing the treasure hunt leaflet to try to entertain a five-year-old. I guess it was a bit, well, worthy. From the Mrs Heelis side of Beatrix's life, rather than the Miss Potter side.

Back by the front door, the girl said, "That was quick."

"Well, we're on a bike ride really. Otherwise we'd have stayed longer."

We had taken our children to the World of Beatrix Potter Attraction in Bowness when they were little. I remembered a life-size Peter Rabbit model and a Mrs Tiggy-winkle. I'm sure that would be too much for a historic house, but, well, how about a life-size Renée Zellweger? Is that too much to ask?

We turned right out of Hill Top. Which was wrong. We were too busy chatting.

"Do you remember us reading Beatrix Potter books to you?" I asked Richard.

"Not much. I recognise the pictures, but couldn't tell you what the stories were about. I don't think many of my generation would know them, to be honest."

"Different in Japan, apparently," I said. "Now, there should be a right turn just ahead,"

There wasn't a right turn.

We pedalled on, and there still wasn't.

I pulled in to a gateway and looked at the map.

"Ah," I said. "This may not be the right way."

The right turn had been before Hill Top, not after.

A man and his dog, elderly and fairly slow (and here I mean walker and dog), were pottering towards us.

"Excuse me," I said, "I was looking for the road that would lead us round the bottom of Esthwaite Water and then south."

I showed him on the map.

He peered. "There's another road. Up there." He pointed up the hill facing us.

I looked at the map, and there was a lane that dropped to the shore of Windermere, meandered near it for a couple of miles, and then joined the original route.

I wasn't sure why I hadn't seen that on the map before. It looked a much better route, right by the lake. "How about it, Rich?"

"Go for it."

"Thank you," I said to the dog walker, but he had lost interest by this time, and was scanning the sky. I thought of all the Japanese tourists at Hill Top. Maybe, just maybe, he sees quite a few lost visitors.

After a stiff little hill, the road curved and dropped, with Lake Windermere appearing through trees. A sharp twisty downhill, brakes on, and there was the right turn, a tiny lane that headed lake-wards. Once at shore level, it was a fantastic road, looping and twisting down and up for a mile or so. Under trees and out, the water at times close, with the sight of a green opposite bank across a wide stretch of rippling water. And not a car in sight.

Richard and I rode alongside each other, marvelling.

"Just brilliant, Rich," I said.

We reached the quiet High Cunsey, not really very high, and then Low Cunsey, presumably lower. Both were a scattering of houses along the road with views down to the lakeshore and woodland behind. A perfect place for a bit of peace, though just a short hop from the honeypot of Bowness. The map showed a footpath right alongside the lake. I would have to come back and investigate that.

And then suddenly we were climbing, and this was a real hill. The sign at the bottom said 16%.

"Wasn't this meant to be a flat day?" Richard said, already pulling away from me as I slowed and changed gear.

"Yes, well, that was ... the ... plan." He was very quickly getting further ahead. "I'll ... see ... you ... at ... the ... top."

He was gone, and I settled down to pedal myself and those panniers of clothes, food, wash-stuff, tools and maps slowly up.

We have different hill-climbing techniques, Richard and I. His is the more usual, standing up on his pedals to put his full body weight into climbing, the bike leaning left and right. It is effective, and quick. My technique is different. I stay sitting down, the strength to turn the pedals coming from my upper legs. It's possibly a balance thing: a distinct tendency to fall off the bike if I stand up to pedal. And maybe because of that, the muscles that I'd be using to pedal standing up just aren't there.

Anyway, I stayed sitting down to pedal slowly through woodland to the top, my lungs sucking in as much as they could, my heart beating hard, my thighs tightening and filling with lactic acid, but I made it, and Richard was there waiting.

We had cycled the C2C together when he was 15, and when I cycled the length of England a year later, he joined me for the last couple of days. Two years later he joined me for the final two days of my ride the length of Scotland. When he announced that he was taking a gap year before university, and that he planned a long cycle ride, I helped plan a route around France, including the Pyrenees and the Alps. But really, it was his route.

We had waved him off on to the ferry at Poole, and he looked much younger than his 18 years and, well, a bit scared. When he came back five weeks later, having survived endless torrential rain in the Pyrenees and snow and ice in the Alps, navigating nearly 1,000 miles through a foreign country with no great knowledge of the language, having his bike stolen, camping by himself or negotiating a cheap hotel room, making every decision for himself, he looked a different young man.

The 20-year-old Richard was certainly quicker and stronger than me on a bike.

"You OK?" he asked.

Was I OK? I should probably have done some more training. In fact, I should also probably have been younger.

"Will be," I said, pedalling past him, body slowly starting to recover.

We turned south, and just before a right turn there were wide wrought iron gates, with twirly scrolls and two shields showing a coat of arms. I looked it up later. This was the Graythwaite estate, home to the Sandys family for generations. Today, the gardens are open to the public, there are holiday cottages and a wedding venue, there's fishing and a sawmill, and there's even a Segway route.

We pedalled over to look at the coat of arms. It had a couple of white towers and some white deer, harts I guessed, on a red, blue and gold background.

"It would be cool to have a coat of arms," Richard said.

"We do. Well, not us personally, but there is a coat of arms for our name. There's even a motto in Latin. 'Fide et Amore'."

"What does that mean?"

"Fidelity and Love. Gives you something to live up to, doesn't it?"

"What's the shield?"

"Arrowheads."

He nodded. "That's good."

The road fell and climbed, fell and climbed. We were crossing the grain of the land, which I supposed was the penalty for missing the original right turn by Hill Top, and for having such a lovely ride by the lake. Here we were cycling mostly through old-looking woodland, no doubt used for the Graythwaite sawmill.

This was probably home to the deer shown on the coat of arms. We didn't see any. They were probably peering at us riding past.

I wasn't entirely sure where we were when we came to a cross-roads, but guessed at right. "That should mean a left then another right," I said.

25

To my surprise, there was.

At Force Mills, we turned up the wide Grizedale valley, with pasture on either side of the lane, and woodland on the hills beyond the fields.

"Watch out for red kites," I said. "They've been releasing them into the wild here."

We didn't see any.

The little village of Satterthwaite was peace and quiet itself. The name is Norse, so this was a Viking village.

With the end of Roman control of Britannia, Lakeland had reverted to its Celtic roots, with links northwards and to Wales. The Celtic Kingdom of Rheged then came under pressure from the Anglians arriving from the North East, for whom Westmorland was their western border. Much of the evidence is in place names. The Celts gave us Derwent, Esk and Blencathra. The Anglians gave us Askham and Westmorland.

Then, via the Isle of Man and Ireland came the Norse, not raiding Vikings, but probably second and third generation settlers fleeing a new invasion from Norway, and coming to the nearest coast to escape. Moving inland, they must have become the dominant people of the hills and valleys, because most of the place names in Lakeland are Norse. 'Fell' means mountain; 'beck' is a stream; 'thwaite' means clearing in a forest; 'dale' is valley; 'sty' a steep pass; 'lath' or 'laithe' a barn; 'rake' and 'gate' mean a path, and so on and on amongst Lakeland's valleys and mountains: Scafell, Seatoller, Ambleside are all Norse, and here, Satterthwaite - 'summer huts in a clearing' according to 'Place Names in Cumbria'.

Much of the spoken Cumbrian dialect is also very Norse. Yet in spite of that, the Celtic sheep-counting system survived. Yan (one), tan (two), tethera (three), methera (four), pimp (five), sethera (six), lethera (seven), hovera (eight), dovera (nine) and dick (ten) are Celtic. Did that suggest that the Norse incomers in Satterthwaite and the other valleys kept on the Celts as their shepherds up on the high fells? It was a theory anyway.

Our road climbed gently and, with the sun shining down, it was idyllic cycling, with fields of cows and sheep on our left, woodland on our right. Forestry Commission signs showed us that we were pedalling along next to the large Grizedale Forest, the name another hint of the Vikings - valley of the wild boars. Today the forest is largely known for its mountain-biking routes, walks, sculptures, high-ropes trail through the forest and visitor centre.

Lunch, I thought.

We arrived amongst a range of buildings that I recognised.

"I think this is where we came when you kids were little, and we walked around the sculpture park. There were wooden sculptures spread along a trail. It was good."

There was, though, no sign of a café.

A man came around the corner holding the arm of, presumably, his mother. They were strolling slowly and looked to me as though they might know where to find the café.

They did.

A courtyard of older buildings had been converted into an exhibition area, shop and café. The café had glass walls looking out over a central area busy with couples and young children, and with muddy mountain bikers. The muddy-ness was quite impressive: dirt streaked up bums and backs, while fronts and faces were liberally spattered with mud. And that was just the children. Actually, not really. With the kids, it was ice cream.

The café had really quite large slices of pie available.

"Rich," I said, "man-size pies."

There was no choice really, and we joined the queue.

Feeling full a short time later, I pulled out our map.

"Looks downhill into Hawkshead from here," Richard said.

The map we were using was a little light on contours, but I was happy to believe him.

We wandered into the Visitor Centre, where a thought occurred to me. "How long," I asked the lady behind the counter, "would it take us to walk around the sculpture park?"

"About two days," she said.

"Two days!"

"Well, the sculptures are spread around the footpaths, but the latest thing is to put new ones along the mountain bike trails, so some of those are quite a long way from here."

I picked up a leaflet, particularly liking the 'clockwork forest'

- a large clock key embedded in a tree trunk.

"We might need to come back another time," I said to Richard.

It was deliciously warm in the courtyard, and we pedalled out on to the road confidently. The road, though, was now enclosed by forest, with tall larches cutting out the light, and it was cool by comparison.

"What do you think about jackets?" I asked.

"Good idea," Richard said. "We're going downhill in a minute, so it will be cold."

We stopped by the high-ropes trail, and pulled jackets on. Above us, children were shrieking at the height above the ground as they swung or crept from tree to tree.

The road climbed.

"I thought you said it was downhill," I said.

Then the road climbed some more. And some more.

It wasn't steep, not after the lane up from Cunsey, but, well, "I can't half feel that slice of pie in my stomach," I said.

Two cyclists flew past us, heads down low over their drop-handlebars, legs pumping.

"Do I look like that?" I asked.

"Only if I squint."

Cyclists are more and more common in Lakeland. There's a tendency to think of mountain bikers in the Lake District, and it's true that as well as the man-made trails like those in Grizedale Forest, there are a lot of bridleways open to mountain bikers throughout the Lake District. Even the route up Skiddaw is a bridleway, and I have known someone who cycled that, though to be honest, I'm not sure it's a good idea.

But road cyclists are a regular sight on Lakeland's roads now, far more often than in recent years. There are some great challenges for the fit club rider, the most famous being the Fred Whitton Challenge, 112 miles including all the big passes. I had once had a whole raft of cyclists overtake me as I struggled up Whinlatter Pass, a good few wearing Fred Whitton Challenge bike shirts. One pedalled with me for a few minutes chatting, but I think he was struggling to go slowly enough. This ride was, clearly, a personal challenge, but not one that a really fit cyclist would consider a challenge. Well, not unless he or she was doing it over three days rather than nine, with compulsory scone-and-cappuccino stops. Now that might challenge a Fred Whitton rider.

We came out on to a ridge, suddenly leaving forest behind us. A sign said, 'Try Your Brakes', and we dropped down a steep twisty descent, brakes definitely on, the bikes swinging left and right around sharp corners.

One bend was very sharp, and I nearly didn't make it.

"Ooooh," I said.

I think the view ahead of us was fantastic, but, to be honest, I was much too busy looking at where my front wheel was going to see anything else.

We dropped right into Hawkshead, passing Hawkshead Grammar School, where a young William Wordsworth was educated and where he scratched his name, alongside many other pupils', into his desk. The desk is still there, in the Grammar School founded by the Sandys family from down the road at Graythwaite.

Wordsworth, the future Poet Laureate, learned his Greek and Latin here, as well as the sciences and arithmetic. He was to go away from Lakeland for some years, but his return to Grasmere, where he lived during his most prolific period, was in itself a draw for tourists in the early 1800s. Some came to stare at the famous poet, others drawn to visit the area by his 'Guide to The Lakes' with 'directions and information for the tourist'.

More poets followed him to Lakeland, including Samuel Taylor Coleridge and Thomas De Quincey, and Wordsworth came to be regarded as the leading light of the 'Romantic Poets'.

Painters came too at just this same time, such as J.M.W. Turner, who painted Lakeland with his usual moody and dramatic style: great heads of cloud and shafts of rainbow above dark fells and even darker lakes. Alongside the poets, Turner's work also encouraged tourism into Lakeland, even if some of his work here had, well, a touch of artistic licence.

Hawkshead, a tourist hot-spot of course, looked gorgeous as we pedalled in, a picture-book Lakeland village of whitewashed stone cottages and pubs, with slate roofs, mullioned windows and hanging baskets. The square was traffic-free, and the tourists - there were plenty of them - were mooching and wandering into gifts shops and cafés.

A Japanese couple emerged from the Beatrix Potter Gallery. We weren't too surprised.

We were looking for Hawkshead Hill, leading us up to Tarn Hows. There were several exits from the town square, but no signs that helped.

"Tell you what," I said. "If we go around the ring road, there must be signs."

We retraced our route, turned down past the car park, and on to a wide and very un-Lakeland-like ring road. Around the bend was a signpost for Coniston.

"That must be it," I said. "I think this must be Hawkshead Hill."

I was straight into my lowest gear, as the hill was instantly steep and looked as though it went on quite a long way.

"See you at the top, Rich," I said, but he was gone.

Half way up was a house: another Hill Top. Hill 'Top'! Half way up the hill!

I struggled past it, the second part of the hill not feeling any the less steep for my having been misled.

Hawkshead Hill was actually the name of the village at the top of the hill. Descriptive, really.

Richard was waiting for me. "OK?"

"Will... be."

We turned right, and climbed and climbed again, the road through woods topping out in the open. We stopped to look. You couldn't do anything else with that view.

Dropping away from us was a wide expanse of ferns, the pale green broken by the pink flowers of foxgloves on their tall stems. Beyond the ferns was the lake of Tarn Hows nestling into the dark green forest behind. Beyond that, darker again, were mountains - the distinctive coned tops of the Langdale Pikes. To their right, further off, was a darker ridge of fells, maybe the heights of the Helvellyn range. To their left, the Old Man of Coniston.

Tarn Hows isn't quite a natural lake. There were three small tarns here until the 19th century, when the owner dammed the out-flow to make one larger tarn that would supply his sawmill. Rather than destroy the loveliness of this hollow in the fells, the result is one of the most beautiful of the Lake District tarns.

The road twisted and turned downhill through the ferns, and we pulled in again just above the water, where footpaths led down to the shoreline. There were couples and families milling around, taking in the views, but not so many as there might have been earlier in the day; time was getting on in the afternoon, and visitors would be heading back to hotels, guest houses and caravans to eat. It was probably time for us to get to Coniston and our hostel.

Our map showed a road continuing on down past the car park towards Coniston, but the only signpost at the car park exit was back the way we had come.

"We don't want to go right down there," I said, "if we can't get out at the end. What do you think?"

Richard looked at the map.

"I think we should go for it."

"Fine."

The road was fantastic - for bikes; I wouldn't recommend it for cars. It was steep and narrow with hardly a passing place. And it just dropped and dropped. We went reasonably fast, though watching out for potholes and for fallen branches from the old woodland around us. The road was wet under the trees as well. It was a touch tricky if you went too fast. We hit a patch of gravel. Then there was a sudden sharp twist in the road.

"Maybe we'd better slow down," I shouted.

Richard carried on ahead, a bit braver than me.

We came out on to the Hawkshead-Coniston road.

"That," Richard said, "was brilliant."

So much, I thought, for a flat first day in the soft centre of the Lake District.

A short way down the road, and we were looking along Coniston Water. The lake was quiet, with no sign of tourist launches and no sailing boats or kayaks. Waves rippled towards us in the breeze.

The lake was long - long enough for water speed record attempts, and the awful tragedy when Donald Campbell's attempt to better his own world record in 'Bluebird' ended in his death. The images on television still seem fresh: the craft powering across the water, the front lifting - almost in slow motion, and then the horrific devastation of the boat and its occupant. That was 1967. 'Bluebird' was finally lifted from the lake bed in the year 2000, and Donald Campbell's remains the following year. A sad end.

We pedalled towards town with the lake on our left to begin with, and then cycled into the centre. The town was busy, and a thought occurred to me.

"I think it's the Coniston Marathon tomorrow," I said.

In fact, the town seemed busy with fit young people.

"The hostel will be full," Richard said.

We cruised slowly past gardens, pubs, shops and church, a mix of whitewashed and grey slate buildings, with the Black Bull Inn standing proud with its back to a river. Immediately behind, so close you felt you could touch them, were buttresses of rock looming over the village - dark hummocks of stone above green grass and ferns. This was real mountain country, and tomorrow's marathon runners would be right up in those fells.

We cycled along to Lake Road and down past houses towards the shore. Beyond parked cars was a shale beach and the ferry terminal. It was grander than I had expected. I had thought there would just be a pier, but there were slate-roofed buildings housing ticket office, waiting area and a café. A wooden jetty projected into the lake, and a launch was pulling away. It was not the National Trust's restored Victorian gondola, but one of the regular little launches, with a smart cabin to keep spray from the unwary visitor. It was empty, going home for the night.

Sailing boats were moored around the lake on our right, and a couple were rowing back from one of them to the shore.

This must be a busy place on a warm summer afternoon, but just now there were more ducks than people. At least I think they were ducks. I don't think they were ring ouzels.

We cycled back up Lake Road, through town and out the far side. We passed the Ruskin Museum, where on another day we might have stopped to see the Bluebird exhibition.

"I don't think it's far to the hostel," I said, and I was glad of that. I was tired.

A large-ish building appeared off to the left, and a lane led us up to the Youth Hostel Association's Coniston Holly How hostel.

I like staying in youth hostels. If you are on a budget, they are great, and the chat is always good. There is a downside, in that generally you are in a dormitory, though at many hostels there are also private rooms if you are flush for cash.

Sometimes you can turn up at a hostel to find there is virtually nobody there, and you find yourself alone in a dormitory for twelve. Tonight, with the Coniston Marathon on the following day, that was a little unlikely.

A narrow corridor led us to a reception hatch, where a couple were checking in with their small dog. As we waited, the little terrier licked at my fingers and rolled on to his back. A chef walked past and stopped. "Aaahhh," she said, and tickled the dog behind his ears. "Don't worry," she said with a smile. "I'll wash my hands."

There was a cheery lady at the desk, who wrote us in her book, checked my YHA card, and gave us a key to our dormitory and another to the bike shed.

We were in an eight-bed dormitory, already filling with fit young marathon runners.

"What sort of a route is the marathon?" I asked one young guy.

"More or less straight up into the fells, and then circle round Coniston Water in the hills."

"Wow. And is it a full marathon?"

"Yes. That's what I'm doing. The marathon race. There's also a marathon challenge and a half-marathon."

"How long will it take you?"

"About three and a half hours."

That seemed very impressive. I wondered if I was talking to a potential winner.

We made up our beds, me choosing the bottom bunk on the basis that Richard's young legs could climb down easier in the night, and set off back downstairs. We needed food, and while we could have eaten at the hostel, the Black Bull had looked inviting.

I picked up my bike's front light to take with us, tossed it up and caught it.

"Have I told you about the time with my mate Nigel and the torch?"

"Um, no."

"Well, we were staying in a bed and breakfast in Little Langdale to do some walking. We were both - I suppose we would now admit - fairly wet-behind-the-ears townies. Anyway, we'd had a day's walking and decided to walk down to the Old Dungeon Ghyll in Great Langdale for a pint or three. It's down a long, twisty road. As we were leaving - early evening and broad daylight this was - I said, 'Shall we take a torch?'. Nige said, 'no need,' so we didn't."

"Ah."

"Anyway, by the time we came out of the pub at closing time, it was pitch black and we couldn't see a hand in front of our faces. We were also probably a little the worse for wear from being in the pub all evening, and we had to make it up that twisty path back to the B&B."

"So...?"

"Well, we had to hold hands, so that when one of us fell off the side of the road into the ditch or whatever, the other one could haul him back on to the road. I vaguely remember us losing each other at one point, which I suppose is a bit alarming. It did take us quite a long time, but we made it. Just."

"You know," he said, "you've never told me about your disreputable past. I guess now I'm away at uni, you feel you can."

"I'm thinking it might be a bit too late to be a bad influence on you. Still, it's worth a try."

The Black Bull was not just a pub. It was attached to a brewery, the Coniston Brewery, makers of Coniston Bluebird Bitter, Old Man Ale and Oliver's Light Ale. I chose the Oliver's Light, never having had it before, and had sip at the bar of the hoppy, sweetish beer - very nice, I thought.

I also had the fish cooked in Bluebird Bitter batter and, while I couldn't actually taste the Bluebird Bitter in the batter, it felt appropriate.

"Can I get you another Oliver's Light?" Richard asked.

"No. One's enough. I'm a bit of a lightweight these days. You?"

"No, I'm good."

We walked back to the hostel in daylight still, with no need of a torch, and looked in the lounge, where a couple of people snoozed in armchairs.

I fancied a cup of tea, so we headed into the dining room. The chefs were just clearing up, but the young woman in chef whites who we had met at the reception came across to the door, and said, "Yes, of course," to my request.

I liked this place.

While we waited, we checked our route for tomorrow. Fifty miles, roughly. Could be a long day, though we were going south again, so surely - surely! - tomorrow would be the flat day that today had not been.

Our friend brought a tray over with tea. This was indeed a good place.

"How are your legs?" Richard asked me.

"Tired, but OK. You?"

"Fine."

I jotted down the distance and speed for the day.

Distance for the day: 30 miles / 48 Km
Height gained: 3,244 feet / 989 metres
Hardest hill: Hawkshead to Tarn Hows
754 feet / 230 metres
Average speed: 9.7 mph / 15.5 Kmph
Fastest speed: 32.4 mph / 51.8 Kmph

A more proficient cyclist than I might think we had not exactly been over-fast, and I guessed they were probably right. Then again, we had cycled over the height of Scafell Pike, carrying panniers full of gear, and it was our first day. Richard would no doubt have gone quite a bit faster if he had not had to wait for me, but I had enjoyed it, and we weren't in a race.

An older and a younger man further down the room were looking at their own map.

"Are you walking or running tomorrow?" I asked.

"He's running," the older replied. "Him and his brother - my nephews. I'm supporting. And you?"

35

"Cycling," I said. "Heading south and then looping back up to north of Kendal."

"Sounds good."

"How long should the run take?" I asked.

"About three and a half hours."

"Oh," I said, thinking that maybe the other guy's time was not the winning time.

I asked his name. "I'll look up the results," I said.

Later, I did look up the results. He was in the top ten finishers out of over three hundred runners that completed the course. Not bad for a marathon through the Cumbrian Fells. To be honest, just completing it seemed impressive, let alone coming in the top ten. There were some seriously fit people staying at Coniston Youth Hostel that night. I clearly wasn't one of them.

"Good luck for tomorrow," I said.

"Same to you. Enjoy it."

"We will," I said. "We definitely will."

DAY TWO - TAN

CARTMEL AND KENDAL

Coniston – Brantwood – Haverthwaite
Cartmel – Grange-over-Sands
Sizergh Castle – Kendal – Staveley

50 miles

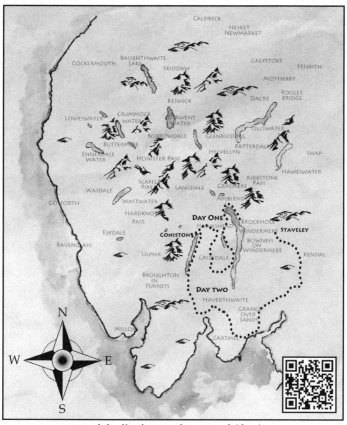

www.lakedistrictgrandtour.co.uk/day/two

The sound of runners getting into running kit woke me, and we had a longer ride today, so I pulled myself out of bed.

Richard was awake.

"I've booked us breakfast," I said. "Thought I'd need a Full English to see me through fifty-odd miles."

In the YHA's dining room the same lady was on duty and serving bacon and eggs.

I said to her, "You've been up early to get that ready."

"Actually, I've just arrived." She indicated the team working behind her. "These guys have been doing all this."

"Looks good though."

We parked ourselves by a window, on the other side of which was some damp-looking rain. A notice was taped on the inside of the window: 'Swimming Pool Closed For Cleaning.'

"Swimming pool?" Richard said, through a mouth of bacon.

Outside on the veranda was what looked like a blue plastic oversized paddling pool with a cover on it. It didn't look like it was particularly in the process of being cleaned, though I suppose the rather persistent rain might be giving it a rinse.

"You don't fancy it?"

He shook his head. "Full stomach."

It was going to be a long day. Down the eastern shore of Coniston Water, then on south towards the coast. There would be a stop at Cartmel before reaching the sea at Grange-over-Sands, and then heading north to Sizergh Castle, Kendal and Staveley.

The weather didn't look too bad until we went out to the bike shed to pick up our bikes. Outside it was pretty obvious that we were going to get very wet. We decided on full waterproofs: jacket, trousers, overshoes and helmet cover. Not cool, maybe, but dry. Or so we thought.

We coasted down to the road back into town and then headed out around the north end of the lake. The wind was blustery and the lake fairly rough, but that didn't stop a couple of anglers from spending their Sunday morning in boats on the lake. There was also a small group of kayakers skirting the shoreline, trying to avoid the worst of the wind.

"So," Richard said, "how do you think the ring ouzel spotting in Coniston went?"

"Not as well as it might," I said.

We cycled on around the lakeshore, heading down the east side of Coniston Water and stopping outside Brantwood, former home of John Ruskin. In Victorian times he was one of the country's most famous writers and thinkers, said to have influenced thinking on the National Health Service, pensions, the minimum wage, and the National Trust - a man before his time. He was a leading art critic, promoting painters such as J.M.W.Turner and defending them against critics of the modern artistic style.

My favourite quote of Ruskin's explained his opposition to allowing the railway to build a new line that would carry trippers from the Lancashire factories northwards from its Windermere terminus: "I do not wish them to see Helvellyn when they are drunk."

Brantwood is open to the public, though was definitely not at nine o'clock on that Sunday morning. Beyond the gate with its closed sign, a large-ish house stood high above the road, caramel-coloured with climbing plants trained up the walls. There was a large corner window, which on a good day must give a fabulous view. Today, the cloud was so low and the rain so dense that we could only just make out the woods on the far shore, and couldn't see the fells beyond, though we knew that The Old Man Of Coniston was right opposite, somewhere high in the cloud.

On a better day, The Old Man would have a good sprinkling of fell walkers going up, most often on a route past the disused copper mines in the valley. From the high stone cairn at the top they would have a wonderful view all around - back over Lakeland, over Morecambe Bay to the south, and towards the Isle of Man out at sea.

With time to spare I might have taken in Brantwood and its gardens as part of our day. As it was, we used the house's drive as a brief stop to try to close any nooks and crannies of our water-proofs that the rain could get through.

"I think it might be a clearing-up shower," I said.

He looked at me.

I said, "I have met someone who hadn't heard of the concept of a clearing-up shower."

He looked at me. "Hard to believe. You know, I feel very wet. I'm really not sure if this jacket is waterproof. Specially my arms. That might be a problem if it's not just a clearing-up shower."

I examined a sleeve. The raindrops were not beading on it at all.

"I think it might be going straight through."

"I've re-proofed it a few times, but it doesn't seem to help."

"Could be time for a new jacket. We're staying in Staveley tonight and there's a massive bike shop there. Could be the place to get one."

"I might have to."

We pedalled on, dodging puddles while trying to glance at Coniston Water. The lake was high by the side of the road, with trees standing in water, while full-to-bursting streams were flooding down through beech woods on the left. There was no traffic at all, and with just a few ups and downs, it was a lovely road to cycle.

A couple of miles along the lakeshore brought us to little Peel Island standing proud of a promontory and, just beyond, we stopped by a reed-filled bay to look back. We were in Swallows and Amazons country.

I had never read Arthur Ransome's books as a child, but thought I ought to before this ride. After all, Swallows and Amazons, the children's adventure story he published in 1930, was said to be based on some of the features of Coniston Water and some of Windermere. Almost in spite of myself, I enjoyed it very much. I read about John, Susan, Titty and Roger sailing their boat 'Swallow' through the night; about the sisters - the Amazons - with their skull and crossbones flag on their own sailing boat; and about their battle with Captain Flint on his houseboat. It was all a jolly good adventure, and Wild Cat Island, where most of the story took place, was based on Peel Island just here - even if it had been transplanted in the book to Windermere.

Arthur Ransome was a story in himself. He was a reporter in Moscow at the time of the Russian Revolution, becoming friendly with Lenin and Trotsky. He fell in love with Trostsky's secretary and spirited her out of the country to Estonia through the battle lines of the civil war. The couple eventually came to live near Windermere, where he was inspired partly by a friend's family learning to sail on the lake (three of the children being called Susan, Titty and Roger), and partly by his own childhood holidays at High Nibthwaite, just a few miles ahead of Richard and me. From there, they could row to Peel Island for family picnics, and clearly the little island was a special place for him.

I could see why: there was definitely a romantic, adventuresome quality to the place, and Arthur Ransome's books encouraged more than one generation of children – and parents – to come to the Lake District for their own adventures.

Coniston Water drains out into the River Crake at High Nibthwaite, and our road followed the river, rolling up and down. Woods and cow pastures accompanied us on either side.

We ignored river crossings at Lowick Bridge and Spark Bridge, which would have taken us on to the main road south from Coniston on the far bank of the river, until a right turn took us towards Penny Bridge which is presumably the name of the bridge we then crossed, but is also the name of a village.

We crossed the busy A-road and settled ourselves to gradually climb the long hill stretching straight ahead of us through Penny Bridge village. We were looking for signs for the Walney to Wear cycle route, which we would be following for the rest of the day.

The Walney to Wear cycle route, or W2W, is one of several waymarked coast to coast cycle routes built by the cycle charity Sustrans. The W2W stretches from Walney Island near Barrow-in-Furness around the southern edge of Lakeland, across the Pennines to County Durham, finishing on the River Wear at Sunderland. It looks a great route altogether, 153 miles, but it must be one of the least ridden.

I was looking forward to seeing the first of the neat little blue-and-red W2W signs that should lead us from Penny Bridge right around the coast and inland almost as far as Kendal.

We had gone some way up the hill before I thought to look at the map. After some slightly hazy squinting, I rifled through my front pannier for my glasses, and in a moment of clarity realised that I had missed a turning, and we were now cycling the wrong way on the W2W. Not just the wrong way, but up a serious hill the wrong way.

"Rich," I said, "I think we should have turned off at that last junction."

He looked at me for a moment. "So," he said, "how's it going with the map reading?"

"It's been worse," I said. "At the moment, we're only averaging getting lost once a day."

"Fair point," he said.

"Besides, this hill is clearly good training for you."

We turned back on ourselves, and going down the hill could clearly see the W2W sign leading off to Greenodd - which was the right direction - and down towards the sea.

In Greenodd itself, the W2W sign seemed to suggest that we go down a rough, stony lane at the back of a row of terraced houses. It seemed a little unlikely, but we rattled our way down the little hill, and there was another sign, this one leading to a sandy underpass below the dual carriageway from Barrow-in-Furness as it bridged the estuary for the River Crake.

The road above sounded very busy, so we were grateful for the little diversion. Thank you, Sustrans.

Beyond, the path led us up on to the dual carriageway bridge, but behind barriers and not on the road, and then led us away to the right and to a footbridge across the main estuary, where Lake Windermere's River Leven meets the sea. It seemed an odd place to have a footbridge, the sign being not just for the W2W but also for the Cumbria Coastal Way, a 182-mile long-distance footpath around the edge of Cumbria. I wondered if the footbridge had been built for that purpose in the 1980s, since it looked too old to have been originally meant for the cycleway, which was a much newer venture. Either way, I suspected there were not a lot of users.

We had reached the sea, but were still in the Lake District National Park, and from the middle of the footbridge could see dark mountains under black clouds on the horizon in the north.

On the far side of the bridge a gravelly path followed the bank of the estuary and then came to a crossroads. A farm at the very end of a driveable road had a sign advertising free-range eggs. It seemed unlikely to have a lot of passing trade.

We cycled down the farm's lane and came into woodland. A

large notice-board beside an area of felled forest told us that the Holker Estate was replacing the commercial forestry with deciduous woodland, just leaving the Scots Pines standing, since they were indigenous. The idea was to encourage the local wildlife, such as woodpeckers.

We didn't see any. They were probably watching us from the Scots Pines.

We did see bullocks. The lane was blocked by a Land Rover and, on the far side, a farmer was trying to call a dozen bullocks out of a field and along the lane away from us by beating on a bucket in front of them. He wasn't being very successful.

In fact he was quite unsuccessful for about ten minutes.

As we waited astride our bikes, the rain stopped.

"I told you it was a clearing-up shower."

It was quite a relief, and we got off our bikes to remove our waterproofs.

We were also starting to feel hungry. I looked at the bike computer. Sixteen miles.

"It would be good to get a scone or something and to dry off a bit," I said. "Haverthwaite is just coming up. There's the Lakeside and Haverthwaite Railway. They have steam trains that take tourists up to the bottom end of Windermere. They must have a café."

"I might change my shirt as well," Richard said. "I feel very wet."

The farmer was clearly unhappy about going into the field to chase the bullocks out, or even to send his dog in, but finally he did both, though a little gingerly, and when, finally, the bullocks started moving, he dashed behind the Land Rover to make sure he was out of the way. The bullocks careered down the lane away from us, the farm dog at their heels.

"Thanks," the farmer said to us, a bit out of breath, and he followed the beasts along.

"I worked on a farm for a while when I was a teenager, Rich," I said. "I remember one time I was working with the cow man, and he said, 'Never turn your back on bullocks'. I reckon that guy has reason to be wary as well."

The W2W signpost pointed across a crossroads, but another

sign said left for Haverthwaite. We went left, and climbed a hill into a small village of cottages and old farm buildings. There was no signpost or any sign of the railway.

"Are you sure it's here?" Richard asked.

"Well, I'm sure there's a Haverthwaite Railway. But I must admit there's no railway just here."

If I had taken out my glasses to look at the map properly, of course, I'd have seen that the station isn't in the village, but is about half a mile beyond. I didn't do that though.

"Rich," I said. "Muesli biscuit instead?"

We had one each.

"Chocolate bar?"

We had one each of those as well.

It's a shame we didn't find the café. Their website says they have Giant Homemade Scones and Mouthwatering Apple Pies. They might have had slightly fewer left if we had found the café that day.

We cycled back down to the crossroads, and back on to the W2W. The road instantly climbed. It got steep, and then steeper again, and was long. I didn't get it; we were meant to be in the flat south, by the coast. I checked the map between breaths as my legs pulled me slowly up in Richard's wake. There were arrows on the route, showing a steep hill. They were right.

"Dig deep," I said to myself. "Dig... deep."

Finally we came out on to a sort of a plateau, with limestone outcrops, little hillocks and small fields and copses, and my heart rate returned to somewhere near normal.

Then the road dropped, long and wonderful, through fields and gentle farmland. We sped downhill, but wondered, really, had it been necessary to go up so high in the first place?

We moved inconspicuously out of the National Park, but there was a reason for it. Cartmel lay just ahead, and I couldn't miss Cartmel, partly because of the place itself, and partly because of the role of the abbeys and priories in making the Lake District that we have today.

We had been to Cartmel once before. Richard had run in a trails race from Cartmel Racecourse and, as we approached the village, the Racecourse came up on our right. We could hear the voice of an announcer from a loudspeaker, but could not make out the words. There was clearly an event taking place though.

"Rich, I think there might be races on. Shall we see if we can go in?"

There was no barrier or ticket-collecting going on at the gate, so we rolled down the slope past tents and cars towards the race track and the grandstand building, the announcer's voice getting louder and more animated as we got closer to a small crowd facing away from us.

Now there was a banner, and it wasn't a horse race that was going on, but the Race For Life. Supporters, some in pink, but most wrapped up in coats, lined the white railings of the race track, a few with their own little banners bearing the names of those who had been the victims of cancer.

The grandstand was empty, so we wheeled our bikes round, and climbed a few steps to get a view of the grassy track, with woodland just behind. It was a lovely little racetrack, though just now, quite noisy.

"GIVE ME A CHEER IF YOU'VE A RUNNER HERE!" came from the loudspeakers. "I CAN'T HEAR YOU! COME ON AND SHOUT OUT FOR THE RUNNERS! I CAN'T HEEAAR YOU!"

Richard said, "I think he must be from local radio."

"I WANT EVERYONE CHEERING AS THE FIRST RUNNERS COME IN. HERE THEY COME!"

And they were. We had timed it so that the first lady runners were just appearing. There was one lady in front, with another, ten yards behind.

"I don't suppose," Richard said, "people really race in a Race For Life?"

The loudspeaker echoed Richard's words: "REMEMBER, IT'S NOT THE WINNING, IT'S THE TAKING PART."

The lady in second place, ten yards behind the leader, clearly didn't have quite the same view. As they passed us, she put on a sprint, overtaking the lady in front, and ran full pelt for the finish line, leaving the previous leader in her wake.

It was, of course, a great cause, and just the running itself, the taking part, so good.

More ladies followed, many in pink, some with t-shirts bearing names. There were sporty-looking ladies to begin with, and then the joggers and the non-sporty, some gently loping in, others clearly having given their all. We clapped them all.

The announcer, meanwhile, was going into overdrive.

"YO LADIES! YOU MADE IT! SHOUT OUT FOR THE LADIES! YO LADIES!"

"Yup, definitely local radio."

We pressed on into the village, and by now we were in need of some food.

"Pub?" I said.

"Sounds good."

We locked our bikes outside a likely looking eatery, only to realise that it looked a little well-heeled for two wet and probably smelly cyclists.

We hesitated and looked around for alternatives in this pretty square. On the far side of a village pump and an obelisk in the square was the whitewashed Old Post Office announcing Cartmel as 'the home of STICKY TOFFEE', and there were lovely houses, some with wisteria (or similar - I'm not good on plants; well, nature generally, I suppose) growing up the outside. There was a very old stone building with a tall arched gateway, and more to the point, there was a pub.

From the outside, it was certainly pub-like. Inside, it too seemed a little posh for us, and we were a little under-dressed, but the oak-beamed bar area was almost empty, so we settled ourselves at a corner table.

We were just about to go to the bar to order soup and a roll, only to find an attentive waiter at our table, ready to take our order. And when soup and a roll arrived, the roll was not on a plate, but on a rather large piece of slate adorned with a truly splendid salad.

"Don't get too used to this," I said.

The bar filled up, and it became clear that we were a bit out of place amidst the Sunday lunch-time diners. It was a good pub though, even offering a pile of newspapers next to the large fireplace. So we finished off our soup and caught up on the Tour de France news. The riders had started the day before, and there were high hopes for Bradley Wiggins.

"Do you realise, Rich, that they only cycled 6.4km yesterday?"

"We did much more than that."

"Wimps."

"How far are they doing today?"

"Um," I said, reading. "198Km."

"A bit more than us then."

"Well, I suppose so. Actually, I reckon the Tour de France is a bit like us. Or me anyway. Will it be the traditional glorious British failure, as I have to resort to pushing Scott over the big passes? Or will there be a triumphal reaching of summits on two wheels?"

"Same with me, but I want to be able to cycle over them without stopping."

"Bit beyond me. Just not pushing would be my triumph, I reckon."

"Glad we're not doing 198Km."

"That might be a challenge too far."

We finally abandoned our comfy pub, but I wasn't ready to leave Cartmel just yet. We hadn't yet got to the main reason I had wanted to come.

We moved our bikes to the gates of the churchyard. There were quite a few people around, partly because it was Sunday, but also because it was Cartmel Priory, and fabulous.

We went inside, and the effect was immediate. Great stone columns supported a high roof, and beautifully carved arches led through from the chancel into side aisles. After the Celts, the Anglians and the Norse, this was the Normans arriving and making their mark.

There had been a Kingdom of Strathclyde stretching from Lakeland into western Scotland, with the last King of Cumbria, Dunmail, battling the English King with what must have been a mix of the Celtic and Norse inhabitants of the fells and valleys. Then, for a while, the area came under the Scottish crown, but written records are almost non-existent. Even 1066 did not make much of an impression on Lakeland. While the Norman knights wrapped up England as far as the southern rim of the mountains, history is virtually silent about what was going on to the north.

It was only in 1092 that William Rufus took over Carlisle, so only the villages of the far south appear in Domesday Book. As Norman lords gradually established control, they began to give land and money to set up the first of the great Norman monasteries in the south in what was to become Furness, part of Lancashire. The south east of Lakeland became the county of Westmorland, with the county of Cumberland stretching all the way around the west coast, across the heart of the fells, and as far as Carlisle. This area would change hands from England to Scotland and back several times but, in the far south, the Anglo-Norman knights were in control.

The Cartmel area was a gift from England's Henry II to William the Marshall, who would become one of the most powerful men in the country. Building a priory at Cartmel became his pet project.

Richard and I wandered around and marvelled at the building, at the tombs of knights, and at memorial stones for the great and the good over the centuries, while light streamed through a great window and beamed down towards the altar.

At the far corner of the Priory we heard a conversation from the other side of one of the giant pillars. It sounded a bit like a tour, but when we looked around the column, it was not a tour guide speaking, but the vicar. A young man, he was wonderfully enthusiastic, his eyes shining behind his glasses. He told us about William the Marshall, and about Cartmel's link to the greatest and richest of the abbeys, Furness Abbey, which came to own all the land between Coniston and Windermere, plus large parts of Borrowdale and Eskdale.

Other monasteries did the same. St Bees Priory acquired land in Eskdale, Ennerdale and Loweswater, Carlisle Abbey down as far as the Lorton valley, and Shap Abbey much of eastern Lakeland.

It was these abbeys and priories that really changed the face of Lakeland. Woodland had been cleared for pasture before, but the monasteries created vast sheep-walks amongst the fells and dairy farms in the valleys - really the beginning of what we see today.

There was more to abbeys and priories than just the land and the farms though. There was hearts and minds. We joined in as the vicar described how a Priory built as a symbol of power by William the Marshall was taken into the hearts of the locals, and when Henry VIII's men came to destroy it, they petitioned the King to allow the

Priory church to survive, since it was their own parish church as well. The petition was granted, and Cartmel Priory's church was reprieved, unlike the once-great Furness Abbey, now a ruin.

Then, over a century later, the townspeople again defended their church, this time against Cromwell's men who would also have destroyed it, and again the locals succeeded. "There are still gun-shot holes in the west doors," the young vicar said.

He was clearly in awe of the Priory and what it has meant over hundreds of years to the people of Cartmel, and I could see why.

He asked me where we were heading.

"Grange-over-Sands next," I said.

"Ah, well that was the 'grange' - the grain store - for Cartmel Priory. The Priory would have owned most of the land here before Henry VIII. And since then, much of it is the Holker Estate. They own the Priory, in fact. They have been very helpful, I have to say. The building needs a massive amount of upkeep."

"It must do."

"Well, enjoy your ride."

"We always do" I said.

We left Cartmel on quiet lanes, hedgerows on either side, the road rising and falling, passing a sign: Lancaster Over Sands - 15. Until the coming of the railways, the sands were the main route across Morecambe Bay from Lancaster to North Lancashire, which is what the area had been until the creation of Cumbria in 1974.

Wordsworth wrote: 'The Stranger, from the moment he sets foot on those Sands, seems to leave the turmoil and traffic of the world behind him; and crossing the majestic plain whence the sea has retired, he beholds, rising apparently from its base, the cluster of mountains among which he is going to wander, and towards whose recesses, by the Vale of Coniston, he is gradually and peacefully led.'

The Queen's Official Guide still leads charity walks across - though at your own risk.

We dropped down into the town of Grange-over-Sands. We were still outside the National Park but, just beyond the town, we would cross back over the border for the most southerly point of our Grand Tour of the Lake District.

Even if we were just passing through, it was worth it. Grange-

51

over-Sands was a nice little place, busy-ish, with local-looking shops and a feeling of stepping back in time. Bunting was strung across the street, and we rolled downhill past 'Lancasters' selling everything from walking boots to crockery to duvets. There was a pretty town-park with flower beds, a conical-roofed band-stand and even a band assembling for a Sunday afternoon concert.

On the far side of the park was a walkway, and beyond that, well, you would have thought sand, but the tide was in. This was indeed the sea, or at least where the estuary of Kendal's River Kent feeds into Morecambe Bay.

There was still a genteel feel to Grange on the road out the far side, with grand houses, quiet-looking hotels and friendly bungalows. Excellent, I thought, if you were looking for a retirement by the sea, without over-much excitement.

A main road would have taken us up to a dual carriage-way, but we were still following little blue W2W signs. Or at least Richard was. I missed the sign. Again.

A small U-turn amongst the traffic took us on to a very quiet lane, absolutely flat, with a railway line and the sea just off to the right.

"Do you get the feeling," I asked Richard, "that not too much happens in Grange-over-Sands?"

The answer didn't come, because our attention had been drawn to a group walking towards us. The two men in front were carrying boots. Half a dozen more men and a lady in a purple dress were following on. They seemed to have come from the direction of the estuary, and I jumped to the conclusion that they had just done the crossing of the bay. How they could have done that with the tide in did not quite occur to me at the time, so I asked the two in front, "Have you come across the sands?"

They were walking fast, and one glanced hurriedly behind before saying, "Well, we've been in the sea. But… tell you what, you had better ask one of them."

I looked behind him, and the lady in the purple dress appeared to have put on a spurt, and was catching up. The two guys ran past us.

Then the 'lady' got close enough for us to see that, actually, this was a man in a long purple dress. With a big stick. He ran past as well, shouting at the first two, and waving the stick.

The remaining group were in fits of laughter.

"Excuse me," I said. "Your friend said you would tell us what was going on."

One stopped laughing long enough to say, "It's a stag do. We've all just been in the sea and, well…" He dissolved into laughter, leaning on his mates.

I put two and two together, and guessed that the first two men had somehow substituted the bridegroom's clothes for a long purple dress while he was in the sea. Hence the big stick.

I liked Grange-Over-Sands.

The lane bent away from the estuary as we approached what looked like a limestone outcrop. Rather than go completely round it, the road rose over the northern end of the ridge, giving us views back over the Cartmel peninsula, and then dropped back to sea level, skirting the flattest of flat fields and heading north.

An underpass took us to the far side of the dual carriage-way, and the W2W signs led us on to what must once have been the main road, but was now a quiet road pointing us in a north-easterly direction towards Levens.

Several groups of cyclists appeared, some in our direction, some going the other way, all with a 'hello'. This was clearly a popular place to cycle, and I could see why. The map suggested all sorts of flat routes, or if you were feeling fit, some climbs up limestone escarpments. With the sun on our backs, it was lovely.

We crossed the boundary out of the National Park again.

When the Lake District National Park was founded, the market towns around the outside of the fells were deliberately missed out, but we were on our way to Kendal, whose story is tied up with Lakeland, so I could not miss the town out.

At Levens, a long road rose up the front of the hill, lined with smart houses with long views back across the flatness behind us to the hills and sea beyond. I guessed they were pretty good views, but I was a bit consumed by the state of my heart and lungs; this felt a tough hill. We had done about 33 miles, so I was now doing a mileage I had not done in a while. I was flaking.

Richard was cycling with me, rather than racing on.

"Rich," I said. "Sizergh Castle is coming up. I could do with food, and they must have a tea room."

He did not object.

While the fells and valleys of Lakeland were sprouting sheep walks, dairy farms and granges under the ownership of the abbeys, the rim of Lakeland was sprouting castles. Some were major castles, like those at Cockermouth, Penrith and Egremont. Others were defensive towers - pele towers. Many are still there, still lived in as part of a grander house or a farm house, while others are crumbling remains.

They were needed. Devastating Scottish raids came not just into border areas, but right down the coast of Lakeland and around to Furness and beyond. Abbeys, villages and farms around the edge of the mountains were attacked and burned, as Scotland fought for its independence from England in the 14th century.

Sizergh Castle had been one of those pele towers, and grew by additions with Tudor, Elizabethan and later extensions.

I had been before, many years before in fact, and had only the vaguest memories of the pele tower and of a café. The café was to be our first call.

We rode through a gateway and up a long drive through open grassland, until we came to an elongated log cabin of a café with a balcony and picnic tables. Perfect.

It was busy there, and we queued for cappuccinos and scones, which were also really good.

We walked around the back of the café, heading for the castle, past several scarecrows as part of the castle's Summer Celebration, and into the courtyard of the castle. Ahead of us was the pele tower and its additions, and on either side were later wings forming three sides of a square.

Two bare legs belonging to a youngster were emerging from a window in one of the wings. In all, three children in shorts and t-shirts climbed out, peered at us, and then climbed in again. It seemed a little odd for a National Trust house, but we went on inside (the main entrance, rather than a window) and all became clear. The Strickland family, having owned the castle since 1239, gave it to the National Trust in 1950, but with the proviso that they could live in the wings. They still do.

As we dodged quickly from room to room, I overheard someone I had taken for a guide, pointing at a portrait, saying, "And this was my great grandfather."

A Strickland was showing friends around. We tagged along in the background. There was the mediaeval thick-walled pele tower, then the Elizabethan section with wonderful oak carved panelling, and much more. We went round too fast really, partly because our Strickland guide was setting a pace, and partly because we still had a lot of miles to go. But it was good; I recommend Sizergh Castle. And the scones.

We cruised back down the long drive to the road, and then headed east, via an underpass for the M6, towards the quiet village of Sedgwick, and then north, pointing at Kendal.

We had left the flat coast now and the road rolled up and down through fields. Grain fields, it occurred to me. We wouldn't see too many grain fields on our cycle tour around the Lake District.

In Natland, the sign for the Walney to Wear cycle route turned away, heading east. Our road into Kendal was quiet, so we ignored signs for a cycle route that would take us round the back of the town, and opted to follow the road along by the river, past the old K-Shoes factory, now a retail outlet. The River Kent was full and fast-flowing today, and brown with silt which it would no doubt deposit in the estuary behind us at Grange-over-Sands and Morecambe Bay.

Kendal is a grey town, its buildings mostly of local limestone, but in spite of that is a bright, cheerful-looking place, with a wide main street, which we cycled down. Cars are banned from much of the main street, the market place, and the many yards (150 of them) that run at right angles to the main street. By late Sunday afternoon, very few shops were open, so families were meandering across the road, window-shopping, and youngsters practised wheelies on their bikes.

Kendal owes much of its shape - the main street, market and yards - even now, to Henry VIII's Reformation and the closure of the monasteries. The result was to take the business of selling the wool from the Lakeland fells away from the monasteries and into

55

the market towns. Kendal was the gateway to Lakeland from the south, and boomed. Each of the still-numbered yards in the town centre would have been filled with dyers, spinners and weavers producing their renowned Kendal Green cloth. There was Dr Manning's Yard - number 83 - and Tanners Yard - number 39, and the pattern of streets - not particularly car-friendly - became fixed to what it is now.

If Kendal Green is no longer nationally known, another product is, and what's more is on sale in a huge number of shops in the Lake District.

"Kendal Mint Cake, Rich?"

"Um, no. Thanks. I'm not really keen on Kendal Mint Cake."

"What? Edmund Hillary took Kendal Mint Cake to the top of Everest. Shackleton took some to the Antarctic. Even Ewan McGregor took it around the world - the long way round! Surely we have to have Kendal Mint Cake cycling the long way round the Lake District."

"I'd rather have a Mars Bar."

"Call yourself a Cumbrian. I am ashamed."

"Do you want a Mars Bar?"

"Have you got a spare one?"

"Might have."

Pause.

"Oh, go on then."

Kendal has another claim to fame in Lake District terms, in that the greatest of authors of Lakeland guides took a job here specifically so that he could walk the fells more easily. I'm talking of Alfred Wainwright, A.W. as he liked to be known.

A.W. made his first visit to the Lake District from industrial Lancashire as a young man in 1933. The trip had led him up Orrest Head at Windermere and had changed his life; he had been captivated by his first sight of the mountains, the woods, the fields and the lake lying below.

He kept coming back, exploring the fells on foot, travelling everywhere by bus. He eventually managed to move to Kendal, though having to take a cut in pay to do so, and began the first of his guide books in 1952 using his careful hand and eye for detail.

I love his books, entirely written in his own hand, with the words exactly aligned to right and left. The maps and sketches, all again hand-drawn in pen and ink, are extraordinary.

Then there is the coverage. Every single route up every single mountain in the Lake District has been walked and laboriously catalogued, with notes showing the best route, hints as to how to find the way, and the best way off in bad weather.

As a person, he was renowned for his curmudgeonly nature, but he certainly had a sense of humour. Book 6, for example, was dedicated to "those unlovely twins, my right leg and my left leg", which were apparently "unsuitable subjects for illustration".

With over two million books sold in his 'Pictorial Guides to the Lakeland Fells' series, he has quite a legacy.

I have to admit I was quite tired by now, and staying in Kendal might have been nice, but we were booked in at Staveley for the night. Not a hostel, but a bed-and-breakfast. I had found it on the internet, and it seemed the best combination of giving us a good start for the following day and being within walking distance of food at a local pub. Besides, a B&B would have a television where a hostel might not, and just by chance it was the World Cup Final that night.

There was also a brewery in Staveley, and you might by now be suspecting a pattern to events. I don't drink greatly, but a pint of locally brewed bitter in a local pub at the end of a day's cycling is very satisfying. The night before was Coniston Brewery at the Black Bull. The brewery in Staveley was, strangely, the Hawkshead Brewery, but I wasn't complaining.

However, we had another five or so miles to get there, and to be honest, that Mars Bar wasn't really cutting it.

We headed north out of Kendal, and turned right on to the National Cycle Network's Route 6, which looked as though it should take us by country lanes most of the way to Staveley.

It did.

We pedalled past a business area of Kendal, through gentle countryside and into the small village of Burneside. From there we followed close to the River Kent until we reached the main road from Kendal to Windermere. This would have been a bit dreadful, but fortunately there was a special cycle lane next to the road, for which I assumed I should thank Sustrans again.

Thank you, Sustrans.

Unfortunately, Sustrans had not been in charge of the weather. We had been dry all the way from the other side of Cartmel, but now the rain started again.

"I'm stopping to put my jacket on," I said.

"I will as well, though I'm not sure how dry it will keep me."

"Bike shop tomorrow?"

"Guess so."

After a short stretch of the cycle lane by the main road, a new-ish bypass continued on past Staveley, while we turned off, over the railway crossing and into the village. It was raining hard by now, and Richard's sleeves were looking alarmingly transparent.

Staveley was not like many of the villages we had cycled through. Although we were back in the Lake District National Park, Staveley seemed more of a working village than a tourist centre. It had an industrial estate and no tourist attractions. Apart that is from the brewery, a very well-known café (Wilf's), and the largest bike shop in Britain. I suppose those are good claims to fame - at least they are in my book - but I didn't suppose the town was over-run with young Japanese couples looking for life-size models of Peter Rabbit and Mrs Tiggy-winkle.

I had thought it would be very clever to put a map showing the B&B on my phone. It seemed less clever when I realised I had run out of battery.

"I think it's at the far end of the village," I said.

My legs were complaining, really wanting the B&B to be at this end of the village.

A hill started to take us up out of town.

"I don't have a good feeling about this," I said.

"I'm going to blame you," Richard said. "Especially if we miss the football.'

"Ah," I said, thinking I might do the same.

A row of cottages appeared on the right, above the road. One had a B&B sign. It wasn't the right one.

"Ah."

But there was another sign, and this, fortunately, was it.

The lady who owned the B&B was extraordinarily welcoming,

placing a sheet and newspapers on the living room carpet where our bikes could drip happily behind the settees. And the house was wonderful: 400 years old, with the beams in the ceiling to prove it.

Once we were clean, we set off into town, taking our landlady's advice on the pub with the large, cheap meals. I was very hungry.

While waiting to order, I read the notice board by the bar. There was an 'Onion Exchange' where you could take your home-grown fruit and veg, and swap it for others' fruit and veg. The village has other examples of its community spirit. When the council wanted to close the public toilets, a group of volunteers took over the running of them, and Staveley public toilets are now twinned with public toilets in Cambodia.

When it was our turn to order, I chose the Cumberland Sausage, washed down with Cumberland Ale. Entirely for the sake of the ride. Admittedly we were in the old county of Westmorland rather than Cumberland, and Cumberland Ale was brewed in Cockermouth's Jennings Brewery rather than in Staveley, but I was prepared to make that sacrifice.

I was even able to find room for another of Lakeland's culinary traditions, Sticky Toffee Pudding. The things we do for adventure.

The Hawkshead Brewery was open, or at least the beer hall was, when we walked along to investigate. Stairs and a glass-walled corridor led us past offices and brewing areas to a large room with benches and tables. In the far corner, local musicians were taking it in turns to entertain their friends. There was a wonderful atmosphere, with families, teenagers, older couples, and dog-walkers all welcome. A long bar was selling the Hawkshead Brewery's own beers, and again we felt compelled to try one.

We sat by a man with his German shepherd. After a few minutes he stood and said, "Would you watch the dog?"

We agreed to, and while we watched the dog and supped the malty Hawkshead Red, he sat at the microphone and played blue-grass on his guitar.

We set off back to the B&B for the World Cup Final.

Not a bad day at all, I reckoned.

Distance for the day: 50 miles / 80 Km
Height gained: 3,444 feet / 1,050 metres
Hardest hill: Haverthwaite eastwards
551 feet / 168 metres
Average speed: 10.5 mph / 16.8 Kmph
Fastest speed: 30.8 mph / 49.3 Kmph
Total distance: 80 miles / 129 Km

So, double the mileage of my practice rides, more height than the day before, plus Cumberland Sausage and real ale.

I probably snored that night.

I have no recollection.

DAY THREE – TETHERA

GOLDEN EAGLES AND YELLOW EARLS

Staveley – Shap – Bampton Grange – Haweswater
Bampton – Askham – Lowther Castle – Penrith
Greystoke – Motherby

54 miles

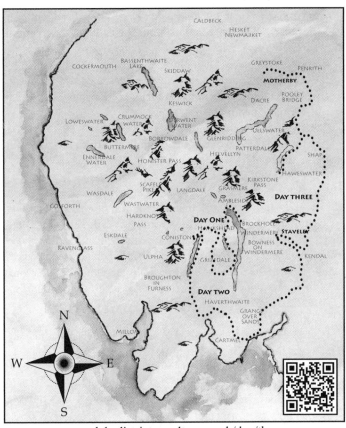

www.lakedistrictgrandtour.co.uk/day/three

"**Y**ou'll want the fell road," the lady who owned the B&B said. I had showed her the route we were looking for to get us to the A6, and asked her how to get there.

Our day would take us over Shap Pass, across to Haweswater, cycling past Lowther Castle before dropping into Penrith, and then looping round via Greystoke to our next stop at the little village of Motherby. Haweswater for the golden eagle. Lowther Castle for the yellow earl. And near Shap, we would be at the furthest eastern point of the National Park.

She said, "It's steep, mind, the fell road."

It was a Cumbrian accent. More, it was a Staveley accent, because she had grown up in this cottage, and the many Cumbrian accents are quite distinct.

"Yes, I thought it might be."

"You want the bridge over the river, then turn right and you'll be on the fell road."

We should not, she said, get lost.

Hm.

We were sitting at her dining table in a living room with low oak beams and a very old dresser set into the wall. The cottage had been part of one longer building, she said, which her father had divided, building on the bedrooms and kitchen behind. He managed, though, to keep the friendly, lived-in atmosphere of the main room.

"I love your house," I said. "How old is it?"

"17th century."

"Wonderful."

We had company at the table, a man of about my age, holidaying in the Lake District for the first time.

"Where is good to visit in the rain?" he asked.

"What sort of place do you like to go to?"

"Well, castles, abbeys and so on."

A man after my own heart.

"Try Cartmel," I said. "It's fabulous."

The cottage would have been built by one of the 'yeoman farmers', owners of their own farms after the closure of Cartmel, Furness and the other monasteries. By the 17th century many of these yeoman farmers were prospering. The great Scottish raids had ended, wool was providing increasing income, and the yeoman farmers began replacing their wooden farms and cottages with stone buildings, like this one.

Wealth was also coming from the ground. Lakeland had become a mining and quarrying region for lead, copper, zinc, graphite, coal, haematite and more. (Even little Natland, the village that we had cycled through on the way into Kendal, had mines, though local legend is that theirs were Treacle Mines.)

The new prosperity increased the demand for stone. On the Westmorland fringe of Lakeland above Staveley, the quarries were for slate, partly for the houses of the immediate area, and for Kendal and other growing market towns, but also for further south. Christopher Wren specified Westmorland green slate for Kensington Palace and Chelsea Hospital.

I had never really paid much attention to the dates above the lintels of Lakeland's farmhouses, but it seems to be true. Very few are before a date of around 1650, and many within just 100 years after that.

Delicious aromas wafted from the kitchen, and when our landlady presented us with a cooked breakfast, toast, cereals and coffee, the thought of a fell road leading us on to the long climb up to Shap Summit was not enticing.

First though, we needed 'the biggest bike shop in Britain'.

We coasted down into town, the day grey but dry, with low cloud hugging the fells above Staveley.

The bike shop was in an industrial unit close to the Hawkshead Brewery, and it was indeed big.

"We're looking," I said to the guy by the counter, "for a water-proof jacket for my son that is actually waterproof, unlike the waterproof jacket he is currently wearing."

"So a waterproof, waterproof jacket."

"Yes, please."

"A cheap one," Richard said.

"A cheap, waterproof, waterproof jacket."

"That's the one."

There was a choice of two that fitted the description. The first was fluorescent orange, and Richard tried it on.

The man serving said, "It's very visible, that one."

He was right. The fluorescent orange jacket would be very

visible. From many miles away.

The other was a mid blue, and looked cool. It would go with his bike, which also looked cool. Drop-handle bars, white frame, touches of blue. Fluorescent orange just wouldn't have worked.

He held the orange one up. "Might scare the eagle," he said, and bought the cool blue one.

So we were set up for the day: waterproof jackets, shorts and waterproof overshoes. Our legs, we reckoned, would be waterproof enough if the rain came on.

We didn't get lost in Staveley. We crossed the bridge and headed off in the direction of the fell road. No, we got lost after that.

The problem was that the signposts on the ground seemed to bear no relationship to the village and hamlet names on the map. There was a left turn towards the fells into a lane bounded by ancient moss-covered stone walls on either side. But was it a farm lane or was it the fell road?

We didn't turn left, but instead cycled on through pleasant countryside eastwards, rather than north east around the edge of the rounded, green-grey mountains now receding behind us. The road seemed to be getting increasingly flat, with hedges rather than dry-stone walls.

"Does it seem to you that the fells are getting further away?" Richard asked.

We looked at the map. It was looking like we had missed the fell road altogether.

"Tell you what," I said. "Let's just head east. We must hit the A6 at some point, and then we just head north."

It was good cycling, with farmland around us, and a distinct lack of significant Lake District hills, but there was some doubt in our party as to whether this heading east idea had been a good one.

Signs appeared for the A6. Fine. We would be back on track, though, from the map, it did look as though we had gone almost back to the edge of Kendal.

At the A6 we turned left, and north, on to a steadily rising road, single carriage-way, but wide-ish. This was good, because occasional lorries stormed past us on the damp road. To begin with, there were low hills on either side - fields with hedges and lone trees, and the occasional larger copse. Sheep were scattered cream across the green.

Farms and little rows of cottages made appearances, the farms advertising rough-fell lamb for sale, 'naturally bred on Shap Fell'.

The road climbed, with an occasional dip to bridge a stream, but after each dip the climbs were longer again. Now the hill tops were not fields, but wilder country. Pale uncultivated grass, and forestry in dark blocks.

Climbing again, we were in real fells, not just hills. Rugged backbones of ridges, with just the odd tree silhouetted against the hillside, and the road stretching out ahead of us as it climbed towards the watershed. Nearly all the north-south traffic was on the M6 away to the east, so cars and lorries were few, and they all seemed to take a wide berth around us.

There had not always been a road here at all. Until the 18th century there were no proper roads in Lakeland at all. To bring wool and ores out of the valleys and hills, the only option was a packhorse track. Even carts and carriages were impossible.

Commercial and military pressures changed that. This gap between the Lakeland fells and the Pennines had become a drove road for the thousands of Scottish sheep driven south to English markets after the Union of the Scottish and English Crowns with James I and VI, but it was not a road that we would recognise. Then Bonnie Prince Charlie led his Scots army down this way in the 1745 rebellion. The Duke of Cumberland chased the Prince back north again, pretty much along this route, and no doubt damned the packhorse tracks, the bogs and the rocky fellsides for slowing him down.

The solution was toll roads - turnpikes - built under permits from a government that wanted its army to be able to get to Scotland more easily, and which would be paid for from the tolls paid by merchants transporting wool, ores, wood and charcoal out of Cumberland and Westmorland to help fuel Britain's industrial revolution. The new turnpikes included the road Richard and I were on, linking Kendal and Penrith, and the first stagecoach on the route, 'The Flying Machine', reached the frightening speed of six miles an hour.

More turnpikes followed, such as Kendal to Keswick and on to

Cockermouth, and within fifty years, most Lakeland valleys could be reached by cart and carriage for the first time. These brought the early tourists - the 'lakers' who used small mirrors to frame 'picturesque' views of the beauty and majesty of a quiet Lakeland. Mocked by some even at the time, they were still pioneers of a sort. Until now, Cumberland and Westmorland had been seen as dreadful places, the mountains frightening rather than welcoming: Daniel Defoe in 1726 wrote of Westmorland as, 'the wildest, most barren and frightful of any that I have passed over in England.'

The numbers of visitors arriving by carriage and stagecoach increased even more with the presence in Lakeland of the great poets, Wordsworth, Coleridge, Southey and De Quincey in the early 19th century. They became an attraction in their own right and changed the perception of Lakeland to that of a place of romantic beauty, finally accessible to the traveller.

Our A6 turnpike hugged the right-hand side of the valley wall, rising towards the ridge. Very few parts of the route had been over-steep, despite the overall height: they clearly knew how to build turnpikes.

We were looking down on the valley on our left, and for some way we could see a farm lane below, whitewashed and lonely in a long, long cut in the mountains.

"Long way to go for a cup of sugar," I said.

A thin drizzle came on, and if truth be told, it was a little bleak. The fields were tussocky and boggy on either side, with black-faced sheep munching away at unappetising-looking grass, and dry-stone walls chasing straight-lined over fells and hillsides. These fell walls would not be as ancient as those in the valleys, no matter how they looked. In the 19th century landowners began asserting ownership rights on common land by ordering the building of walls.

You can often see the difference: ancient valley-floor walls looping and curving around tiny fields, and seemingly intended to clear the land of rock, while the newer walls were built straight and true, marching up fellsides. Presumably they looked sensible on a map of ownership, but on the fellside itself, they can seem mad.

Most of high Lakeland still is common land, with the commoners - the hill farmers - having the right to graze their sheep beyond the intake walls on fellsides high above the valley floors. The farmers don't usually own the land, but their rights are ancient.

We reached the top in a blustery rain, fortunately coming from behind us. We knew it was the top, because in a lay-by on the other side of the road there was a stone obelisk with a plaque: 'This memorial pays tribute to the drivers and crews of vehicles that made possible the social and commercial links between north and south on this old and difficult route over Shap Fell before the opening of the M6 motorway. Remembered too are those who built and maintained the road and the generations of local people who gave freely of food and shelter to stranded travellers in bad weather.' It made you think: here we were on a July day, in damp weather; how would it have been for a traveller in the depths of winter, perhaps with snow on the ground and fog all around, and his vehicle breaking down? Not good, I thought.

Still, it was our first proper pass at 1,350 feet above sea level, and even if it didn't appear in '100 Greatest Cycling Climbs', it felt like a first stage had been accomplished. Tomorrow would be the Kirkstone Pass though, and that might be a very different task indeed.

From the top, the view across to the Pennines in the east was surprisingly undramatic. No sudden drop from the heights of Shap Summit, but rather moorland scenery stretching into a soggy distance, with a bank of cloud settled over the line of mountains.

On the west side, electricity pylons lent an un-Lakeland look to the domed hills, again a scene the Tourist Board will probably miss out of next year's calendar.

We zipped up zips and toggled toggles. It might be chilly on the way down.

"On?" I said.

We pushed off, and now it was downhill, pace increasing, wind, rain and spray in our faces. Richard led us down from the top of the pass. I slip-streamed along behind him, occasionally needing to touch the brakes as my momentum, without wind resistance, threatened to take me into the back of him. We reached 32 miles an hour with barely a pedal, much slower than a Tour de France racer of course, but feeling good. A reward for the climbing, and a pretty good way to tick off the furthest eastern boundary of the National Park as part of The Challenge.

We passed forestry and quarries, used and disused. Shap Pink Quarry was a great scar of granite beyond a rusting gate, and did indeed seem to have a pink tinge, but Shap Blue Quarry was out of sight, so I can't report the accuracy of the name.

We began running parallel to the West Coast rail line, with Shap Summit the legendary highest point of a railway line in Britain.

It was the railways in the middle of the century that changed the scale of tourism. Trains had come as far as Kendal and Windermere in the south, Penrith and Shap in the east, Keswick and Cockermouth in the north, and right around the coast of Cumberland and Furness.

Wordsworth, and Ruskin after him, wanted no more, and both campaigned to prevent more railways through the centre of Lakeland.

Even so, from a time when even carts and carriages could not make their way to the lakes at all, by the 1880s a quarter of a million people a year were getting off at Keswick station alone. The focus of Lakeland had changed from the pastoral and the mineral to tourism: visitors to the towns and fell-walkers coming specifically to walk Lakeland's mountains.

Just as that thought came to me, we pedalled past one of the exceptions - a set of large industrial towers on our right disgorging steam into a sky with more than enough water in it already. Shapfell Lime Works, just outside the National Park boundary, uses limestone from the local quarry to produce lime for the steel industry, and the constantly steaming towers are a landmark to drivers on the M6 a few hundred yards from where Richard and I were cycling.

It had been a very quick downhill ride from the top, and it seemed a matter of minutes before we had arrived at the town of Shap, just outside the National Park border.

"Rich," I said, "that's twenty miles. A break would be good, do you think?"

"What sort of a break? Café or just a bench and biscuit?"

I realised that the rain had stopped.

"Bench and biscuit would do me."

So we didn't stop at the pub on the edge of town, but pedalled on down the long and dead-straight main road that mostly constitutes Shap. The town had plenty of amenities, even an outdoor (heated) swimming pool. It doesn't any longer have a railway station, despite the trains thundering through not so far from the town. But there was a bench from which - we soon found - we could observe the very particular type of tourist who comes regularly through Shap.

A bandy-legged walker approached along the pavement, maybe in his sixties, with a long cagoule, a medium-sized rucksack, and two walking poles. He shuffled past, rather than strode, head down.

One muesli bar later, there was a couple approaching down the pavement. Two walking poles each. Rucksacks. Bandy legs. Well, the man anyway.

I had to ask.

"Excuse me," I said. "Are you walking far?"

They stopped, but there was something about the stopping that said, 'I may have trouble starting again.'

The lady said in an Australian accent, "We're walking the Coast to Coast."

"Oh, of course." I had forgotten that the Coast to Coast Walk, from St Bees on the Cumbrian coast to Robin Hood's Bay in North Yorkshire, would cross our own route just here. "How has it been?" I asked.

"The weather has been awful," she said.

"Ah, yes, I suppose it has. But have you been enjoying it?"

The man spoke for the first time. Another Australian accent. "Put it this way," he said. "We've been walking for seven days and in all that time, we've seen less than fifteen minutes sunshine."

Seven days. That would have included the previous Thursday, when the Lake District had torrential rain for hours, 'Thunder Thursday' as the weather-forecasters had dubbed it.

"Right, yes. Well, it's stopped raining now," I said, trying to add some cheerfulness to the deep depression forming overhead.

"Huh."

He walked on. Maybe the rain was our fault. Could easily be.

The lady watched him go for a moment, then said, "It's been OK really. Just, well, wet. Better press on. You're cycling? Going far?"

"A tour of the Lake District," I said.

"Well, stay dry."

190 miles on foot, starting at St Bees on the Irish Sea, up and over the hills of the Lake District, the Pennines and North Yorkshire, finishing at Robin Hood's Bay on the North Sea. A route designed by Alfred Wainwright, crossing some of the most spectacular of England's landscapes. And quite a challenge, I thought.

We finished snacking and drinking, and cycled up the road, coming to our turn-off towards Haweswater and our almost inevitable sighting of the golden eagle.

At the end of a lane was a small crossroads, with two lady walkers consulting a map.

They looked up as we approached, and one said, in an American accent, "Is that Shap down there?"

"It is. And it has shops and pubs."

She smiled. "Oh, good. Just what we need."

"I assume you're on the Coast to Coast?"

"We are."

"So you would have been walking last Thursday in those torrential downpours?"

"Yes. Up on the tops. Lightening and everything." She smiled again. "A pub, you said?"

"Yes."

They headed off into town, the sun peering out from behind clouds and sprinkling light on the wild flowers lining the verges of the lane. Pinks, yellows and whites, against green and stone. It was a picture.

"I hope the sun's shining on the Australians," I said. I suspected it was not.

I consulted our own map. "It's surely too far for them to have walked from Patterdale today. I suppose they could have stopped at the Haweswater Hotel last night."

"They've still come quite a long way from St Bees."

"Explains the bandy legs. The men, I mean. And I think I understand that guy. Imagine all that rain, that far walked and so much more to walk to Robin Hood's Bay."

"The ladies were OK."

"Sterner stuff."

I ignored the signpost for Shap Abbey. It was a ruin, thanks to the Reformation and Henry VIII. I suspected it might be a disappointment after the beauties of Cartmel the day before.

A lane took us along to the top of a turn-off that should have dropped us down into the valley and along to the hamlet of Bampton Grange, back inside the National Park. A tractor was making a meal of reversing up the road as two cars came up, so we edged around it, and headed along the top road, which would get us there as well. More cars appeared. And more.

"This Bampton Grange," Richard said. "Is it big?"

"Well, no."

"So where are all the cars coming from?"

"There's Bampton as well down there. Could be a real metropolis."

It seemed unlikely from the map, but it was a theory.

The view from the top road, when we weren't avoiding approaching cars, was tremendous. We seemed to be in limestone country, and ahead of us was what I took to be a limestone scarp, a plateau with a short, sharp cliff and a long green slope down to the valley floor. In the valley bottom would be the mighty conurbation of Bampton Grange and Bampton, while across the valley, way off to the left, we could just make out Haweswater's dam wall set into the more rounded fells of Lakeland proper.

Bampton Grange and Bampton turned out not to be a conurbation. Bampton Grange was a tiny hamlet nestling in the valley of the River Lowther, with the white-painted Crown and Mitre coaching inn looking very tempting.

I guessed that like Grange-Over-Sands for Cartmel Priory, Bampton Grange was originally the grain store for the White Canons at Shap Abbey. Anyway, it was very pretty, and had absolutely no sign of any people. Clearly they had all driven up out of the village just as we were arriving.

Word gets around.

We pedalled across the bridge, and then climbed gently through woods and fields, popping out almost unexpectedly right at the Haweswater dam. A long concrete wall disappeared off towards the far shore, melting into a grassy and wooded ridge topped with

73

domes of rock. On the left of the surprisingly thin top to the dam, the dark and uncomforting water was very close to its rim, ruffled and pock-marked as the wind blew down the valley carrying threats of rain to come.

The reservoir was opened in 1935, built after it became clear that the Victorians' Thirlmere Reservoir, with its pipeline to Manchester, was not going to be enough. Haweswater now supplies about a quarter of the water used in North West England. The price was the dismantling and flooding of the village in the peaceful Mardale valley - church, pub, farms and homes.

Looking along the length of the dam, and up the valley, the reservoir seemed so big. Bigger than I had expected. I had seen it on the map, but not really taken in that the expanse of water was nearly half mile wide. When the reservoir is full, the remains of the villages are under nearly 100 foot of water, and the reservoir runs four miles back up the valley. By comparison, that thin wall of concrete seemed inappropriate for holding back such a vast volume of water.

I spoke my thoughts to Richard.

He pondered and said, "I wonder if the people who live in the valley worry about that at all?"

"I don't know. I suppose they've grown up with it."

The length of the reservoir was about to test me. I had sort of expected the road alongside to be flat.

The road was not flat.

We overtook a puffing lady cyclist part way to the hotel, and her partner, puffing less, a couple of hundred yards ahead, and exchanged hellos with both.

Two miles from the dam wall we came to the Haweswater Hotel, and it was very tempting. A sign showed a Gastro Pub while another sign showed burgers and fry-ups. The two seemed a bit incompatible.

"Perhaps they have two eateries," I said. "The Gastro Pub and the burger-and-chips café for wet walkers, bird-watchers and cyclists."

"I could do a burger."

"The thing is, will the weather get better or worse? If we're going to cycle to the far end and spot the golden eagle, do we go now in the drizzle, or afterwards and take a chance on either rain or no rain?"

"How about getting to the end first, then we can dry off inside if we need to?"

"Good plan. Golden eagle, then burger and chips in the bit of the Haweswater Hotel that isn't the Gastro Pub. They might not let us in a Gastro Pub in our state."

The road dipped towards the shoreline and rose again, all the time with a stone wall on our right, beyond which we could see across the width of the water to ridges of grass and heather, rising to rocky tops. Ahead of us, the fells were higher, their tops cut off by cloud. Somewhere up there was Harter Fell and also High Street, a mountain named after the Roman road that ran its length.

It was extraordinary to think that the best route for the Roman legions from their base near Penrith to their fort at Ambleside took in a fell-top ridge, rather than a valley route. I had once walked up on to High Street from this car park with a friend who was a policeman and a group of his police colleagues. It had been a sunny day and, after we had eaten our sandwiches at the top, they had started to lie down, settling their packs as pillows, and closing their eyes.

I must have looked bemused, because my friend said, "We always have a sleep after lunch when we're out walking."

And they did.

For half an hour I had sat taking in long, sun-drenched views of the eastern fells, contemplating that I had around me a group of sleeping policemen on Lakeland's High Street.

Richard and I stopped at a high point on the shore road. A wooded promontory from the far side prodded out into the reservoir, and just off it, a small island poked out of the water. Directly opposite us, a rocky valley dropped down to shore level.

"I think," I said to Richard, "that the valley over there is the one with the golden eagle nest."

There has been a golden eagle presence in Riggindale valley since 1967. To begin with, the RSPB guarded the site and kept it secret to prevent attempts to steal eggs. More recently there had only been wardens stationed at a hide through the spring and summer to help visitors see the beautiful bird. The current male eagle (number three) had not had a partner for a few years, so there were no eggs to steal. That also meant that there had been no young since 1996.

I'd have liked to see him really, but with my naturalist skills, I had low expectations.

"It's also been known to fly across the reservoir here, according to a bird-watching blog I found."

We both peered.

"I can't see it."

A large black bird flew diagonally across the lake, close above the water.

"Could be a black eagle." I said. "A new species."

"What about that flock of birds on the water near the island? Honking like Canada geese. Rare Canada eagles?"

"Could quite easily be."

We coasted downhill, and pedalled into what was becoming proper rain, pulling to a halt at the end of the lake. A half dozen cars were parked in the car park, with no sign of occupants. Presumably they had either walked around to the RSPB hide to try to catch a glimpse of the golden eagle, or they were walkers heading up to Harter Fell or High Street no matter what the weather.

"Do you want to walk round to the hide?" Richard asked.

I weighed up the chances of us seeing what the online bloggers had seen, a raven mobbing the eagle, or even just the daddy of raptors perched on a boulder, against the higher likelihood of burger and chips in a warm café. The rain came on that bit more.

"Or else we could go on a hunt for burger and chips."

There was a really good painting of a golden eagle on the notice board - a fearsome creature with compelling amber eyes, a hooked beak and brown plumage with a hint of gold at the neck.

I took a photo. It was a bit raindrop-spattered, but I could probably Photoshop the drops out.

"Burger?"

We started back up the slope from the car park, and the cyclist couple came down the other way. He was still a couple of hundred yards ahead.

The cycle back to the Haweswater Hotel involved some more hills, but whether it was the wind behind us or the food ahead of us, they didn't seem as high, and we were pedalling up the driveway very, very soon.

"Hey," Richard said, as we parked our bikes by the door, "look."

A red squirrel was wandering about the little garden, tail up, nose sniffing, as he scampered from one smell to the next, before sitting on his haunches to look at us, and turning back to scamper off the other way.

Fantastic.

I love red squirrels, though they are not rare where I live. Families of them live in the cemetery, and the main worry is that the greys are getting steadily closer, and their squirrel-pox might kill off our gorgeous locals.

We approached the hotel's front door, and it did look slightly more Gastro Pub than burger-and-chips. I took off my overshoes, and realised that while the parts of my bare legs that had been under the overshoes were quite clean, above that I was filthy. Really filthy. I looked at Richard's legs. So were his. In fact we were both so impressively dirty at shin and knee level, that we spent several minutes photographing our legs.

Well, we thought it was funny.

It's not impossible that our photographic session was being watched, because as we dripped our way into a quite-grand hallway, we were met by a young man.

"Do you," I asked, "have a café? Burgers. Chips. And so on."

"We have a bar."

"And are you doing food?"

His eyes seemed to flick to my legs. "We are not serving for another half an hour."

This was disappointing. Having failed to spot a golden eagle, spotting a burger and chips at a place that seemed to advertise them on the outside had not seemed too hard.

"We have scones," the young man said, and almost instantly regretted it.

"Ooh. Scones. Yes please. And jam. And tea."

We sat in the Gastro Pub, the only guests. It was really very smart, except for the corner where our coats were dripping from the backs of chairs and where our mud-spattered shins were only partly hidden under a table. Tea came in a proper china tea-pot, with matching cups, saucers, sugar bowl and milk jug. We felt a little out of place, but the scones and tea were good, and if it weren't for two wet and muddy cyclists dripping away in a corner, the Gastro Pub was very nice.

Fifteen minutes later, we saw the cycling couple come past the window, and overheard a conversation in the hallway.

"Are you doing food?"

Pause. The look at the legs, I thought.

"We are not serving for another half an hour."

I called through. "They've got scones."

"Ooh, scones. Two scones please."

Ah, cyclists.

We dropped down from the reservoir, this time heading north, and arrived in Bampton, another pretty and quiet village. Like Bampton Grange, there was probably not a large enough population to explain all the cars heading out of the villages.

They were due to have a Sports Day, a notice board announced.

"Must be huge rivalry with Bampton Grange," Richard said.

The day had dried up again, and the cycling was fun, the lane dodging past fields and small copses, hills on our left, and the surprisingly flat valley of the River Lowther on our right.

Through the village of Helton, and then into Askham, which was wonderful. It seemed a village as they were in days gone by, with two pubs, a shop, a church, and another open-air heated swimming pool.

At a crossroads, a left turn would have taken us up on to Askham Fell where wild horses live. Not small ponies, but grand beasts, capable of standing Lakeland's winter with a little feeding from the friendly locals.

Our road dropped down the other way, with wide stretches of grass on either side, and beyond these the most lovely houses. All were old, though varying hugely. Some stone, others with white-washed plaster, one with a columned porch to the front door. We passed a sign for Askham Hall Gardens. Askham Hall was the home of the Lowther family, formerly of Lowther Castle, where we were heading.

If it had not been for a sudden heavy shower, I would have loved it in Askham.

"Come on," I said. "We can shelter in the café at the castle."

We put on a spurt, down over a bridge, under trees, and then out and up through the gates of a stately home that at one time was the stately home of stately homes. It was a long driveway, twisting through parkland, and climbing, until we finally had a view across to Lowther Castle itself.

Built in the early 19th century at the height of the Lowther family's wealth, it was abandoned more or less as Haweswater was completed, at a time when the Lake District was metamorphosing.

The Lowthers, the Stricklands at Sizergh, the Curwens in West Cumbria, the Cavendishes at Holker Hall and other great families had owned great swathes of Cumberland, Westmorland and Lancashire North of the Sands. The Lowthers in particular were immensely wealthy. A castle here had been the home of the Lowther family for centuries, with footnotes relating to Edward 1 and to Mary Queen of Scots. They owned the coal mines of West Cumbria, and had built the port of Whitehaven to export the coal to Ireland.

In the early 1800s the Lowther Earl of Lonsdale built an enormous gothic mansion - Lowther Castle. Towers, ball room, picture gallery and glorious gardens.

But by the end of the century, the spending out-ran the income. Especially the spending of the 'Yellow Earl'. Spanning the 19th and 20th centuries, he threw massive parties, bringing in his guests using his fleet of yellow cars, to be met by his servants in their yellow livery, and the Earl himself, dressed in yellow.

You're spotting a theme.

He was a founder of the AA (hence their yellow vans), Chairman of Arsenal Football Club (hence their yellow away strip), and donor of the Lonsdale belt for amateur boxing (I guess the boxers rebelled against it being yellow…).

Meanwhile, the sheep and the ores of Cumberland and Westmorland were no longer providing the income that the land-owning families had become used to. Mines had closed as ores dried up or became too expensive to dig, and the coarse wool of the sheep that would survive a Lake District winter was not fine enough for a changing world.

Under the Yellow Earl, the Lowther family fortune was decimated, just as the institutions and the nouveaux-riches were taking over Lakeland. Manchester Corporation had built Thirlmere and now Haweswater, and bought up the surrounding fellsides to ensure the water stayed clean. The Forestry Commission was also buying land and planting the conifers needed to make pit props, or that an army might need as trench posts for any repeat of the First World War's more deadly scenarios.

Meanwhile, the trains were bringing the wealthy of Lancashire north to build mock castles and stately homes, and the hoteliers were coming into the towns with an eye on the massive number of visitors. The National Trust, by this time, was fighting a rearguard action, also buying property, but trying to preserve rather than alter.

The old landed families changed with the times or capitulated.

The Lowthers moved out of the grand castle. Tanks trained in the grounds in the Second World War, and in the 1950s the roof was taken off. Gradually the house fell into ruin, with trees and shrubs growing from towers, and floors and staircases collapsing. The grounds turned to jungle - or at least that part that was not covered with chicken sheds.

We pedalled down the large concrete slabs that made up the car park, thinking that they were probably linked to the Second World War tanks, then pushed our bikes through a gateway into the old stable yard.

It had been transformed. The stable blocks on each side had been, or were in process of being, renovated. Directly ahead, behind glass walls, was yet another source of tea and cakes. Lowther Castle's brand new café had huge slabs of cake, baked in their own kitchen, with tables behind those glass walls allowing us to look out on the work going on to stop the castle collapsing altogether.

"You know," Richard said, "I went spinning for the first time the other day. It was exhausting, and they didn't even stop for cappuccino and cake."

"Shocking," I said.

Afterwards we had the quickest of looks in an exhibition of

photos of how the garden had been in its jungle state, and the work being done to return it to some of its former splendour. We also chatted to the lady at the gate through to the gardens, a jolly lady, pleased to talk about the gardens and the progress they were making. Placed in a Trust, the castle and gardens were being renovated for public access by grants and donations, and by volunteer help. Richard and I had cycled there early in the process, and it could be a long job.

The Yellow Earl's successors have been making up for his excesses, and they are still the largest private landowners in the Lake District. Clearly they have the commercial touch that the Yellow Earl did not.

With the day turned dry again, we cycled out past the estate houses and offices for the Lowther Estate, and then it was a straightforward ride into Penrith, coasting down a long straight drive to the A6, and turning north. The A6 zigzagged past a pele tower and Norman church at Clifton and on to Eamont Bridge, with its prehistoric earthworks and its welcome sign telling us that the last battle on English soil had been fought there in 1745. Much of the village, trailing alongside the old turnpike road, seemed old: thick-walled houses and cottages, and the single-file stone bridge itself. The road was busy here, but then it was five o'clock on a Monday, and we were heading into Penrith.

We had cycled over forty miles, and I was tired. Then again, maybe it was all the cake and scones.

After Yellow Earls, tiny perfect villages and golden eagles, the outskirts of Penrith catapulted us back into the 21st century. We crossed a dual carriage-way at a traffic-light controlled round-about, then cycled into town along with queues of traffic, passing DIY stores and supermarkets. The town centre was not modern though, and we pulled off the road by a clock tower, which the traffic flowed around.

I needed a bank, and we were surrounded by them, deciding which was the poshest building. HSBC came an honourable second, with magnificent arched windows and a sort of a bell tower. But in first place we named Barclays, built in the local pinky-brown sandstone - as was much of the town - with mock-Elizabethan windows and copper-sheathed little spires on the roof.

The pinky-brown sandstone was everywhere in Penrith. Not just the banks, but houses and the shops. My favourite building was that of James and John Graham, Family Grocers, four storeys of sandstone built to supply the Victorian farmers of the Eden Valley with 'agricultural seed cake and manure', but today a delicatessen with stock including Penrith fudge and Cartmel sticky toffee pudding. My sort of shop.

We pedalled uphill from the Victorian town centre along the Corn Market, past the Market Cross with its round slate roof supported on a dozen wooden posts, and then up again past the sandstone ruins of Penrith's grand castle, and out of town on the Greystoke road.

We crossed a bridge over the M6, the main route to the Lake District from the rest of the country of course, rather than the railways; the Penrith to Keswick railway line was closed in 1972, a decision which nowadays seems perverse.

Of the sixteen million tourists visiting the Lake District every year, the vast majority will arrive either by the motorway exit here at Penrith or by its sister at Kendal. As a result, traffic in the summer in Lakeland is a real issue for the local councils and the Lake District National Park Authority.

The Park, founded in 1951, was intended to protect the landscape and beauty of the fells and valleys, and to promote recreational usage. The founding was part of a grander movement over the previous decades led by groups like the Ramblers Association and the Youth Hostel Association. Those seekers of the solitude of the fells might well look at that phrase about promoting recreational usage and think, 'Be careful what you wish for' if they could see, in the 21st century, the long queues of cars through central Lakeland on sunny summer weekends.

The 21st century. In our first three days it seemed that we had ridden through a potted history of Lakeland. Romans, Vikings, monks and yeoman farmers; turnpikes, railways and motorways; the National Trust and the National Park. Over the next six days, it would be good to fill in the gaps.

Richard and I were to stay that night at the small - and quiet - village of Motherby, and from there it would be the shortest of cycle rides back over the border into the National Park.

As we cycled into a drizzle, Motherby didn't seem to be getting any closer. The road rose and fell through farmland, not steeply, but enough.

"You alright?" Richard asked.

"Well," I said, "I'd quite like to be there now. But I'll be OK if you don't mind going at my speed."

My speed by now was slow.

"No. That's fine."

After a long four miles we were cycling past Fort Puttnam, one of three 'folly farms' built in the 18th century by the Duke of Norfolk who owned Greystoke Castle. This one was quite clear from the road, with its mock battlements. Just a bit strange for a farm, but perhaps the Duke was a bit strange.

Greystoke itself seemed to be a lovely little village. The green had a large church and a shop on one side, a pub on another side, plus a cycle café and the entrance gates to Greystoke Castle.

Greystoke Castle had been built and destroyed and re-built over time. The Howard family - here for fourteen generations - don't open their grand home to the public, but do have weddings and other major events. The most well-known person related to Greystoke Castle though was fictional: Tarzan was the son of Viscount Greystoke in Edgar Rice Burroughs's Tarzan books.

And so up the hill to Motherby.

My friends, Dave and Jacquie, had a guest house there, and were more than used to cyclists. After all, the most popular long-distance cycle route in Britain runs very close to Motherby: the 'Sea To Sea' or 'C2C'. The Sustrans route runs 136 miles from the Cumbrian coast at either Whitehaven or Workington to the North Sea at either Sunderland or Tynemouth. Thousands cycle it every year, and a common end to Day 1 is the Greystoke area, including Dave and Jacquie's excellent guest house.

By the time Richard and I turned into their yard, we had cycled 54 miles, and my legs could feel them. I was tired and muddy and wet. Jacquie looked me up and down and diagnosed tea and home-made fruitcake. We probably hadn't had enough cake that day.

Once we were clean we walked the mile to the pub at Penruddock. Over food and a pint of Jennings Cocker Hoop, we talked about the Mountain Rescue Service. Dave and Jacquie had been in the Patterdale Mountain Rescue for thirty years, with Dave as leader for much of that time. They will have helped countless people from the fells in that time, some lost and some hurt. And not just people.

"I remember you telling me about the bull rescued from a ravine by RAF helicopter, the beast in a harness swinging out over Ullswater."

"We had another animal rescue as good: herding cows out of a river using kayaks. Though I'm not sure health and safety rules would allow that now."

Human call-outs had been increasing as walkers with mobile phones and sat-nav devices realised too late that a map and compass, plus a knowledge of how to use them, might have been a good idea. But this year, call-outs were down, because visitor numbers in the Lake District generally were low.

Partly it was the recession, partly it was the weather: the whole country had had a wet summer, hardly encouraging tourists to have a UK holiday, and in particular, to come to the Lake District.

"It's not the people who booked a long time ago," Jacquie said. "They've still come to the Lakes. It's the last minute bookings that haven't materialised. The campsites and hotels are quiet. Everywhere is quiet. So there are fewer walkers on the fells, and fewer call-outs."

As if to prove it, there were no other visitors staying with Jacquie and Dave that night, though the following day was different.

"A group of C2C cyclists," Jacquie said. "We'll be full."

Well, we'd left them a little of the home-made fruitcake.

Back at the guest house, I sat in bed and wrote up the day's details:

Distance for the day: 54 miles / 86.4 Km
Height gained: 5,768 feet / 1,731 metres
Hardest hill: Shap Summit 1,148 feet / 350 metres
Average speed: 11.7 mph / 18.7 Kmph
Fastest speed: 32 mph / 51.2 Kmph
Total distance: 133 miles / 214 Km

It had been a quicker day, but tomorrow would be more of a challenge.

I put my light out, thinking about the route. The Kirkstone Pass, a 7/10 in '100 Greatest Cycling Climbs', plus poets and bears.

"Tomorrow, Rich," I said. "we're going on a bear hunt."

"Are we going to catch a big one?"

DAY FOUR - METHERA

POETRY CORNER

Motherby – Dacre – Pooley Bridge – Aira Force – Glenridding
Patterdale – Kirkstone Pass – Ambleside – Chapel Stile
Great Langdale – Grasmere – Rydal – Grasmere

44 miles

www.lakedistrictgrandtour.co.uk/day/four

The plan today was only partly to go on a bear hunt. This was also going to be Poet's Day.

We would cycle alongside Ullswater, then up and over Kirkstone Pass, dropping into Ambleside, and out into Great Langdale. Then another up and over to Wordsworth's Grasmere.

Bears were going to be first though, in the churchyard of the small village of Dacre, tucked away in the north-easterly corner of the National Park.

"What do you mean by bears?" Richard asked.

"Well, I'm not really sure. Best to see them and then make up our minds. If they are bears or not, I mean."

"Bears. In the Lake District?"

"Exactly."

We said our goodbyes to Dave and Jacquie, and our thanks for man-sized cooked breakfasts, and set off down the hill towards Penruddock in, perhaps surprisingly, sunshine. There were meadows either side, and at the bottom of the hill, a tiny stream trickling under the road, the Petteril, close to the start of its wiggly journey to join the river Eden in Carlisle.

"I used to work in Motherby," I said to Richard, "and my business partner used to call that 'The Mighty Petteril'."

Richard looked at the little beck.

"Right," he said.

"And we once liberated a bucket full of frogs in The Mighty Petteril when our neighbours filled in their pond."

"I hadn't realised till now how into animal liberation you are."

I raised a fist. "Free Willy." I said.

Beyond little Penruddock, we were confronted by the busy A66 taking traffic to and from Keswick and the west coast of Cumbria. It took a few minutes to get safely over as streams of cars, caravans and lorries drove past, but once over, we were into a network of country lanes. It was very lovely: sun shining, no crowds, no cars, relatively flat cycling, occasional farms and cottages, and hedges with dog roses and honeysuckle bound into them.

There was a possibility I would get us lost, as the map didn't seem to tally with the lanes, and although we began to come across signs for Dacre, the village didn't seem to be getting any closer.

Until suddenly we were in Dacre, where there were wonderful old stone houses, a whitewashed 18th century inn with narrow, little windows, and a lane leading to where the bears should be - the church, or at least the churchyard.

We parked our bikes in the lane, and I told Richard what I had found out about the Dacre bears on the internet.

Dacre, I had read, has four stone effigies in the churchyard, one in each corner of the original churchyard. They are ancient, and nobody yet seems to have come up with an explanation. In the 19th century the vicar decided that the four carvings were bears. The first shows the bear asleep with his head on a pillar. The second shows the bear with a small cat or a lynx having jumped on its back. The third has the bear struggling to shake off the cat. While the fourth has the bear with a smile on its face, having eaten the cat.

Inside the gate, the first bear, about three foot high, was obvious on our left. Obvious in the sense that there was a carving, not that it was a bear. The second was to the right, and this one was definitely a creature of some sort.

"What do you reckon, Rich? Bears?"

A voice came from the gate. A man was leaning on it.

"There's a theory," he said, "that they're lions. Roman lions. Or even before that. Not bears at all."

"You're from here?"

"Aye. Saw you cycle up. Where're you from?"

"Cockermouth."

"Cockermouth? I always think you're a bit cut off in Cockermouth."

Richard and I exchanged a look. Dacre didn't seem to be the epicentre of excitement, but there you are.

"So," I said, "do you think they're bears or lions?"

He shrugged. "You can see better with t'other two on far side of church."

We walked around the church, with a glimpse through trees to Dacre Castle, another pele tower, and a twin of one that is part of Dalemain House half a mile away. This must have been a vulnerable area to Scottish raids.

We found the next bear / lion, and this did clearly have a cat or some small creature on its shoulder, while with the other effigy you could make out a face better. This one might also have had a tail.

"They don't look like lions or bears to me," Richard said. "More like sloths."

"Sloths! A new theory. I like that one."

The inside of the church was wonderful and clearly much loved, both by the locals and by visitors on a bear hunt. I could see why: it had a Norman tower, 13th century stone arches, and a carved knight on a tomb, plus wall-plaques dedicated to the parish's gentry over centuries, particularly the Hasell family of Dalemain House and Dacre Castle. There had been a monastery here in Anglian times as well, and there were the remains of Viking crosses, including a stone carving of Adam and Eve.

Not everything was ancient though. An intricately etched window by Sir Lawrence Whistler illustrated a view over Dalemain House and towards Ullswater, just a few miles beyond. I also liked the colourful, stained glass window in honour of politician Willie Whitelaw - Margaret Thatcher's 'everybody needs a Willie'.

In fact, the church had such a long history that the bears / lions could really have come from any period. I picked up leaflets to read later, and we left, really with no more clue than the 19th century vicar and his bears theory. Unless of course they were sloths.

We pedalled out of the village, swinging around the lanes, until a hill with a warning sign: 12%. I slowed to climbing mode.

"I might save myself for Kirkstone Pass," I said.

Richard pulled ahead.

He was waiting at the top.

"Look," he said, and gestured to the warning sign pointing back the other way: 8%.

"Hah. So hills really are steeper going up than down."

We pulled on to the long main road leading from Penrith down to Ullswater. As we dropped, glimpses of mountains began to appear between the rolling green hills more close at hand, and then we turned a corner and the lake appeared. There was no blue sky above, so no blue lake, but steel grey water stretching away to the right, beneath the rounded ends of green ridges on the far side.

"Left here, Rich, and we can nip into Pooley Bridge."

The road followed the lakeshore, woods on the left, water on the right, past the jetty and ticket office for the lake steamer. A small group of tourists waited for the next steamer, either to take them to Howtown on the south side for a walk along the lake's edge, or to Glenridding near the far end of Ullswater, where we were heading.

Pooley Bridge seemed to be just waking up for the day, with a handful of tourists looking at the Millennium Fish in the square - a flash of silver from a leaping fish on a pink-red sandstone monument, or picking out postcards from outside the gift shops. It was a pretty little square, and we circled and headed back along the lake road.

Ullswater, seven and a half miles long, is second only to Windermere in length, and some say the most beautiful of the lakes, though there is plenty of competition for that accolade. Wordsworth called it 'the happiest combination of beauty and grandeur, that any of the Lakes affords.'

Woodrow Wilson, before he became President of the USA in 1912, had several cycle tours of the Lake District and made life-long friends here. In 1899 he wrote that the road alongside Ullswater 'must surely be the most beautiful road in the world.' Once I had completed this ride, I thought, I might be clearer on that in my own mind.

Certainly, when early versions of tourists came to the Lake District in the 18th century, Ullswater was one of the great draws. Some didn't come for the peace and quiet, though. Some came for the cannons. Out there on the lake was apparently the perfect spot for echoes, so a mini tourist boom developed, with locals taking visitors out on boats to fire cannons and to marvel at the echoes bouncing around the fells.

I wondered what the Lake District National Park Planning Board would make of that nowadays.

We rejoined the main road along the lakeshore, but it wasn't busy, and there was room for the occasional car to skirt us.

Hotels with glorious views across the lake were sprinkled along the road or down by the lakeside, some of them grand buildings, some older inns. We pulled in outside The Brackenrigg Inn at the top of an incline to take in the view properly without having to worry about cars. Directly across the lake a marina of white sailing boats rocked on the water with, behind it, the green humpback of Barton Fell. The Sharrow Bay hotel and restaurant was in one of the inlets there - one of the modern gourmet tourist's destinations of choice.

Looking further down the lake, the fells began to coalesce darker against the sky, and beyond lower hills was the Helvellyn range, high and graceful.

"Fantastic," I said to Richard, and it would be hard to disagree.

The road dropped back down to the lakeside through Watermillock, and the land rose steadily on our right as we came under the hill of Gowbarrow Park. From Gowbarrow, the views across Ullswater were even more stunning than our roadside views. Gowbarrow is National Trust owned, and was the backdrop to our next stop, perhaps the most renowned waterfall of Lakeland.

We pulled into the Aira Force car park, and locked our bikes to a fence rail. The car park had a good few cars in, with families and couples gathering themselves for the walk up to the falls.

We walked past the National Trust van on the path under the trees, through grassy glades and over a bridge above the rock-filled stream. The path climbed steadily with oak trees and ferns all around, the sound of the racing stream below and a moist, mossy smell to the air. A young family gambolled down past us.

At the viewpoint at the bottom of the falls, a mother and her seven-year-old were taking a photo of themselves, giggling their faces into the phone she was holding, as she tried to capture the white torrent behind as well as the two happy faces in front.

The viewpoint was a moss-covered stone bridge over peat-brown rushing water, with a fine spray coming from the white spume falling fast and high through a gorge into a deep pool. Above the waterfall, another bridge spanned the gap between rocks, but the route was closed, the rain having brought down part of the path to the top.

Back at the bikes, I said, "I enjoyed that."

"Pretty impressive after the rain," Richard replied.

"Hungry now though. Muesli bar before the next stretch?"

"Seems a good idea."

So we munched, and I contemplated the first major pass of the Lake District, a slightly alarming 7/10, and the highest road in Lakeland.

The road followed the lakeshore for a way. To begin with, a few trees and bushes screened the lake and the green hillside of Place Fell on the far side, itself dotted with trees. On our right, thin woodland and bracken ran up to hills above. It was a tremendous route and, when we found we had just a low wall separating us from a view across the water, I wondered if the American President had maybe been right.

We were at Glencoyne Bridge, said to be the spot that had inspired Britain's fifth most loved poem. Spring daffodils somewhere near the lakeshore here had inspired Dorothy Wordsworth's prose description, which in turn is said to have inspired her brother William's poem. Even I - acknowledged poetry philistine - knew it:

> I wander'd lonely as a cloud
> That floats on high o'er vales and hills,
> When all at once I saw a crowd,
> A host of golden daffodils,
> Beside the lake, beneath the trees,
> Fluttering and dancing in the breeze.

Well, I knew the first verse anyway.

Actually, it was good. It rhymed, and I liked rhymes. Like the way A. A. Milne rhymed foxes, boxes and, er, sockses.

We twisted up through trees to the top of a small promontory, where there was a lay-by above the lake.

"Stopping," I called to Richard, and pulled in. The sun was streaming through a copse of oaks, lime-green and fresh, and rippling off the wavelets on the lake. It really was wonderful.

We dropped down lakewards again, rocks and bracken close to

the road, and found ourselves coming into Glenridding. There were houses of dark slate, a grassy area, a car park and visitor centre on the right. On the left, with lawns running down to the shore, was the large and very grand Inn on the Lake, a feature of the valley here, almost as much as the hills around. Beyond a bridge over Glenridding Beck were tourist shops with postcard stands crowding a covered pavement area.

Behind the village we could just make out the Glenridding valley with, on the north side, the rugged Sheffield Pike, while on the south was the ridge that would lead to the classic route up Helvellyn - Striding Edge.

We were in an oasis amongst the rocky wilderness around.

Striding Edge itself was hidden from view, but was one of the main draws for hikers in the Lake District. The breathlessness of the climb, the awe-inspiring views over the teardrop of Red Tarn one thousand feet below, the nervous taking of the 'bad step' as part of the rock-strewn challenge of the ridge, are all talking points each evening in the picture-postcard guest houses and hotels of Glenridding.

Glenridding has not always been a picture-postcard tourist village. Up the valley are scattered remains of quarries and mines. This had been another of Lakeland's mining villages, and Greenside Lead Mine had only finally closed down in the 1960s.

We turned into the lane to the steamer ferry pier, cycling parallel to the beck on its way into the lake.

A slate-roofed ticket office led on to the jetty and, tied up on the far side, was one of the steamers for Howtown and Pooley Bridge, its wide red funnel poking above the white railings of the pier. Passengers were making themselves comfortable on seats under an awning as a union flag billowed in the breeze, and the crew made ready.

A handful of motor and sail boats were tied up on our side of the jetty, and there were kayaks and Canadian canoes bobbing on the water, their occupants in reds and yellows against the dark blue of the lake.

We pedalled back up the lane, where groups of five or six teenagers in brightly coloured cagoules were gathering, their rucksacks of truly Himalayan proportions.

"Duke of Edinburgh?" I said to Richard.

He had done Duke of Edinburgh Award expeditions when he had been at school, and he too recognised the look.

"Definitely," he said.

A short way beyond Glenridding, the lake ran out and Patterdale village began.

There were stone-built houses with their original emphasis on keeping out the weather blowing down from a wintry Kirkstone Pass, a white-painted White Lion Inn, and a post office, but not much more than that. Patterdale had a different feel to Glenridding. Equally little, but somehow more rugged. The start of Kirkstone Pass rather than the end of Ullswater.

The road did not immediately start to climb, but hugged the west side of the valley, a steep fellside on our right. To our left were small fields surrounded by dry-stone walls and with little copses of trees. Beyond was another steep fellside, green and bouldery.

The road switched valley sides to run under Hartsop Dodd, and there was a turn-off signed to the hamlet of Hartsop in a side valley. Then we were cycling past Brothers Water, and the road began to rise. Not steeply, but enough to give us a view over the tarn. The water was dark and still. No fishermen, no kayaks. There were very few cars on the road either. It was all very quiet.

Past Brotherswater Inn and Sykeside Farm with its campsite, the valley began closing in on either side. Still the road was barely climbing, but High Hartsop Dodd on our right and Stoney Cove Pike on our left were narrowing the route through the mountains.

Then it began, with the road now at an angle to make me change gear and say to Richard, "You can get the teas in at the top."

"You're on," he said, and he began putting distance between us rather faster than I had hoped, but not, I should say, feared.

In bottom gear, I persevered. Kirkstone wasn't the steepest I had cycled up, I decided, but it did go on a long way: 5.3 Km according to '100 Greatest Cycling Climbs', with the last kilometre 'where things start to get serious'.

Beyond dry-stone walls on either side, the grass became less, the rocks and boulders more. A sheep followed my progress, with eyes that had seen it all, though probably quicker.

My legs became tired just as the road became steeper. Thoughts came into my head of the gear in my panniers, and I began to consider what I should perhaps have left out.

A family came walking down the road - father, mother and two young teenagers. "You're doing great," an American accent said.

"Thanks. Did you see... a much younger... and fitter... version of me... up ahead."

"Yup. I think you're catching him."

Actually, it was starting to get quite hard now, but American observers and what might possibly be the top ahead of me, gave me impetus. "Dig deep," I said to myself. "Dig... deep."

It wasn't the top, and then there was another top that wasn't, and another.

Finally the slope began to lessen, and the pressure on my muscles began to ease. I was going to make it without stopping. A last push, past the big boulder - the steeple-shaped Kirk Stone - the road now flattening, and there was the Kirkstone Pass Inn, all whitewashed stone and slate roof, with car park and picnic tables on the opposite side of the road.

Lying on the ground was a bike stacked with two reasonably substantial rear panniers, while Richard lounged at one of the tables.

"You made it!" he said.

I eased alongside him and got off.

"I did," I said. "And without stopping, amazingly."

I was pleased. A 7/10 and the highest pass under my belt. Though I suspected nowhere near as hard to cycle as some to come.

"Fantastic."

"Hey, where's the tea then?"

"Ian's getting it."

"Ian?"

"Ian."

Ian was a friend who I had left my itinerary with, and who I only now recalled had said he might go for a run here and try to time it with us getting to the Kirkstone Pass Inn.

"As I got to the top," Richard said, "Ian was just running down off the fell."

"Wow."

And here he was, appearing with a tray of teas.

"How did you manage that?"

Ian was in fell-running gear - shorts, t-shirt, knobbly running shoes, and with a small bum-bag, a contrast with the Duke of Edinburgh groups down at Glenridding. Ian had his own challenge going on - running over all of the 2,000 foot high fells of the Lake District (known as 'Wainwrights') in a year. He was fit, Ian. By my standards anyway.

"I just guessed when you might get here, and guessed how long I might take."

"That's good. Mind you, I'm going to expect you to appear at the top of every pass with a cup of tea now. You've raised expectations."

"It could be arranged. For a small fee."

Fell-running has a long tradition in the Lake District. From the time that guides took wealthy tourists over the fells in the 19th century, there have been 'guides races' to find the fastest, the winner getting a small cash prize. Many of these traditional races still exist, based on village and town shows, with competitors racing up and down the local fell. Up being a case of hammering out the height; down being a fast and furious descent, leaping over boulders without much thought of a safe landing.

Other races and challenges, especially long-distance ones, have grown over the years, the most famous of them the 'Bob Graham Round', the challenge being to cover 42 peaks, 27,000 feet of ascent, and 72 miles in 24 hours. The original route was set by Bob Graham in 1932, the runner training on the fells barefoot much of the time, partly to toughen his feet, and partly so as not to damage his plimsolls. It was another 28 years before the next successful attempt at the 'Bob Graham', but the club of successful runners has (at time of writing) reached over 1,700.

Names like Kenny Stuart, Billy Bland, and especially Joss Naylor are well known locally, and with huge respect. Their achievements in running in these fells are almost legendary. I had happened to be in Buttermere when Joss Naylor ran through as part of his '60 at 60' challenge. He was running over 60 Lakeland peaks in 36 hours to celebrate his 60th birthday.

I had also been to a talk where he had spoken matter-of-factly about being driven back from a major race and dropped in Borrowdale, running over the fells to his farm in Wasdale, dealing with his sheep, and then setting off to run a section of the 'Bob Graham' to support a friend. Joss had run it himself in 23 hours and 11 minutes. He had also run the 214 Wainwrights - Ian's 12 month challenge - in 7 days, 1 hour and 25 minutes.

There was 'fit' and 'fit'.

I took the tray back into the Inn, its low ceilings and doors fitting with its 15th century age, when it was presumably a refuge for packhorse drivers heading over Kirkstone Pass with their loads. I wondered if Joss had stopped by on any of his runs for a cup of tea.

Our route down to Ambleside from here was going to be quick. We were going off down 'The Struggle' towards Ambleside, rather than the main road towards Windermere town. Both were steep downhills, but The Struggle looked particularly so from the map.

We walked down the slope to the junction to look down over The Struggle. A ribbon of road twisted and turned across the fellside heading for the waters of Windermere at the foot of the valley. Up on the right was a slate quarry, with gravel tracks showing it was still a working site, while on the left side of the road, the land fell away into a valley before rising again steeply to Wansfell Pike.

A breeze was blowing up from the valley bottom, with a fresh, clean feel in the lungs. This was what the Lake District was about.

"I'd better be off," Ian said. "Some way to go yet."

He was heading up first to Stoney Cove Pike and ticking off another batch of Wainwrights from the list. Head down, legs getting into a rhythm, he set off past the inn, while Richard and I mounted up for a few miles down The Struggle that would not be a struggle at all.

Even so, we had just cycled up Kirkstone Pass, so maybe the cycling down was the reward.

"I don't know about you," I said, "but I reckon we deserve this."

The road dropped fast and steep, swinging a little to take in contours, Raven Crag high up on the right, the valley falling away towards Stock Ghyll on the left. Beyond, Wansfell Pike was a green hogsback, heading down to the lake ahead of us.

A flatter stretch and then down again. We stopped twice to take in the view, and it was worth it. The reflected blue waters of a corner of Windermere set amongst the greens of field, forest and fell. Two sheep eyed us from behind stone walls, their heads raised from the poor-looking grass of the fell. One was grey and unshorn, a Herdwick; the other, shorn to a pale cream, with twin red splodges on its back. As I raised a camera, both turned their backs on me and headed away downhill.

The steepest section of all was the final one, brakes on, into Ambleside. Slate and stone houses rose to meet us, and then we were emerging into the busy main street. There were cars and people everywhere. Civilisation, I supposed, as we negotiated real traffic for the first time since Penrith.

"Let's park up and walk," I said, and we skittered across the road to an outdoor shop with railings outside that looked good for chaining up the bikes.

The sun was out, and there were families with ice creams, hikers with rucksacks, dog walkers, and teenagers with clipboards.

"School project?" Richard asked.

"Must be."

By common consent, we avoided them, and headed instead for the café opposite that looked like it might do the largest sandwiches. Walkers' and cyclists' sandwiches.

Of the sixteen million holiday-makers coming to the Lake District each year, a good proportion would spend at least part of the time here in Ambleside. We took seats at a bench looking out of the window on to the main street, people-watching while we ate. The pavements were crowded, a mix of shoppers on a mission for new walking gear, and potterers taking in the ambience of the town.

Ambleside was perfectly placed for the tourist or hiker or anyone enjoying the Lake District; almost central within the spokes of Lakeland's valleys, it was a certain draw no matter what the weather or the time of day. It had a wealth of outdoor and bike shops, oodles of cafés, restaurants and pubs, and a smattering of food shops, book shops and banks. Most of all I liked Zeffirellis cinema and restaurant.

I had first been to Zeffirellis when I had been Richard's age, in the Lake District for a walking holiday with my old school friend, Nigel. We had stayed in Little Langdale at a guest house and come in to Ambleside one night, discovering Zeffirellis. At the time, it had been a greasy-spoon restaurant with a flickery movie screen through a curtain. Modern Zeffirellis was different - six screens, including 3D, two very, very nice vegetarian restaurants, and jazz evenings.

I made the first of a sequence of errors at that point. "We're staying at a hostel outside of Grasmere tonight, Rich," I said, "and I'm not sure what other food shops we'll pass before then. Maybe buy something here that's easy to carry in the panniers and that we can heat up later?"

First mistake: there was no need to shop here; we could pass a shop in Grasmere.

Second mistake: that shop would probably have some proper food.

Third mistake: "These cans of soup-meals look OK."

"Fine by me," Richard said.

Fourth mistake: "What about some pasta to go with them?"

"Sure."

Clearly he was not aware that occasionally I needed a kick up the backside. And that this was one of those occasions.

Grasmere, our destination, was not far up the main road, but this was a Grand Tour, not a straight-line ride.

We set off westwards out of Ambleside, initially on the same road as on our first day - the road towards Coniston – crossing the River Rothay. Where the Rothay and Brathay rivers join to reach Windermere, otters could be found. It's extraordinary to think that it was only in 1978 that hunting otters with dogs was banned, and that otterhound packs in the Lake District were disbanded, but thankfully the lovely creature is making a come-back.

We didn't see any.

Instead of turning off almost at once at Clappersgate, we carried straight on, the wooded base of Loughrigg Fell on our right, rough fields and the River Brathay on our left. Cars backed up behind us, with nowhere to overtake, so we pulled in at a gateway, and set off again once the backlog was gone.

We were going into Great Langdale, a fat arm of a valley thrust into the fells, with the Langdale Pikes on the northern flank, and a mass of mountains to the south and west – Pike of Blisco, The Band, Bow Fell, Crinkle Crags and beyond them, Scafell Pike.

At Skelwith Bridge, a fork took us on to the Great Langdale road, and out of the traffic, or most of it, anyway. The road narrowed through trees, with gentle downs and ups, and then opened up for a fabulous view over the little lake of Elterwater, tree- and field-lined, the sun reflecting off the water. Pleasant riverside footpaths followed the River Brathay downstream towards Skelwith Bridge, and upstream along Great Langdale Beck towards the village of Elterwater.

Elterwater village looked extraordinarily pretty in the valley just below the road, its houses dotted amongst woodland. Sitting neatly in the entrance to Great Langdale probably also contributed to the village being three quarters holiday homes, and only one quarter lived in. The Langdale Estate timeshare and hotel complex was also on the edge of the village, with Scandinavian-style lodges, a spa and hotel rooms that were 'contemporary, eclectic and country chic'. Langdale had come a long way since the valley's main draw was the big fells and rock climbing routes on Raven Crag and Pavey Ark. Some of the valley's rough edges had been knocked off, but it was clearly still quite a place.

A short way along the road, the village of Chapel Stile seemed different to Elterwater. With green-slate terraced houses built originally for quarry workers, and with a school, a church and the Langdale Community Village Store, the village just seemed more a local village still. Set into a hillside of boulders and ferns, and looking down on surprisingly flat fields through which the valley's beck pottered, the village no doubt had a good proportion of holiday cottages, but the impression was of a traditional community.

We pushed straight on through Chapel Stile, the road hugging the north side of the valley floor, which was still almost flat, with lush grass for the sheep in their higgledy-piggledy walled fields, and the occasional giant boulder. It was a real contrast to the increasingly rugged fells around us.

The valley took a kick north west before curving round west

again, so we found ourselves pedalling towards the distinctive domed heights of the Langdale Pikes, rising dark against a pale sky. As we got closer, the New Dungeon Ghyll hotel appeared at the base of the footpath up Stickle Ghyll that would lead via Stickle Tarn on to the tops. And beyond that was the Old Dungeon Ghyll hotel, host to generations of climbers - Chris Bonnington, Joe Brown and Don Willans were names I knew, but previous generations back to the 19th century had stayed here to climb or to train for expeditions around the world.

Even now, above the ODG on Raven Crag, we could make out a group of climbers part way up the cliff face. We stopped to watch, but were too far away to make out more than small figures on a ledge. And time was moving on.

We pedalled on to a right-angle turn in the road. To the left, the lane wiggled up over a pass to Little Langdale and Wrynose Pass, but that was the wrong way for us. We were heading back north, not south.

Straight ahead of us was a kissing gate into a meadow sprinkled with golden flowers amongst the emerald green of the tall grass. At the far end of the valley, a long ridge of fells broke the haze of cloud - Crinkle Crags and Bow Fell.

A sign said 'no through road for cycles', so this was as far as we would go down Great Langdale. We took in the view, then turned our bikes around.

Back at Chapel Stile, we turned off the Langdale road into the village. I have to admit I was starting to flake, so when we came to a small, grassed area outside Langdale Church, with the sun shining on it, I voted for a lie down and a chocolate bar. The vote turned out to be unanimous.

So there we were, horizontal, when a head poked out from one of the whitewashed cottages overlooking the grass. The face was quizzical more than anything, and clearly decided we had not passed out and were probably not camping there for the night. The face disappeared.

As we mounted up to move on, four youngsters on bikes appeared, heading uphill just behind us. I would guess they were aged about ten.

One of them whispered to his mates, and they zoomed ahead of us up the slope, glancing back at us. It was a clear challenge.

Now, we had panniers, they had not. We had cycled some miles that day. I guessed they had not. But the gauntlet had been thrown down.

"Come on, Rich."

It's possible I took Richard by surprise, but soon we were hauling them in, and when one had a chain come off, we were away.

"Yes!"

"I can't believe you just did that."

"I have some pride. Not much, but some."

The lane was soon amongst bracken and boulders. Still climbing, the road was a struggle, but I made it in my usual slow and methodical way, with Richard waiting for me at various points. My pride didn't stretch to challenging Richard. I would stick to ten-year-olds with dodgy chains. More my level really.

We stopped at a bend in the road with an open view down over the valley. A swathe of ferns in summer green dropped away to Elterwater village, white and slate-grey houses tucked amongst full-leafed trees. On the far side of the village, the woodland spread over two small hills, and beyond them, a longer stony ridge stretched away. Through a gap in the hills, there was the suggestion through haze of something higher, possibly Coniston Old Man.

Langdale, I thought, was magical, and could probably do with a poet to do it justice. Cue Grasmere.

At the top, the road ran behind a large building which we reckoned must have amazing views towards Windermere. It was only as we were going past it that we realised it was a YHA hostel, a grand Victorian mansion converted into dormitories for generations of walkers, cyclists and climbers.

There was a 25% steep hill sign for the way down into the village of Grasmere, and the Red Bank road zigzagged darkly through trees. Glimpses of the lake began to appear and then there was a full-blown view over the water. I hauled on the brakes, maybe a little too much for a damp-ish road under trees, and the back wheel slid a little but righted itself. Richard disappeared ahead of me before I could think to tell him I was stopping.

It was worth the stop. On the far side of two meadows, the waters of little Grasmere gave a shaded reflection of the hillside opposite, and those hills disappeared northwards into a haze. I could make out a large hotel on the water's edge, while away to the left behind a copse must be Grasmere village.

I dropped down more slowly now, so as to be able to sneak looks over the lake as I rode. Richard was waiting for me.

"Are you alright?"

"Yes. Fine. Just stopped to look at the view."

"I thought perhaps you had come off. I was about to pedal back up."

"Sorry," I said. "Should have shouted. Shall we go on into Grasmere?"

"Sure. Where's the hostel?"

I showed him the map, and pointed out the hostel on the road north of the village.

"Hang on," he said. "Aren't we missing out Rydal Water?"

"What?"

If part of the ride was to see every lake, then we had to see Rydal Water.

"Tell you what," Richard said, "we could cycle back down the main road to it. It's not far."

He was right. It wasn't far, and the route would be incomplete otherwise.

It occurred to me that we had seen just one car on the road over from Chapel Stile. It wouldn't be quite the same on the road to Rydal, but there was no choice.

We pedalled on past the Faeryland rowing boat hire and tea shop. After seeing the lake from the high Red Bank road, a rowing boat sounded wonderful, or even bringing kayaks and paddling not just around Grasmere, but down the River Rothay to Rydal Water and on into the waters of Windermere.

We cycled past the garden centre and turned right at the old grey church whose churchyard has the remains of Wordsworth. The Storyteller's Garden was also here, home of Taffy Thomas MBE, collector and teller of tales and stories from Lakeland and elsewhere, and a legend in his own right. I have never met Taffy though I am sure he will have told his stories to my children at their school or on a visit to his Garden, wearing his grand 'Tale Coat' and matching hat, each with beautifully embroidered images that can be the start of a story: a hare, a snake, an owl, and many more.

In 2010 he was made the first Storyteller Laureate. Alongside the honorary title he was given a 'bag of dried beans, a simple compass, a packet of love hearts, a clear glass bottle, a tall white candle, a silver lucky charm bracelet and a whistle.'

Excellent.

Taffy seems to me to represent two themes about Cumbria and the Lake District. Most obviously there is the story-telling. But then there is the fact that, like me, he is not Cumbrian, but an off-comer drawn here by the love of the place, who has become a part of the community. And although Taffy will never feel truly local, his children will, and always will, wherever their work or families might take them.

We pedalled out of town, passing Grasmere Sports Ground, where every year the Grasmere Lakeland Sports are held. The fell race - called the Guides Race - is a major event in the fell running calendar.

There is also hound trailing, a great Cumbrian tradition. When a visitor sees hounds careering across the fells, it's a natural assumption that this is fox hunting. There's a good chance it's not.

For at least a couple of hundred years folk in and around Lakeland have kept dogs for racing across the fells - hound trailing or in local dialect: oond trailin'.

It's often a family thing, spanning generations of owners, and generations of hounds. The dogs are mostly lighter than foxhounds, having been bred over the years for speed and agility across rock and moor: the dogs, not the owners, in case of any misunderstanding.

The owners, you'll usually spot leaning on Land Rovers, binoculars trained on the fellside.

The trail might once have been a dead cat (we're talking 18th century here), but today is made using a mix of aniseed and paraffin. A race is targeted at about 30 minutes, in which time the dogs can cover about ten miles. Prize money is generally just £5 to £10, though the bets placed on dogs can make winning a bit more lucrative.

I once asked a hound trailer if there was any connection with hunting.

"No," he said.

The other great draw at the Show is the Cumberland and Westmorland Wrestling. Traditionally, the wrestlers have worn white long-johns and tops, with trunks round their middles, all embroidered with designs by mothers, wives and girlfriends. No longer compulsory, they are still worn, and there are separate trophies for best costume.

There is a possibility that Cumberland and Westmorland Wrestling was brought here by the Vikings. The wrestlers grip each other behind the opponent's back and have to throw their opponent to the floor like that, a style closer to Icelandic wrestling than other older English styles.

I certainly like to think that as well as Viking crosses, Viking place-names and Cumbrian dialects, a Viking sport has passed from father to son (and today daughter) right up to the present day.

We pedalled, father and son, out to the main road, and did a little circuit of the buildings that hide Dove Cottage from the main road.

This had been William Wordsworth's house during his 'golden years' at the start of the 19th century. He, his wife Mary and his sister Dorothy lived here, often with guests. Wordsworth was a superstar of his day, and his presence here attracted other poets, such as Samuel Taylor Coleridge and Thomas de Quincey, and even sightseers. As William and Mary's family expanded, the house became too small for them, and they moved to Allan Bank on the other side of Grasmere, then to the Old Rectory in the village, and later to Rydal Mount in Rydal, but it is Dove Cottage that most people associate with the poet.

I had visited Dove Cottage and the museum earlier in the year with my wife, Claire. The house is deceptive, from the front looking like a small cottage, but at the back, the upstairs rooms run back along the hillside. It wasn't quite as small as I had been expecting. I had gathered that Wordsworth had hordes of visitors staying in a one-up one-down cottage. In fact, it was really quite pleasant, especially the upstairs bedroom which, in Wordsworth's time, would have had a quite wonderful view across the lake.

Wordsworth was clearly not poor, living off a legacy left him by an admirer of his talent who wanted the poet to have time to write.

Wordsworth had liked to compose outside, and Claire and I had climbed to the gazebo at the back of the hillside garden and looked across to the hills beyond. When Wordsworth lived here, there were no houses to block the view. It must have been stupendous. Poetic, in fact.

Wordsworth was prolific, writing huge quantities of poetry, though the poem most studied by school pupils these days, The Prelude, was only published by Mary after his death. The Prelude is long, partly autobiographical and partly philosophical. It was originally intended to be the prelude to an even longer poem, the great work of his life, though now it seems that The Prelude itself is that great work.

A confession. I haven't read it. Perhaps one day I will, but I suspect I may well still prefer foxes, boxes and sockses.

I know. I am a Philistine.

I am ashamed.

A bit.

The road to Rydal was the same main road that Richard and I had started our journey on at Brockhole, and just as unpleasant for cycling.

In Wordsworth's time, carriages and carts would have made their slow journeys up the toll road over the hill. Wordsworth vehemently opposed the building of the new road alongside the lake in the 1830s, rounding a wooded promontory, twisting through ninety degrees and cutting through woods to Rydal Water. In the summer these days, queues of cars make their slow way along, and for two cyclists in amongst them, it was not ideal. The road is one of those that tempts a driver to pass, even when there is not really enough room nor enough visibility around corners.

So this is a plea to the Lake District National Park and to Sustrans. How about creating a nice, wide cycle path along the south sides of Rydal Water and Grasmere, joining up with the bottom of the hill at Red Bank? Now that would be a lovely route. An asset to Lakeland.

We cycled as far as necessary to get to Rydal Water. I had a count up. We had now ridden to eight of the sixteen lakes on the Visit Cumbria website: Windermere, Esthwaite Water, Coniston Water, Haweswater, Ullswater, Elterwater, Grasmere and now Rydal Water. It was very pretty, with reeds around the edges, a tiny island and low fells behind, but spoiled on this side of the lake by all the traffic right next to it. The other side, I knew, was wonderful.

We turned back, anxious to get off the road as soon as we could.

Back at the junction close to Dove Cottage, we had the choice of looping around through Grasmere village or staying on the main road to head north to the hostel. The main road was wider here, so we opted to stay with it. It was shorter. Quicker. And at this stage we were still looking forward to our meal-soups and pasta. Clearly, we hadn't cooked them as yet.

Of course, had we looped back around through the village, we might have gone past the shop and bought something to cook that would be tasty to eat. But that didn't happen.

Grasmere Independent Hostel was half a mile north of the village, up a little drive, quiet and with fantastic views up and down the valley.

"I've put you in the room just by the door there," the friendly owner told us when we checked in.

"Will we be sharing?"

"No. Not tonight."

He gave us a tour, showing us the large dining room and the kitchen with its modern stainless steel equipment. Then there was the generous number of showers, and the sitting room with its round window looking right down the valley. Our own room had two sets of new-looking wooden bunk-beds and an en-suite toilet. The hostel clearly was great. Unfortunately for our host, it seemed empty. It deserved more people. Really, it was very nice. Go there! Take friends!

I found him later enjoying a beer on a bench in the garden. He told me his plans for more work on the place.

"Have you run the hostel for long?" I asked.

"No, we bought it just recently."

"Well, I really do wish you well with it."

"Thanks," he said, and despite the lack of customers, he seemed very relaxed, though I have no way of knowing if that was the beer, or the fact that he was the owner of an independent hostel just outside Grasmere with stupendous views of Lakeland.

Probably the beer.

Richard and I had the kitchen to ourselves as we heated up our meal-soup and our pasta.

It was rubbish, but at least we were not having to smell the aromas of other people's delicious evening meals, prepared with fresh herbs and spices, with real meat and vegetables, with...

Oh, I give in.

We watched TV in the lounge.

What we really should have done is gone to the pub and eaten there.

"I blame you," I said. "There's a pub down the road, and you didn't insist we go and eat there, and instead you ate that meal without complaining."

"Cup of coffee?" he said.

"Go on then."

Distance for the day: 44 miles / 70.4 Km
Height gained: 4,481 feet / 1,366 metres
Hardest hill: Kirkstone Pass 958 feet / 292 metres
Average speed: 10.7 mph / 17.1 Kmph
Fastest speed: 32.8 mph / 52.5 Kmph
Total distance: 177 miles / 283 Km

So, a shorter day. A Poet's Day.

Actually, it felt more than 44 miles, but then we had done some reasonable height over the course of the day. We hadn't wrestled in long-johns, raced over countless fell tops or even composed poetry, but it felt good to have cycled over the highest pass in Lakeland. That was one down of the six Great Cycle Climbs in the Lake District; five to go. Plus, we had seen Langdale and Ullswater and Grasmere. Oh, and a long time ago, sloths.

DAY FIVE - PIMP

AROUND SKIDDAW

Grasmere – Thirlmere – Castlerigg – Mungrisdale
Hesket Newmarket – Caldbeck – Bassenthwaite
Braithwaite – Whinlatter Pass – Cockermouth

56 miles

www.lakedistrictgrandtour.co.uk/day/five

111

I was hungry.

Probably Richard's fault.

I levered myself out of my bunk and pulled back a curtain. Outside it was pouring with rain.

Richard was awake.

I said, "I reckon it's about a mile back to Grasmere in the wrong direction. But we could get ourselves a cooked breakfast there."

"Worth it then," Richard said.

We packed, thanked our host and went outside to release our bikes from the bike shed. It was warm out, despite the rain, so we both decided on shorts rather than waterproof trousers. Jackets, helmet covers and overshoes seemed like a good plan though.

I consulted the map with my glasses on. A rare moment, admittedly.

"Do you realise," I said, "we didn't get lost once yesterday?"

"Your average is going down then."

"I'll see what I can do about that."

A lane, Helm Close, went off almost opposite the bottom of the drive.

"We can take that lane and get into Grasmere without going on the main road at all. It comes out on Easedale Road."

The Easedale Road led from Grasmere village to Easedale Tarn, an atmospheric little tarn surrounded by rocky fells. The road was also the start point for the walk up Helm Crag, whose two rocks on the summit - one large and seeming to loom over the smaller - are known as the Lion and the Lamb.

I had always assumed that the reference was from the bible: that when Christ returned to earth, 'the lion would lie down with the lamb', but apparently not. In the bible, it's the wolf that will lie down with the lamb. So now I am confused about where the reference comes from. Either way, the Lion and the Lamb are well worth walking up to. A tip though. If you are a young parent walking it with your own parents while carrying your brand new tiny baby, don't climb up on the rocks at the top. It's not popular.

We dropped down to the main road, spray flying out from our wheels, then turned down Helm Close. It was a winding, up-and-down lane with dry-stone walls on either side and, judging by the filthy state of the road surface, it was much used by the local farmers. As we skimmed through dirty puddles and mud patches, it didn't feel like nice clean watery spray that was coating our legs and splashing up on to faces. A grand little lane for a dry day's cycling. Not quite so good that day.

Easedale Road was flatter, with yellow lines down it and with a footpath on the far side of the wall for pedestrians. We were heading back into touristy Grasmere, and very soon we were in the village, suddenly up-market again, with multi-starred restaurants and hotels.

"Why didn't we stay in one of these then?" Richard said.

"On your bike."

We also didn't go to the Grasmere Gingerbread Shop by the church, renowned for baking distinctive gingerbread biscuits using their own secret recipe. The shop usually has a gorgeous aroma of freshly baked gingerbread, so eating warm gingerbread biscuit immediately outside is definitely the best way to experience it. No, we went to the small bakery and tea shop that had a handful of tables and sold giant sausage-and-bacon butties and large mugs of coffee. On balance, more what I needed.

As the lady at the counter went to cook the bacon and sausages, we sat at one of the tables and discussed the day.

We were heading north over Dunmail Raise, past Thirlmere, then taking a loop around the east and north of the Skiddaw range. I had planned lunch at either the pub at Hesket Newmarket or the mill café at Caldbeck. I might need a large sausage-and-bacon butty to get me there. Then we would go over the hills at the Back O'Skiddaw to Bassenthwaite Lake and over Whinlatter Pass to Cockermouth. It could be a long, wet day.

The man bringing in the day's supplies joined in. "Course, you often get different weather on either side of Dunmail Raise."

Claire and I had been told much the same when we had first moved to the Lake District: "If it's raining in Cockermouth, it's sunny in Ambleside. If it's sunny in Cockermouth, it's raining in Ambleside." Experience had taught us that wasn't necessarily correct, but sitting in the café in Grasmere looking out at the rain, we hoped it would be true today.

The lady brought our sausage-and-bacon butties.

"Are you from Grasmere?" I asked.
She smiled. "No, Liverpool."
"Bit different here."
"It is that."

Suitably filled for a day's cycling, we decided against muddy Helm Close for cycling back to the main road, and instead pedalled back through the village.

We passed the Heaton Cooper Gallery, with its paintings of the Lake District by three generations of the Heaton Cooper family. Our home, like very many belonging to residents and visitors to Lakeland had more than one on the wall - prints that is, rather than originals - of William Heaton Cooper's wonderfully evocative paintings of Lakeland in golden autumn or in a snow-capped winter or with spring breaking over a blue tarn amidst the fells. Some are moody and cold, some bright, with bold blocks of colour that seem unlikely and yet really do appear when the light strikes the fells and tarns of the Lake District in a certain way.

We also passed the Co-op where we could have bought something other than meal-soup and pasta, but we won't go there.

The main road wasn't too busy but, when cars and vans did pass us, there was quite a bit of spray.

The Travellers Rest Inn and the various cottages along the road were almost all whitewashed, and still bright on a grey day. It was something which Wordsworth had railed against. Before then, stone cottages had remained natural stone but, during the time Wordsworth lived in Grasmere, it became common to render the outside and to paint them. Suddenly, houses and cottages of local stone that had blended into the countryside stood out against the fells. Wordsworth was appalled, and that feels strange today, since the whitewashed cottage, with fells behind, has become one of the iconic images of the Lake District.

The road rose gently at first, and we passed the hostel again, before Dunmail Raise began properly. It wasn't steep, not a real challenge, but did go on for some way. We pedalled up nose-to-tail, there being not much point in Richard going on ahead only to have to wait in the rain at the top.

Up on the right was Seat Sandal, with beyond that, Fairfield, Dollywagon Pike, Nethermost Pike and Helvellyn. Wonderful names some of the fells in Cumbria have. We could see nothing of them today, with dense cloud so low that we were almost in it as we approached the top of the pass.

As the road began to level out, it split into a brief section of dual carriage-way, and there on our right was a great pile of stones. Historians say it is a bronze-age cairn, but I prefer the legend of King Dunmail, 'the last King of Cumbria' in the 10th century.

Dunmail was the son of King Owain (a very Celtic name for a King of a mixed Norse-Celtic people) who, alongside the King of Scotland, signed a peace treaty with Saxon England's King Athelstan at Eamont Bridge. A few years later the Scots were defeated in battle, and both Owain of Cumbria and Constantine of Scotland recognised the English King as their overlord, the first 'King of All The Britons'.

Another battle, with Owain killed, and his son Dunmail reasserting the independence of Cumbria. Yet another battle, and Dunmail is defeated by King Edmund of England.

And so to the legend: Dunmail was killed in a battle right here, and as he died, he handed his golden crown to some of his warriors, who fought their way out and took the crown up Seat Sandal. From there they threw it into Grisedale Tarn for safe-keeping 'till Dunmail comes again to lead us'. Edmund blinded Dunmail's two sons and ordered that a giant pile of stones be placed over Dunmail's body.

But the warriors of Cumbria did not forget their leader. Every year since then, Dunmail's ghostly warriors are said to retrieve the crown from the tarn and bring it to the pile of stones. There they bang their spears on the pile, but each time a voice issues from the cairn: "Not yet, not yet. Wait awhile, my warriors."

Historians says Dunmail didn't die in the battle, but went into exile, with Cumbria and Strathclyde handed over to the Scots King, but that's a much less romantic story. In fact, I was tempted to bang my cycle pump on the cairn and brandish my bike-helmet to the sleeping Last King of Cumbria, but to be honest, the dual carriage-way doesn't exactly add to the romance of the area and, well, it was a bit wet.

The road began to slope down and became single carriage-way, narrowing and twisting.

I said, "There's a left turn at the bottom of the hill that will take us around Thirlmere on the quiet side."

"Fine."

We picked up speed, and sooner than an accelerating Richard had expected, a sign appeared

"Rich!!" I shouted after his disappearing bike. "Turn here!!"

He heard me too late, and I waited for him round the corner as he found a spot to turn.

Thirlmere's dam - at the far end to us - was built at the end of the 19th century, the reservoir designed to supply Manchester's water. Even more of an engineering feat, it seemed to me, was the building of a 95-mile long aqueduct all the way to Manchester. We had been cycling past it - after a 4-mile tunnel under Dunmail Raise, the aqueduct is mostly a concrete channel, covered over with concrete and soil, and contouring around the hillsides. It bypasses Grasmere and Ambleside to the east, runs under the River Kent at Staveley, then takes a loop around Kendal before heading on south. Rivers are tunnelled under or piped over, with the average fall in height of twenty inches per mile enough to take the Lake District's water to Manchester in thirty hours.

Richard rejoined me as we cycled past what is left of the village of Wythburn, one of two villages flooded by the reservoir. The flooding of the valley was vehemently opposed by many, including Ruskin, who is said to have preferred that Manchester be drowned under the rising waters. Not all were opposed; Manchester clearly needed a good, clean water supply.

Today, the reservoir was full, and was being rapidly topped up from the sky and from the streams-turned-torrents flowing down from the Helvellyn range on our right and from the Wythburn Fells and Armboth Fell on our left. Not that we could see the fells. The cloud level was only about a hundred feet above us. It wasn't on a day like this that Wordsworth had written:

> Thou has clomb aloft, and gazed,
> From the watchtowers of Helvellyn;
> Awed, delighted, and amazed!

At least we were on a good, flat cycling road, very quiet, with all the traffic staying on the main road, apart from the odd few here for the start of a walk or a run. We pedalled alongside each other, content in each other's company.

"We brought you kids here with your bikes when you were little," I said.

"I think I might remember that."

"It was great fun. You could go for ages along here, just keeping half an eye out for cars."

Today wasn't really the weather for families with bikes.

Across on the other side we could make out a Victorian turret: the outflow of the reservoir.

On our side of the reservoir, we cycled past woodland. Thinned trees ran down to the water's edge on our right, while thickly-planted forestry climbed the fellside on our left.

The thinned woodland is due to a court case in the 1980s. The original Act of Parliament permitting the building of the reservoir had included the proviso that only native woodland could be planted around the waters. That had been ignored, and for decades a drive or a cycle ride next to Thirlmere would be entirely through a corridor of thick, dark conifers. The court found that to have been illegal, and now the removal of conifers and re-planting with broadleaf trees makes the whole valley far more pleasant.

Well, pleasant when it is not heaving down with rain. There were certainly no picnickers at the tables in the parking areas today.

A herd of red deer live in and around the forest west of Thirlmere, around 150 of those beautiful and graceful creatures. I gave the occasional scan of the woods as we rode, looking for a magnificent nine- or ten-pointer of a stag, or even a group of does. Really, I would have been happy with any sighting.

Three or four miles of absolutely flat cycling - the first since Grange-over-Sands - brought us on to the dam. We stopped by the impressive coat of arms of Manchester Corporation and looked back down the reservoir. On another day, the waters might have reflected a blue sky, with the green fells on either side running down through forested ridges to the shoreline.

Today though, the lake disappeared into cloud, and close up, the water was a choppy, graphite bleakness. We were not unhappy to head off the dam wall in the direction of the gloriously-named St John's-in-the-Vale.

We crossed the main Ambleside-Keswick road, and a small lane took us into the narrows at the start of the valley, with High Rigg on our left beyond little St John's Beck, and higher, more rugged buttresses on our right leading up towards Watson's Dodd and Great Dodd.

Then something strange happened. It stopped raining. In fact, the sun came out as we rode on to drying tarmac. Perhaps the guy at the bakery in Grasmere had been right about the weather changing at Dunmail Raise.

Gradually the valley widened, with flat grassy meadows, and steep bracken- and grass-covered slopes on each side, punctuated by rocky outcrops and fallen boulders. Back behind us, black clouds loomed over the fells, and ahead of us in the distance, the tops of Skiddaw and Blencathra were cut off by a layer of grey cloud but, above us, the sky was blue.

A C2C sign pointed away to the right. This was the 'Old Coach Road' alternative route for mountain bikers, a rough off-road track, but we turned the other way at the sign for St John's-in-the-Vale Church and followed a narrow lane. At a bend in the road, an even narrower lane headed off, where it would cut up between the two low fells of High and Low Rigg for the little Victorian church. Across to our left was Bridge House, the home in the 19th century of John Richardson, a local builder, then teacher, but who came to be known for his poetry. He partly wrote in Cumberland dialect, such as his poem, 'It's nobbut me!', which I think has to be read aloud to be understood. So please do so now. Imagine you are a daughter of marriageable age living with the family in St John's-in-the-Vale, not far from where a young John Richardson lives. The poem is written in her voice.

Ready? Here you go:

Ya winter neet; I mind it weel,
Oor lads 'ed been at t' fell,
An' bein' tir't, went seun to bed,
An' I sat be messel.
I hard a jike on t' window pane,
An' deftly went to see;
Bit when I ax't 'Who's jiken theer?'
Says t' chap, 'It's nobbut me!'

'Who's me? says I, 'What want ye here?
Oor fwoak ur aw abed?' -
'I dunnet want your fwok at aw,
It's thee I want,' he said.
'What can t'e want wi' me,' says I;
'An' who the deuce can 't be?
Just tell me who it is an' then'
-Says he, 'It's nobbut me.'

'I want a sweetheart, an' I thowt
Thoo mebby wad an' aw;
I'd been a bit down t' deal to-neet,
An' thowt 'at I wad caw;
What, can t' like me dus t'e think?
I think I wad like thee'
-'I dunnet know who 'tis,' says I;
Says he, 'It's nobbut me.'

We pestit on a canny while,
I thowt his voice I kennt;
An' than I steall quite whisht away,
An' oot at t' dooer I went.
I creapp, an' gat 'im be t' cwoat laps,
'Twas dark, he cuddent see;
He startit roond, an' said, 'Who's that?'
Says I, 'It's nobbut me.'

119

An' meanny a time he come ageann,
An' menny a time I went,
An' said, 'Who's that 'at's jiken theer?'
When gaily well I kent;
An' mainly what t' seamm answer com,
Fray back o' t' laylick tree;
He sed, 'I think thoo knows who't is;
Thoo knows it's nobbut me.'

It's twenty year an' mair Sen than,
An' ups an' doons we've hed;
An' six fine barns hey blest us beath,
Sen Jim an' me war wed.
An' many a time I've known 'im steal,
When I'd yan on me knee,
To mak me start, an' than wad laugh
--'Ha! Ha! It's nobbut me.'

Just great.

The road climbed slightly, with the flat green fields of the valley
left behind, and instead the tussocky end of Low Rigg's ridge to
cross. Some ups and downs, and then there was a trail of cars
parked in a layby along with a Luchinis ice cream van out of
Keswick, just a couple of miles down the hill. This was a popular
place. We were at Castlerigg Stone Circle, which must be one of
the most photographed stone circles in the country.

Standing in open country on a slight dome of a hill, and with
fells all around, it is hugely atmospheric. Any decent Lake District
calendar must, just must, have an image. It might be of the stones
with snow on their tops and a sun-lit view across to the white tops
of Skiddaw and Blencathra to the north or Helvellyn to the south
east. Or maybe a misty, autumnal scene, with a dew-speckled
sheep strolling past a giant boulder. Or even a summer-time view
of the stones picked out against the greens of a Lakeland June day,
and someone in a red jacket perched on a stone.

Legend has it that it is impossible to count the number of stones. The National Trust says 40, and I was prepared to believe them.

Families were picking their way around the stones, watching out for puddles in the grass, the largest right in the centre of the circle. The sun had disappeared behind cloud, but a photographer had his tripod set up and was eying a view through his camera over the standing stones towards Helvellyn, even though the tops were invisible in cloud. He was wearing a photographer's waistcoat with copious pockets for lenses, and appeared to be waiting.

"Do you need some sun on the fells?" I asked.

"Hoping for it," he said in a Liverpool accent.

"Are you here on holiday?"

"I come up two or three times a year. For this," he said, gesturing at his camera. "It's my main hobby."

I took my own photo in the same direction his camera was pointing. I thought I might as well follow the lead of a proper photographer, even if mine was a little digital camera, rather than a brute of a thing with a long lens.

I looked at the result.

Grey stones against a background of grey mountain and grey cloud.

The Liverpudlian photographer was still waiting patiently. I found the delete button.

Castlerigg Stone Circle is very old - 5,000 years or so - and that makes it one of the oldest stone circles in the country. There are lunar and solar alignments to some of the stones, but the jury is out on whether they are coincidental or whether they were part of a great calendar of the skies. I must admit I quite like the thought that neolithic people were producing their own Lakeland calendar featuring Castlerigg Stone Circle.

From Castlerigg we retraced our route and then headed north, crossing the busy A66, and pedalling into the little village of Threlkeld hard up against the slopes of Blencathra, or Saddleback, as it is also known. The mountain dominates the village, a great wall of rock, with sharp ridges rising severely from either side. The steepest, Sharp Edge, is round the back and out of sight, but those at the front make a stunning backdrop to the village.

Looking back southwards, the view was towards Clough Head, the most northern of the fells that make up the Helvellyn range. The mountain itself was mostly in cloud, but in front could be seen the back of the Threlkeld quarry - now an excellent Quarry and Mining Museum, but which had provided granite chippings for the building of the Thirlmere dam we had just cycled over.

It wasn't part of the plan to stop off at all in the village, but we were diverted by the most amazing topiary. We were not at any sort of stately home, but just outside a domestic house. The hedge along the front of the house had a car carved in it, as well as a figure playing football with a dog, while on top of the hedge I thought I could make out giant versions of a squirrel, snail, peacock, dog and so on.

The owner pottered out of his gate. He looked of retirement age, but then, I thought, you would have to be retired to have time to create and keep going such a feat.

"This is fabulous," I said. "Did you make these?"

"Ay. Can you recognise them?"

"I think so."

"The hare on the tortoise?"

"Ah, yes. I see it."

"The snail?"

"Yes. Got that one."

"And the Herdwick sheep?"

"Oh, I thought that one was a dog. Sorry."

"No. It can be a dog if you see it as a dog. And along the side here, that's me with the ball, and that's my wife with her umbrella."

"I really do think they're great. It must take you ages."

"Aye. About an hour a day."

"What about round the side? Is that next?"

"Well. Could be."

Just by the house, a sign for the main section of the C2C showed our route out of the village, eastwards up a country lane with the mass of Blencathra on our left. A couple of guys with bikes pored over a map.

"You OK?" I asked.

The younger of the two men replied, "Yes. Fine, just showing my mate where we're going."

He was riding a fine-looking bike, was dressed in cycling lycra, and was probably a very quick cyclist. His mate, if we're honest, didn't seem to fit into the same category.

"Are you doing the C2C?"

We were back on the coast-to-coast route, which headed from here north to Mungrisdale before turning eastwards to Greystoke, though we would be leaving it at Mungrisdale to cycle north.

"No, I'm from Keswick and we're doing a circuit of Skiddaw and Blencathra. You?"

"Oh, we're on a bit of a tour of the Lake District for a week or so. We started this morning in Grasmere and we're finishing in Cockermouth. Much the same route as you today."

"What's the whole tour?"

"Well, er, all the passes, all the lakes, and as far north, south, east and west as you can go in the National Park."

He looked thoughtful. "I hope you're going to put the route on the web?"

"Well, I suppose so."

"Good. I'd like to do that."

The sun came out as we spoke, and was warm. I was very warm, still wearing my jacket. So as the two cyclists headed away from us up the lane, Richard and I removed layers and ate biscuits. The day was entirely different to the one we had started in, sunlight filtering through the trees that lined the road as we set off uphill.

In a few minutes we had caught up with the pair of cyclists, the one clearly finding the hill easy, the other not so. We cycled with them for a few minutes chatting about cycling routes in the Lake District, and then we carried on. This was a quiet lane, a farm lane with a gate to open before the C2C signs dropped us down to the A66 where a cycle lane by the road kept us away from the traffic. At Scales we were off on a lane again, still hugging the skirts of Blencathra.

Again we were on the quietest of roads, even though the traffic of the A66 was busy below us. We were in a different world.

The lane rose and fell along the side of Souther Fell, an outlier of Blencathra. The tarmac was dry now in the sunshine, and on our left, bracken-covered slopes rose steeply, with foxglove spikes pinkly dotting the green hillside while, above them, poked a series of large boulders. On our right, a dry-stone wall separated us from flatter fields and marshier ground where sheep were grazing, with the low hills of Greystoke Forest in the distance.

Souther Fell has a good ghost story. In the 18th century there were several sightings of an army of ghostly soldiers marching five abreast across the summit on mid-summer's day.

We didn't see any.

In one dip in the road, a long puddle remained, with no way around. We cycled slowly through, our pedals dipping into the murky water at each down stroke. Once through, I looked up and an enormous bird of prey was circling quite low above the fellside, great wings outstretched with finger-tip feathers at each end. It dropped suddenly and flapped madly in mid-air before rising again and circling. It was so large that if we had been at Haweswater I would have called it a golden eagle, but here I assumed it was a large buzzard.

The two cyclists caught us up and they too stood to watch. It was a truly awesome sight, this magnificent bird so close above us. It circled higher, then higher again, drifting away over the fell.

Mungrisdale, the next village along, nestled up to the fells above it and straddled the river, with the pub on one side and the village hall on the far bank.

We would miss the village's annual 'Family Fun Day' on the following Saturday: the sack race, Punch and Judy, magician, welly throwing, face painting and wheelbarrow race. Just listing them makes me smile.

We stopped on the bridge behind the pub to eat a muesli bar each, the water rushing underneath us in a mini gorge and, as we did, the pair of cyclists went past us, the speedier-looking guy in coasting mode, the companion (by now I was thinking brother-in-law) struggling a little.

After a five-minute break we pedalled onwards, the road still hugging the fellside, to Mosedale, which was no more than a handful of houses at the entrance to the bleak Mosedale valley. Black-faced sheep stared at us through a wooden fence from a rough-grassed field, with the green Bowscale Fell dipping down to one side of the valley and the rocky slopes of Carrock Fell on the north.

Carrock Fell is best known for its hill fort on the very summit, with thick, but tumbled down walls surrounding a large open area. There is a theory that it was a tribal headquarters before the arrival of the Romans, and that the legions demolished it. But it's just a theory. Either way, I had an image of those thick walls not being tumbled down, but with Celtic warriors patrolling and looking out across the forested plain towards the distant Pennines in the east. It would have been quite a place.

We cycled on, with great boulders right along the side of the road under the steep side of Carrock Fell. Then the fells came to a sudden end, and on either side was moorland rather than fell - grassy, brackeny and sheepy.

The bracken was bright green and beautiful in its own way, though a menace to the farmers: bracken is poisonous to sheep, horses and cattle, and it spreads easily in poor soil, overwhelming other plant species. The European Union is banning the one chemical which is effective against bracken (apparently because it is unsafe when used on crops of spinach...), and unless resistance to the regulation is successful, it seems that more valleys and fellsides will be covered in the ferns.

A group of cars was parked in the middle of nowhere ahead of us with various people milling around.

I pulled in by them. A man and a woman in mud-stained waterproofs were talking at the back of a Land Rover, while studying a map. Others seemed to be marching into the bracken on either side.

The pair looked up at me.

"Oh, hi," I said. "I thought maybe you were hound trailing, but..."

The lady smiled. "No, we're trying to get rid of the bracken from the archaeological sites here."

"Ah. Right. The hill fort up on Carrock Fell?"

"No, that's too high for bracken. Just around here. This was an iron smelter in the 1800s," she said, gesturing into the bracken.

"The roots interfere with the archaeological remains unless you dig them up."

So it was not just farmers that objected to the spread of the bracken.

"That's good to do then."

"You could join us if you like."

"Um, thanks, but, well, we're on a bike ride really."

"Another time."

"Definitely. Yes, another time."

A young couple on a tandem slowed briefly, edged past us, then stormed ahead of us at speed.

"Better go then," I said. "Thanks though."

There were various dips and hollows in the land around that I had not noticed, but these, I thought, could easily be the remains of old miners' pits. The whole area had been a great mining area over the centuries, including for lead and tungsten ores in Carrock Fell's mine, and that mine only closed in 1981.

The road had a little dip just afterwards to a ford, with a foot-bridge next to it. The couple with the tandem were just extracting themselves and their bikes from the narrow footbridge.

"Rich," I said. "What about it?"

"The ford?"

"At speed I reckon."

"Go on then."

And so we did, the couple with their (dry) tandem and (dry) legs watching us.

We both hit the water, plumes of spray flying, and stood on the pedals to pull out on the far side.

"That was good," I said, inspecting a wet bike and wet legs.

"I'm very wet."

"Worth it."

We went straight into the short, sharp hill rising up from the ford, only to find the tandem cruising past us as though it weren't a hill at all. By the time we got to the top, they were disappearing.

"Now is that because they are on a tandem and have two lots of legs to push? Or are they just very fit?"

"No panniers," Richard said. "Makes a difference."

At the top, the moorland was quite flat and open, the home,

apparently, to wild ponies.

We didn't see any.

The moorland ran out and we were cycling through farmland, hedges lining the single-track road with sheep-filled fields behind them. It was great cycling, and after a mile or so, we jinked through a collection of farm buildings and were in Hesket Newmarket.

A village green runs the length of the centre of the village, with one large tree in the middle and a covered-over market cross. Down either side of the village green are two roads that run parallel. The green is like that at Askham, but the houses around the green here are less grand, mostly cottages, some of stone, some painted. It's a homely place, and the pub would generally make it more so.

The Old Crown is home to Hesket Newmarket Brewery, one of the early microbreweries in the tale of the revival of real ales. Started in 1988 by the owners of the village pub, it was taken over as a cooperative of enthusiasts on their retirement. There's now about one hundred members, each with an equal share in the ownership, and with a waiting list for new members.

And they also make very good beer: 'Blencathra', 'Skiddaw' and the wonderfully named 'Doris's 90th Birthday Ale', amongst others.

However, it was a weekday lunchtime, and despite the presence on the doorstep of the pair of cyclists from Threlkeld and the tandeming couple, it was closed. No liquid lunch there today.

Not that I would anyway. Today was going to be a long enough cycle ride without beer wallowing in my belly. Richard might have, but he was young, and probably I would have at his age. He would certainly have found it hard to resist a taster of Doris's 90th Birthday Ale.

We rode up the slight hill past the green, turning the corner at the top, and here was the one larger house of the village, Hesket Hall, built 400 years ago like a series of boxes leaning against each other. There are countless corners, and the story is that it was built to be one large sundial.

The road climbed up a hill out of the village, which was a disappointment to legs that had expected a sit down in The Crown, and they had a bit of a go-slow until we crested the hill, and were cycling through hedged farmland on the way to Caldbeck.

The farms around here were one of the areas most badly affected by Foot and Mouth Disease in 2001. Thousands of cows and sheep were slaughtered as the authorities tried to prevent the disease spreading across the county and further afield. It was an awful time.

Vets trained to save animals' lives found themselves not relieving suffering animals of pain, but 'culling' whole herds of healthy animals as a quarantine around infected farms. Lambs born in the morning would by the evening have been culled alongside their mothers. Slaughtered stock would lie dead in farmyards for days before collection, within sight and smell of farmers and their families trapped in their farms, unable to leave. From here north to Carlisle, and in many other parts of Lakeland, hardly an animal was left in the fields.

Those reliant on tourism suffered hugely as well. Visitors were told to stay away from the Lake District, fell footpaths were closed, and another set of businesses was devastated. Hotels, guest houses, tea rooms, attractions and holiday businesses throughout Cumbria all saw an entire season's income disappear overnight. Staff were laid off and some businesses did not survive.

You wouldn't know it to look at the lovely countryside here, to breathe in the clean air, and to hear the sheep call to each other, but the scars must run deep amongst those who suffered most.

We dropped down into Caldbeck. My legs, I knew, would not be disappointed here.

Caldbeck was strung out along the roads that lead into the village, with many of the buildings old mills lining the Cold Beck from which the village gets its name. Today, some are houses while others have been converted to businesses. Caldbeck has, as well as a pub, church and school, a proper local shop, a gift shop for tourists and Priest's Mill, where my legs were heading for.

Priest's Mill was down a rough lane next to an impressive church whose cemetery has the grave of John Peel, as in 'D'ye ken John Peel?'.

'D'ye ken John Peel?' is one of those songs that takes me back to school days, along with rousing ditties about the sinking of the Titanic, mine disasters and railway crashes.

John Peel was a huntsman from Caldbeck, famous in his own lifetime for his fox-hunting and his wild lifestyle centred around the hunt and the inn. A farmer, he was one of thirteen children, with thirteen of his own, and his wife must have been more than a little tolerant.

The words of the song are said to have been written as a bet in a pub, though the song itself became famous as the tune of the Border Regiment, and then as one of the great songs to instil Britishness and stiff upper lips into the children of the land. Our own kids, learning songs about cabbages green, have definitely missed out.

Lake District hunting is quite different to fox hunting in most parts of England, and not as associated with the gentry as it is elsewhere. Here hunting is on foot, often up amongst the high fells, the crags and the bogs, where horses would definitely struggle. There is a long tradition of a pack of hounds being kept to keep down the fox population and farmers have traditionally taken part, following the hounds led by the huntsman as they find and chase down a scent.

'The Blencathra' pack, based at Threlkeld, is out several days a week through the winter, mostly around Skiddaw and Blencathra, though their territory runs as far as Helvellyn and Scafell Pike. Five other fell packs divide the rest of Lakeland - the Coniston, the Eskdale and Ennerdale, the Lunesdale, the Melbreak and the Ullswater. There is a lot of support for hunting as a means of controlling foxes. The Blencathra has around 750 members.

Of course, times have changed, and so has the law. As things stand at time of writing, it is illegal to purposefully kill a fox with a pack of hounds. Instead, two hounds can be used to flush the fox out, and a fox can then be shot. If a pack accidentally comes upon a fox, and gives chase, again that's not illegal. Anti-hunt groups claim that the fell packs get around the law by various means and that they still manage to hunt foxes with dogs, and there have been attempts at monitoring and sabotage.

There isn't a lot of middle ground between those who see fox hunting as cruel, and those who support it both as a practical means to control foxes and as a traditional country pursuit.

We coasted down the little bumpy lane to the two-storey, stone-built Priest's Mill, and locked our bikes up. A couple of shops occupied the bottom half, including The Wool Clip, specialising in local wool yarn and products, while up a ramp was the café, atmospherically built into the roof space of the old mill building. Two chairs were free by a window looking down on the wooden mill-wheel and the gushing mill stream below. After nearly thirty miles, and with another twenty-odd to go, I needed proper food. And a cappuccino.

While we ordered, the pair of cyclists came in.

"You know back there," I said to them, "the bird of prey. It was just a large buzzard, wasn't it?"

Not, I was thinking, a golden eagle.

The sporty-looking cyclist deferred to his brother-in-law (if such he was). "You're the expert. Was that a buzzard?"

"Yes," he said.

So I supposed that settled it.

Caldbeck was the furthest north we would ride in the National Park, the boundary a few hundred metres away on the Carlisle road. Close enough, I thought, with South, East and North borders under our belts, because now we would be heading westwards on our circuit of the Skiddaw and Blencathra fells. We said goodbye to the two cyclists, half expecting to bump into them again at some point, unlocked our bikes and joggled up the stony unmade lane into the village again.

The cottages were built higgledy-piggledy, some white, some creams and greys, a nice little place.

Beyond a cattle grid on the edge of Caldbeck, an unfenced road rose to bleak, blowy fell-country, the Back O'Skiddaw, with barely a tree to hinder the wind.

To our north were low hills, while the fells to the south were grassy and rounded - great humpbacks rising to the heights of Skiddaw and Blencathra. Off to the right was Ullock Pike, arguably the best of the routes up Skiddaw. The most common is 'the tourist route' from Keswick. 'Tourist route' is perhaps unkind.

There are wonderful views behind, down over Keswick and Derwentwater, and right down through the Jaws of Borrowdale, where Castle Crag sits picturesquely in the gap. Skiddaw is still a challenge to the walker, or the fell runner, and from the top of the fourth highest fell in the Lake District, the north Cumbrian plain, the Solway Firth and the hills of Dumfries and Galloway are clear on a good day.

On a good day. Dark clouds loomed over Skiddaw and we could see the rain up there.

A hand-painted sign warned 'COWS please slow' which can be interpreted more than one way. In fact, it was sheep that were wandering around the edges of the roads, shaggy tough-looking beasts, capable of dealing with the weather and surviving on the rough, boggy peatland on the south side of the road or the slightly higher but still rough grasses to the north.

As we turned off on a lane signposted for Bassenthwaite, the rain came. We put jackets back on, and were glad when the road dropped downwards into a little valley for some shelter.

We were heading south-west now, and the lane climbed again, with a view of Overwater, a small tarn really only seen from here or from the delightfully named hills of Little Cockup and Great Cockup off to our left. Above them a bird was circling, large-winged and black against the clouds above, the wrong shape for a buzzard, and I guessed at a raven as it wheeled in the air and headed away.

An impressive farmhouse stood by the road - Orthwaite Hall. 17th century maybe, it had mullioned windows and a solid appearance, despite the pink paint of the walls.

A short way beyond, we turned on to the road down to Bassenthwaite village, almost a continuous downhill for a mile or so, much of it through woodland and with a stream to one side. As good a way of going downhill on a bike as I can think of, and by the time we were at the bottom, the rain had stopped.

Bassenthwaite seemed mostly a working village, rather than a tourist village, though presumably with the odd B&B and holiday cottage, and we rode past the village green down to the main road. Directly opposite, another lane went off, signposted for Scarness, and we followed that.

Slightly longer than the direct route along the main road, we reckoned it would be more pleasant, and it was. The quiet road led us through fields with a view up to Ullock Pike and Skiddaw on the left, and on the right down to Bassenthwaite Lake – the answer, of course, to those quiz questions asking how many 'Lakes' there are in the Lake District: pedantically, just this one.

A gate came up on our right, with a track leading across fields to St Bega's Church, a sublime church dating back to before the Normans. Overlooked by green and slate-grey fells, and itself looking down to the wind-blown lake, it is only reachable across fields and is a peaceful, romantic spot. Poets had not stopped being inspired by Lakeland after Wordsworth's generation, and in the 19th century, Alfred, Lord Tennyson came here.

Tennyson re-told the stories of King Arthur in blank verse, and his version of the death of Arthur is said to have been inspired by the position of St Bega's by the lakeshore. A dying King Arthur, resting in a ruined chapel by a lake, commands Sir Bedivere to throw his sword Excalibur into the waters from which he had been given it by the Lady of the Lake. Twice the knight cannot do it. The third time he throws the sword,

> But ere he dipped the surface, rose an arm
> Clothed in white samite, mystic, wonderful,
> And caught him by the hilt, and brandish'd him
> Three times, and drew him under in the mere.

We pulled out on to the main road again, cycling south past a screen of oak, beech, ash and holly concealing forestry behind, while on our right were fields with black-faced, cream-bodied sheep scattered across them. Beyond were glimpses of the lake, and beyond again the dark green of spruce and firs in Thornthwaite Forest which climbed right over the summit of Ladies' Table (though Lord's Seat behind was clear of forest).

Directly above the lake is Barf, a name which has always amused any American visitors, home to Bishop Rock part way up a slate scree. The rock is repainted white whenever it needs it, as a memorial - it is said - to the drunken bishop in the pub below who bet his friends that he could ride his horse up the scree slope, and who didn't make it. The rock is meant to mark where the bishop met his end. Sadly, it's probably not true, but it's a good story.

We passed Mirehouse, a family-owned manor house that is open to visitors, with gardens that also lead down to St Bega's Church. Tennyson stayed with his friends the Speddings here, hence his knowledge of the church.

On the other side of the road was Dodd Wood. From the top of Dodd, an outlier of Ullock Pike and Skiddaw, the views down the length of Borrowdale are stunning. But Dodd Wood was better known for its temporary summer residents. A sign by the road said 'Osprey Viewing'.

With a wing-span of four or five foot, and talons designed to pluck pike or trout from a lake, they make an amazing sight. Driven to extinction in Britain over a hundred years ago, a pair reappeared in Scotland in the 1950s. Numbers grew in Scotland, and in the 1990s ospreys began to appear at Bassenthwaite Lake. When the Lake District Osprey Project created a nest in 2001, a pair took it over, and there have been nesting ospreys at Bass Lake ever since.

"Look out for ospreys, Rich."

I didn't mention the Lady of the Lake. We wouldn't have seen her either.

The road flattened and widened on the approach to Keswick. At the large roundabout for the A66 we had no alternative to the main road. We needed to go west to go over the Whinlatter Pass to Cockermouth, and there was neither a cycle lane nor any sort of a lane that would avoid us being on the A66 for a short while. We put heads down and charged along it, the flatness making progress quick. The sooner we were off the better.

Fortunately, a cycle lane did appear before too long. We had hit a portion of the C2C again, and we slowed so that we could take in the sight of the fells we were approaching, which were now in sunshine. Directly in front was long, low Barrow. About the same height as the ever-busy Catbells away to our left with its summer queues of walkers, Barrow is generally quiet and makes a lovely walk from the village of Braithwaite, where we were heading. The road swung gently right, and we could see the long ridge of

Grisedale Pike. Green and gentle-looking in the summer, like all these fells it would turn russet from the bracken in the autumn, and would have its share of snow in the winter. With the other fells that make up the Coledale Horseshoe walk, such as Hopegill Head, Crag Hill and either Causey Pike or Barrow, it makes really good walking country.

We turned into Braithwaite, the small village at the start of Whinlatter Pass. I decided I needed sustenance in the form of a Mars Bar and some sort of a sugary drink. I wasn't too fussy at this stage.

We cycled past Braithwaite's campsite and turned left at The Royal Oak (which on another occasion would have tempted us), over a little stone bridge, and found The General Store amongst a clutch of whitewashed cottages with slate roofs. The store had just what I needed.

The lady serving asked after our route and when I told her, she said, "There's not a good forecast for later in the week. Could be floods, they say."

"Ah," I said.

Outside, we mooched around the pretty village for a few minutes to give our legs a break.

The bridge crossed Coledale Beck, flowing out of Coledale valley behind, yet another of the Lake District's former mining areas. Silver and lead were mined here from the 16th century to the 19th century, and the mine was worked on and off until as recently as 1990. Some of the buildings still exist, but it had become a sad, empty place since then.

The day felt warm, and we parked ourselves on the shop's bench for a few minutes. A couple of older men were chatting nearby as they walked by. "Farming has changed, you know," one said. "When I was younger, the farms here were all about rotation. Potatoes one year, kale the next. One farm even had a field of strawberries. Now it's just grass for sheep and bullocks."

He wasn't, I guessed, talking about hill farms, but the valleys, and I supposed it must be common for there to be more specialisation generally, not just in Lakeland. Richard and I were meeting a hill farmer for lunch at Buttermere the following day. That was going to be interesting.

Today though, we had a hill to climb.

"Ready?" I asked Richard.

"Yup. You?"

"I was born ready."

He just looked at me.

The road over Whinlatter Pass was instantly quite steep. We were on the second of the six Great Cycling Climbs in Lakeland. Maybe only a 5/10, but I reckoned they all counted.

With overhanging trees and a rushing stream on our left, a passenger in a car would no doubt think it very pretty. For me, it was straight into slow-and-steady mode, hands gripping handlebars as the whole body helped the thighs turn the pedals. The tortoise to Richard's hare.

Up and around the corner, still just as steep, the lungs now working hard, heart pumping. Past the busy car park for the classic walk up Grisedale Pike, and making our way around cars parked on the road. A few cars coming the other way, a couple my way, several with mountain bikes on the back or on top. Past the white house by the side of the road that must have extraordinary views over the lake to Skiddaw, and then the sign for Whinlatter Visitor Centre: 2.5 miles. Some twists and bends in the road, and then a sudden little extra steepness as the road goes left around the fellside, and the trees on the right disappear leaving an awesome view from a lay-by.

Richard was waiting and I pulled in beside him, breath coming hard. Immediately below the wall, a field of ferns dropped away towards the valley. Beyond the flat green fields on the valley floor rose the Skiddaw range, with Ullock Pike and forested Dodd in front. Ullock Pike's ridge fell away leftwards to the lake. Somewhere down there was a small church, and ospreys.

Directly across from us on the side of Seat How was Whinlatter Forest - a patchwork of dark forest and lighter greens showing the different types of tree grown there by the Forestry Commission, and other patches of bald brown stumps where sections of forest had been clear-felled. We had once had a German visitor who we had brought here, and who had been shocked that we still had clear-felling of forestry. In her part of Germany it was illegal, seen

135

as detrimental to wildlife and the environment.

The Forestry Commission's way of working has changed, of course; once, they would plant continuous forest over every elevation and valley, with no break for wildlife or indigenous trees or recreation. Today, a glance at Dodd Wood across the valley showed that had changed. The forest had gone from the top of Dodd, and the trees on the slopes were more mixed. But looking over to the forest on the west side of the lake, there were still those bare patches, which on the ground look like the scene from the film Lion King after the land has been decimated. I can't help thinking that a policy of selective felling of trees – 'continuous cover' – might be a better one.

Even so, it was a fantastic view. A very good excuse to stop for a pause for breath.

A man and his two children had come out of their car to take in the same view. "Not far now," he said to us. "Only another couple of hundred yards and it's downhill all the way to Cockermouth."

Well, nearly, I thought.

A flatter section of the road took us back under trees and past a fast-flowing beck before we were climbing again, though not as steeply, and it wasn't long before we were close to the top. A long, flat stretch, a short down and then a last very steep up, and we were at the sign for Whinlatter Visitor Centre.

So a 5/10 done. Good, I thought. Though that left an 8/10 and a 9/10 for tomorrow. Hm.

It was late in the day now, so the Visitor Centre was quietening, with cars edging out of the car park. There's no doubt it is a grand place to visit, with forest trails, café, shop and outdoor play area. The biggest draw has become their mountain bike trails.

I have to admit that I had thought mountain biking a relatively recent phenomenon, and I suppose the most recent incarnation is. But then I had read about 'pass storming' in a Cycling Touring Guide to Northern England published in 1947. Harold Briercliffe described how we would carry his bike to the top of Lakeland passes where there was no road and cycle down the rock-strewn footpaths on the far side. It might save him a long round-trip, and he clearly enjoyed it hugely, despite what must have been fairly rudimentary bikes with no suspension. He did have useful advice: apparently it had not been a good idea to cycle over Sty Head Pass on a tandem carrying camping gear with his 'very muscular' girlfriend.

We pushed off and were soon heading downhill, a car overtaking us with a large plastic ice cream tub balanced on the roof.

"Hey!" I shouted, but it was too late. The car was disappearing down the hill. "I reckon we might see that box again on our way down," I said.

"On the first sharp corner, probably."

The road dropped and twisted. No sign of the box.

We were in a valley now, the forest gone from our right, where a great slate and heather slope headed up steeply to Whinlatter Fell. Above the forest on our left emerged the ridges leading up to Grisedale Pike, grass-covered and green in the sun. The road dropped again through trees, and after the entrance to the car park for Spout Force, there was a sharp turn into a steep downhill. A large plastic ice cream tub lay in the middle of the road. I slowed, Richard speeding onwards. Around the tub were scattered cooked baked potatoes, their innards squished on the tarmac.

Crows would no doubt have the potatoes, I thought, but not the ice cream tub. I braked, pulled in and walked back up. I just about managed to get the ice cream tub into the top of a pannier, and set off after Richard, the steep slope twisting through trees and over a bridge above Spout Force's stream, to where Richard was waiting for me round the corner.

"You alright?" he asked.

"Yes. Just picking up the ice cream tub. Did you see what had been in it?"

"No."

"Baked potatoes."

"Bizarre. Did you pick them up?"

"They were a bit far gone."

The road dropped down and down again, and we were going fast now. Past the lane for Lorton, out of the hills and on to the flatter valley floor, but still carrying our speed. We finally slowed and joined the road from Buttermere to Cockermouth, the road gradually climbing, fields around us with just low fells off to our left and right, before coming to a long, gentle hill taking us out of the

137

valley. It was nothing. It will never be mentioned in any book on steep hills. Never. But I was tired by now. Again, Richard waited for me at the top.

Then it was straight, with little ups and downs, out of the National Park and down the hill into Cockermouth.

From Lorton Road, we dropped down into one of the oldest parts of the town, Kirkgate and Market Place. Here the houses and cottages, once uniformly white with black raised borders to the windows, had been painted in almost seaside shades – creams, yellow ochre, pale blue, teal. Above Market Place stood the castle and Jennings Brewery from which tremendous yeasty aromas drift into the town several days a week.

We pedalled over the bridge crossing the River Cocker and into Main Street. This is the iconic view of Cockermouth, with the wide Main Street flanked by trees, a white marble statue of Lord Mayo in the centre, and Georgian shop fronts lining the street.

Most of the shops in Cockermouth are locally owned rather than chain stores, and the town is not yet a huge tourist draw, but did get overmuch national exposure in November 2009, when devastating floods swept all through the low-lying areas of the town. Many of the shop fronts were replaced following the floods, and the town centre is probably looking even better than it did before.

We cycled on to the far end of Main Street, where the National Trust own Wordsworth House, the birthplace of William Wordsworth. If the castle at the other end of town were ever to be opened to the public, Cockermouth might become a real tourist attraction in the summer. For the moment, it's a homely town. In fact, my home town.

We cycled up through town. It had been a long day, and I was tired. But I still had something I wanted to do.

Our house is at the top of one last little hill. Traditionally I race Richard the last section, and he always wins.

"Rich," I said as we approached it. "I'm done in. Don't expect me to race you up this bit."

"Fair enough."

I let him pedal slowly ahead of me, gathered myself, and once he was the right distance away, put the hammer down. True enough, he didn't expect me to race him up that last bit.

I overtook at speed, legs pumping their last.

"YEEESSSS!!!"

"You..."

He was too late. I sped around the corner and on to our drive. I had beaten him home.

On the drive, I was almost bent double getting my breath but managed the last word as well.

"There's a proverb, Rich," I said. "Age and treachery... are more than a match... for youth and skill."

And then I went and sat down for a bit.

Distance for the day: 56 miles / 90 Km
Height gained: 5,406 feet / 1,648 metres
Hardest hill: Whinlatter Pass 758 feet / 231 metres
Average speed: 10.8 mph / 17.3 Kmph
Fastest speed: 36.6 mph / 58.4 Kmph
Total distance: 233 miles / 373 Km

There was a good chance that, on tomorrow's Honister Pass and Newlands Pass, youth would win out. Treachery, I thought, can only get you so far.

DAY SIX - SETHERA

BUTTERMERE AND BORROWDALE

Cockermouth – Buttermere – Honister Pass – Seatoller
Rosthwaite – Grange – Ashness Bridge – Keswick
Newlands Pass – Buttermere – Cockermouth

43 miles

www.lakedistrictgrandtour.co.uk/day/six

141

Today was to be a round trip from Cockermouth over two of the biggest passes in the Lake District, taking in Crummock Water, Buttermere, Honister Pass, Borrowdale and possibly Ashness Bridge and Keswick on the way back to Buttermere via Newlands Pass. All before lunch.

We were meeting Richard's old school friend Eddie at Buttermere for a late lunch in the pub on the way back.

That was the plan.

It was starting to feel ambitious.

Crummock Water was to be our twelfth lake out of the sixteen suggested by Cumbria Tourism, while Honister Pass and Newlands Pass would make it four out of six of the Great Cycle Climbs. Although it was a round trip, it felt like a big day.

Eddie had been in the local paper when he took over the tenancy of a farm in Buttermere at the age of 19, making him the youngest farmer in the Lake District. I had asked Richard to see if we could meet up; cycling all round the Lake District was giving me all sorts of questions that I didn't know the answer to, and I thought Eddie could maybe help.

The forecast had been rain, which was wrong. We set off in sunshine, the sky an azure blue with the odd wisp of high cloud. It was a fantastic day for cycling, if chilly.

We soon warmed up though, and stopped just outside Cockermouth to take off our jackets. The view was stunning. The linked fells of Grisedale Pike, Hopegill Head and Whiteside provided a dramatic ridge line of sun and shade, sharp against the sky. It was as if a perfectly blue page had been torn in half, uncovering a second page behind.

We rode hard down the hill which had been an uphill struggle for me the day before, but instead of turning for the Whinlatter Pass, we carried on into the village of Lorton.

Lorton is almost two villages. Low Lorton straddles the Cockermouth-Buttermere road and has the pub, while High Lorton runs off at an angle and has the village's primary school and tennis court. The church is on its own in middle ground.

We pedalled into Low Lorton, and I said to Richard to slow and stop by an old set of buildings on our right. It was not the buildings

142

I wanted to show him though, but the sign high on the wall. It was a very old AA sign, probably from the time of the Yellow Earl's involvement with the Automobile Association when the AA provided most road signs; it was only in 1939 that local councils were given the duty of providing road signs. This one was a yellow disk with LOW LORTON across the middle, and above and below that the distances to relevant destinations:

BUTTERMERE 6

COCKERMOUTH $3^{3/4}$

LONDON $299^{3/4}$

Ambitiously precise, I thought, given that it was made at a time long before GPS, though later I entered 'Low Lorton to London' on Google Maps and it came up with 300 miles. Hmm.

Under the distances the sign said:

SAFETY FIRST

And that might have been a useful hint, because the sign also seemed to have gunshot holes in it.

Anyway, we clearly had six miles to go to Buttermere, and they were six wonderful miles, starting in the Lorton Valley's network of fields, all grassed for sheep or cattle. We had passed Lorton's pub, The Wheatsheaf, and it occurred to me that the chap in Braithwaite might have had a point about a wider range of farming in the past. Perhaps wheat had been grown here, though it can't have been an easy crop to grow in Lakeland's climate.

Streams ran in gullies under the road, and by each of them were piles of rocks and stones, more evidence of the 2009 floods. Like Cockermouth, Keswick and Workington, this valley had also suffered, with Lorton Bridge washed away completely by the River Cocker, riverside houses flooded, and fields covered in debris, particularly stones washed down the mountains and deposited on the valley floor below.

The hills rose on either side. On our right was the grassy ridge of Low Fell, not a high mountain (the clue is in the name), but the views from the top eastwards into the Lake District are glorious. On our left were the much more substantial fells of Hopegill Head and Whiteside, their steep western slopes in shadow from the low sun in the east.

The road divided and we took the left fork for Buttermere and began to climb. The sun dappled through trees all around us and a busy stream found its way down to the valley below the road on our left.

The trees finished, the land became rougher, and we topped out at Lanthwaite Green just where the ravine of Gasgale Gill forms a gap between Whiteside and the high, rocky bulge of Grassmoor, dark today before the sun had touched it.

"My favourite mountain, that," Richard said.

"Why?"

"Just that I used to run it. You know, cycle out here, run up Gasgale Gill and then up on to Grassmoor. Great views from up there."

"I think mine is Grisedale Pike. For the same reason. When we first came to live here I used to do a lot of running around Whinlatter, and if I was feeling fit, I'd head up on to Grisedale Pike and back."

"Do you remember we cycled up to Whinlatter once, and then ran up Grisedale Pike?"

"I think I walked more than ran, but yes, and you carried on and did the Coledale Horseshoe. I think I went back to the café for a cappuccino and a sit-down."

He smiled. "And this next bit is my favourite bit of road."

We cycled on, the unfenced road falling then rising a little, falling and rising a little, and with each rise a brand new view came to us of the lake that we were dropping towards. Crummock Water was a dark blue reflection of a clear sky, with the shaded triangle of Rannerdale Knotts slicing out into the water, and with the sunlit Buttermere fells on the far side: the high dome of Red Pike and in the distance the more rounded High Stile and High Crag. On our right, straight across the waters, was the rock-strewn humpback of Melbreak. All the while, high above us on our left, the mass of Grassmoor loomed, with runs of loose scree above the lower grassy slopes, and above that, scrambly rock formations leading up to a point, breaking into the cornflower-blue sky.

The air was so clean and clear, the colours so bright. If Woodrow Wilson during his cycle rides around the Lake District had said that the road alongside Ullswater must be the most beautiful road in the world, then today the road alongside Crummock Water was giving it a run for its money.

Several sheep wandered into our path and we slowed to go around them - grey shaggy ewes and black lambs. These were the Lake District's very own Herdwicks, and I was looking forward to talking to Eddie about them this afternoon. Three generations of his family farmed in these valleys - Eddie, his father and his grandfather - so there was a good chance that these sheep were either Eddie's or his family's.

As we got closer to the lake, there were farms alongside the road and stone walls appeared on either side, with sheep in the fields beyond. There were still sheep on the road though, a ewe and lamb lying down pressed against a wall, and by one of the farms there was a sign:

TEK CARE

LAMBS ONT ROAD

The Herdwick is a purely Lake District breed, mostly found in the central and western fells. The breed was possibly brought here by the Vikings and was definitely here at the time of the abbeys and their sheep-walks. They are probably the most hardy of breeds, capable of surviving on the fells through the winter.

They are 'heafed', that is, Herdwicks naturally know their own fells and rarely stray too far, with the lambs learning from their mothers. During the foot-and-mouth-disease outbreak in 2001, whole herds were lost, and the breeding of Herdwicks on the fells had in any case been under threat for a very long time. The wool, once prized, is not commercially viable, though Herdwick meat has a fantastic flavour.

As long ago as the 1930s Beatrix Potter was one of those who campaigned to maintain the traditional breed of Lakeland. As the married Mrs Heelis, she even became a judge at local shows. When she died, she left fifteen farms to the National Trust on the condition that they continue to graze Herdwicks, and the National Trust is still one of the organisations that supports the breed.

A good thing too. The Lake District would not be the same without its black lambs, its grey shaggy ewes and its 'tups', as the farmers call the rams with their horns curving around to pointed tips, proudly displayed at valley shows.

The cliff-face of Rannerdale Knotts was getting closer, a steep wall of rock, its long ridge separated from the slopes of Grassmoor's neighbour Whiteless Pike by the valley of Rannerdale.

Rannerdale has the most gorgeous display of bluebells in late spring, and there is a local legend that the bluebells grow where blood has been spilled; in this case the blood of a Norman army lured into the valley and destroyed.

Here's the story as written by Nicholas Size in his book, 'The Secret Valley: The Real Romance of Lakeland' in the 1930s, which he said he reconstructed from 'local place-names, old ruins and half-forgotten stories' and from the fact that the Norman tax-gatherers were unable to enter the Lakeland valleys at the time of the writing of Domesday Book.

According to his book, the people of Lakeland were a mix of Norse and Celts in 1066 and independent of both England and Scotland. With the Normans moving northwards, refugees arrived in some numbers - Anglians from northern England. Over the next few decades, the Normans took all the land around Lakeland - Carlisle, Penrith, Kendal and the coast, but attempts to take Lakeland itself were repulsed by the combined peoples led by Earl Boethar. One of the reasons for the success of the Earl and his warriors was that they had a whole valley hidden away from the main routes into Lakeland: the valley of Buttermere and Crummock Water, with the only access via high passes or swampy bogs, and kept secret from the enemy.

A final push to take the secret valley came with an army sent down from Cockermouth. When the army arrived at the foot of the Rannerdale valley, a path led them up into the valley itself, and into an ambush, where they were destroyed. Hence the blood and the bluebells.

Nicolas Size's book was a wonderfully romantic version of events, and he used artistic licence quite freely. I particularly like his description of Earl Boethar as a 'kindly, humorous man, with lightish hair and a fresh complexion', (this of a man for whom there are no records from the time), and his dismissal of the 'savage'

Normans as compared with 'the free men of the North'. But is the main thrust of the story true? Did the 'free men of the North' keep the 'savage' Normans at bay for fifty years, and was Rannerdale the site of the final battle that kept the Normans out of Lakeland, and persuaded King Stephen of England to give away Cumberland and 'Westmarieland' to King David of Scotland? Or does Lakeland not appear in Domesday Book simply because at the time it was part of Scotland, with Nicholas Size's book no more than a good story?

I don't know, but personally I like the 'free men of the North' story, and, well, I'd like it to be true.

We cycled around Rannerdale's promontory, the lake close on our right. At a pull-in a small group were preparing scuba diving equipment for a dive in the dark waters.

Once around the point, the valley opened up again and the road ran flat alongside the lake. There was more of a breeze here, coming down the valley, but it was not cold, and we were still cycling through the seeringly bright blues and greens of the valley.

The lake began to run out, and the road rose through woodland. Then there were houses, slate and whitewashed, as we rode down a short hill into Buttermere village. The village's hotels and tea rooms were off to our right, presumably getting ready for another day catering for Buttermere's considerable tourist trade. A coach was pulled in, and a group of Japanese tourists were wandering. You could see why. The village stands between the two lakes of the valley, with the fells opposite broken by the white streams of waterfalls. The walk down to Buttermere lake is easy and popular, and the walk around the lake is wonderful.

"We'd better carry on if we are going to be in time for Eddie," I said.

"Fine by me."

So we were straight into a steep hill out of the village, past the tiny stone church with its little bell tower on one end and stone cross on the other, and past the junction with the road down from Newlands Pass. We would be back down there later on. All being well.

On up through trees and once out, the road began to drop to the lake again. On our left the ground rose steeply, the bracken giving way to the heights of Robinson. At the far end of the lake the long ridge of Fleetwith Pike slid down towards the water and, in the gap between Fleetwith Pike and the three rounded summits on the southern side of the lake, stood the hummocky dinosaur-back of Haystacks.

Not one of the larger Lake District fells by any means, but probably now deserving of being a place of pilgrimage, Haystacks is where Alfred Wainwright had his ashes scattered. Close to the top is Innominate Tarn - 'no name tarn' - and I had been disappointed when the suggestion of renaming it Wainwright Tarn was turned down. It would seem a good tribute.

We cycled on towards the end of the lake, stopping for another of the characteristic views of Lakeland calendars. Alongside images of Castlerigg Stone Circle, Ashness Bridge and Surprise View, you have to have the pines of Buttermere. There's many an image in gift shops of the stately pines on the slatey shoreline reflected in the water of Buttermere, with Haystacks forming the backdrop. There was no reflection for us today, the breeze enough to ruffle the water, but it was still extraordinarily beautiful.

Coming out of the valley at Gatesgarth Farm, Honister Pass had an initial steepness as we climbed towards the base of Fleetwith Pike. But the road flattened in a false-sense-of-security sort of way and moved to the centre of the valley to join the fast-flowing beck weaving around in the bottom of the valley.

A camper van was parked across on the grass by the stream, and the door opened to reveal a tousle-haired couple. They had edged their van off the road between boulders, and there were lots of boulders, ranging from small to enormous and climbable. In fact, as we rode past, a climber was placing a bouldering mat on the ground beneath the overhang of one of the largest boulders to break his fall as he tried his skill on the overhang.

Some of the rocks and boulders had probably bounced their way down from high ridges on either side, (and I wouldn't want to be in the way) but many will have been left by the glacier that carved this U-shaped valley in the last ice age.

Richard and I had been riding together till now, but Honister

Pass was not a 9/10 for nothing, and the road began to rise and get tougher. He went on ahead, his own mission to get to the top without stopping at all, mine to get to the top without pushing - though I would allow myself pauses for breath if I needed them.

Now on the left side of the beck, the hill was more long than steep. I was managing. On either side the boulder graveyard became more dense, the valley closing in, with long scree slopes under rock buttresses.

Then the road crossed the stream on a small bridge, and the proper steepness began. '100 Greatest Cycling Climbs' says this section is a 20% gradient. I thought I could see the top now, though only beyond a steeper section again in the distance - apparently 25%. First I had to get up this one. My legs were slowing, and about half way up I had to take some pressure off. I looked behind - no cars, and then started a couple of zigzags across the road. It seemed to help, and I reverted to the straight up the road very slowly mode, repeating the process when I needed to.

Gradually, very gradually, I was approaching the 25% gradient. I could see it coming. It wasn't as long, but it looked very steep. There was no way, I thought, that I was going to be able to get up there. Was there?

As the road steepened I went into zigzag mode again, but then a car came down and I had to get out of the way. As I did so, my legs just stopped. Well, so did my lungs really, and the heart wasn't much better.

Foot down on the ground, I think I said a rude word. Something pithy expressing the fact that I was a bit rubbish at these big hills. I gulped air, and let my body return to a semblance of normality.

After a minute, I went for it. Legs pummelling down, ignoring the lungs, pushing the bike uphill. The wall for the Honister Slate Mine car park was in sight, and a couple were dangling their legs over the edge and watching me.

Somewhere in my head it occurred to me that they were either non-fit people watching someone who can cycle up Honister Pass, or fit people - probably fit cyclists - who were shaking their heads at this mass of sweat desperately inching his way forwards and likely at any moment to fall off.

Either way, I couldn't stop now. One more push and the road

began to get less steep. Less again, and I had made it to the top of the third of the Great Cycling Climbs.

Richard was perched on a boulder at the entrance to the Slate Mine and he clapped me up to him.

I stopped, leaning across my handlebars, breathing hard.

"You made it," Richard said.

"I had to stop… That was… a bit… rubbish."

"But you didn't push though?"

"No… I didn't… push."

"That's brilliant."

Son, I thought, thanks.

"You?"

"I made it."

"Hey, well done you."

Honister Slate Mine is the last slate mine in England, and has almost closed more than once. Most recently Mark Weir bought the moth-balled mine in 1997 and through what seems to me an inspiring mix of imagination, hard work and guts, made a go of the business.

The mine still produces Honister green slate from shafts deep inside Fleetwith Pike, but the tourism element is a major factor now. They run tours through the mines (I'd been; it was spectacular in there) and have been introducing adventure tourism in the form of their 'Via Ferrata'; those brave enough are harnessed on to fixed cables, and can traverse across the cliff face high above Honister Pass. The latest 'Extreme' version includes a 230 foot wire bridge.

Mark died tragically in a helicopter accident in 2011, and at time of writing the plans for a giant zip wire are still in the balance. I guess if it does get the go-ahead it would be a fitting tribute to the man.

"What do you reckon, Rich? Downhill all the way from here?"

"It might be a bit uphill over Newlands Pass to get back to Buttermere."

"Good point. How about a cup of tea in Grange? I think I might need that."

We pedalled past the YHA hostel next door to the mine, but stopped again by the 20% gradient sign at the top of the road down.

At the far end of the valley we could see a wooded ridge, and further off a long line of hills, grey-blue against white clouds forming in the east. Perhaps the Helvellyn range. It was quite a view.

Up to our left was a steep grass and bracken slope leading up to Dalehead, while opposite us was a short, sharp climb that would lead towards Grey Knotts and eventually Great Gable.

"Good enough," I said, and we set off. I let Richard go first. He's braver than me going down steep hills on a bike. Something about age and bounceability, I think.

The road twisted as it dropped away, and we had to brake to a halt more than once as traffic came the other way, mostly cars but also a white delivery van, who I thought must curse the deliveries to Honister Slate Mine. More of a problem was two vehicles trying to pass each other on the narrow twisty road.

We finally freed ourselves and set off at speed downhill. It was fun.

There was a reasonable incline for most of it, but then towards the bottom it suddenly became very, very steep as the road dropped into trees. Which would have been fine if it weren't for two teachers who clearly weren't safe to be out on their own, let alone with a party of school children. They were all wearing full waterproofs and safety helmets, presumably on their way back from ghyll scrambling - a wet sliding descent of a mountain stream - but perhaps they wanted the extra excitement of walking out into a road without looking.

The children weren't the problem. They were waiting patiently in line to the left of the road. First the lady teacher, without looking uphill, wandered out in front of Richard as he sped down ahead of me. I saw him swerve and manage to miss her.

Which was the cue for the male teacher, watching Richard's departing back and again not looking uphill, to wave his children in a crocodile across the road. I shouted. I hollered. I panicked. I threw on the brakes.

It was the children that saw me, and made a small gap which I snaked through.

My heart was beating as hard as when I had reached the top of Honister from the other side.

"I don't believe that," Richard said.

"To think that those two are meant to be in charge of the kids.

I hope the kids look after them."

We were in the hamlet of Seatoller, originally built for workers at the slate mine, today a pretty little place of slate and whitewashed cottages with hanging baskets and gorgeous views to the fells.

We pedalled on past the turn for Seathwaite to the south of us, at the very end of the Borrowdale valley.

The hills above Seathwaite had been the source of much of the water that caused the floods of November 2009, pictures of which were shown around the world. In a single 24-hour period measurements show rainfall on the fells there of over 300 millimetres (over a foot of water in old money). The ground was already sodden and there was nowhere for the water to go, except down the waterfalls, cliffs and gullies into the valleys below.

Rain falling on Maiden Moor and Bessyboot and Great Gable and the Langdale Pikes coursed into Borrowdale and on into Derwentwater. The becks overflowed from Helvellyn and Nethermost Pike and Armboth Fell into Thirlmere, which fed into St John's Beck, and from there into the River Greta, flowing westwards. More becks joined from the slopes of Skiddaw and Blencathra, before the Greta met up with the River Derwent as it came out of Derwentwater by the pencil factory in Keswick, flooding through the houses by the river.

From there the Derwent took the mass of water into Bassenthwaite Lake, joined by the surging Newlands Beck with water from Robinson and Hindscarth and High Spy and Causey Pike, and by more streams from the great mass of the Skiddaw range.

West of Richard and me here in Seatoller, the streams and falls of Red Pike and High Stile and High Crag and Haystacks and the southern sides of Dalehead and Robinson flooded into Buttermere, and the River Cocker carried the water on into Crummock Water and beyond, with the ravines from Melbreak and Whiteless Pike and Grassmoor and Whiteside adding their waters and their stones and boulders, loosened and washed down into the swirling river. The fells above Loweswater added more, the valley leading to Whinlatter more again.

The flooding Cocker, now carrying pebbles, stones, rock, boulders and even uprooted tree trunks, met the flooding Derwent in the middle of Cockermouth, with a pinch-point of the main bridge.

I was in my office by the Cocker on that Thursday morning, 19th November. We had never flooded before, though other houses and businesses by the Derwent had flooded twice already in the past few years. As the river rose after nine o'clock, water began to ooze in under the door and I thought we might need a dehumidifier to dry off a damp carpet. Around ten o'clock I thought we might need something more and went in search of sandbags. I managed to come back with four. It was nowhere near enough.

When the river crested a little raise behind the office, the River Cocker flooded in, surging around the office, lifting desks and filing cabinets and bookshelves, punching a hole through to the shop in front of us. There was paper everywhere, floating around in the dark water. We gave up trying to lift things out of the way when we realised that the water had suddenly reached waist height, and it was getting dangerous.

From the top of the raise just behind the office we watched as the river continued to rise, eventually reaching two metres high inside our office which was effectively part of the flooding river. The same was replicated all through the centre of the town in homes and businesses, even those well away from river banks. It was not just placid water, but a roaring, surging flood flowing down Market Place and Main Street carrying cars with it, tearing up the road in little Challoner Street. The Mountain Rescue had boats battling against the flow along Main Street to rescue folk, and helicopters pulled people from skylights in the roofs, the buildings themselves shaking and shivering with the pressure of the water.

From Cockermouth, the Derwent took the combined waters on westwards. As the land flattened, the river dropped more of its stones, turning what had been fields of grass by the river into fields of stones. Bridges were undermined, damaged or destroyed completely all the way down to the coast at Workington, where Police Constable Barker was carried away by the waters.

Within a few days, the waters had receded, but left devastation. As I write this, I realise that was three years ago today.

In Seatoller the sun was shining on Richard and me. The village, the valley and the fells around were benign and beautiful.

The road turned northwards and was virtually flat now along the valley floor, though all around were still high fells. There was the wonderfully named Bessyboot to the south, another hump-backed dinosaur, and the trees of Johnny Wood on our left, behind which the summit of High Spy appeared. Fields gave way to woodland and a beck came in on our right on its way to merge with the River Derwent that would feed the lake.

The next village was Rosthwaite, with its two hotels and the farm tea room. I had called at the tea room with my wife Claire and my friend Hugh the previous year at the end of a walk from Grange. Hugh is partial to strong tea, so I had said to the lady, "Three teas please, and could you make one of them really strong. You know, pretty well black. So that the spoon stands up in it."

"Round here," she said, "we call that 'tea'."

Pause.

"In that case," I said, "two weak teas and one tea."

The village of Rosthwaite, and the whole valley, is the home to a grand local community, but house prices are well outside what young sons and daughters of local families can afford to pay. Across the Lake District as a whole, the National Park Authority wants to see nine hundred new houses built for local ownership only. At the same time, new blood can be a blessing for a community, as with Taffy Thomas in Grasmere. Off-comers come and stay, and their children and children's children become local.

Holiday cottages are another local issue; in Borrowdale over half the houses are holiday cottages. Again, it's getting the balance right, because the local community needs the income from visitors coming to the valley; farming alone cannot pay the bills.

North of Rosthwaite the valley narrowed into the 'Jaws of Borrowdale' with the road running through rock-strewn woods. Many of the trees here and in the rest of Lakeland are ash trees, and it would be a tragedy if disease were to destroy great swathes of them.

The River Derwent was below on our left, and on the far bank the woods marked the base of Castle Crag, by no means one of the largest of the Lake District fells, and the smallest in the Wainwright guide books, but the views from the top are just great. You climb through old slate quarry workings, needing a sense of balance on the scree path. From the top, you see right down Derwentwater to Skiddaw.

We stopped at the car park for the Bowder Stone and a quick charge along the path. The Bowder Stone was massive. A roughly cube shape, and resting on one edge, as if a huge dice had been thrown down from one of the fells and had somehow contrived not to fall flat on one side. A ladder runs up to the top on one side and a mother was waving to her son and partner from the top.

There were also two climbers with bouldering mats under an overhanging open side. The stone's tiny ledges had coverings of chalk that the two young guys occasionally tried to clear a little, before re-chalking their hands and climbing, leaning outwards and searching for the next move.

On the far side was a stone building amongst the trees that surround the Bowder Stone, a climbing hut, one of many scattered around Borrowdale, Langdale, Patterdale and Wasdale, and belonging to climbing clubs. The Fell and Rock Climbing Club of the English Lake District alone has 1,200 members and five huts, though this one seemed to belong to the Northumbrian Mountaineering Club.

Rock climbing, as opposed to walking up mountains, began in the Lake District with Victorian professionals able to reach the area by train. The original base was Wasdale Head, but Borrowdale and Langdale soon attracted rock climbers as well.

It was dangerous. Modern safety equipment was unknown. Rock climbers wore boots, with or without nails in the soles, or they took them off to climb in their socks or with bare feet. Ropes were of hemp, and the early climbers only used them to rope to each other, and not to the rock face, so a fall by one climber could - and did - bring off all the climbers. While Keswick's Abraham Brothers introduced a better system of nails in climbing boots, it was not till the 1920s that more modern footwear - 'rubbers' - were invented, plus newer rope belay systems that would hold climbers to the rock face in case of a fall - or should anyway.

Rock climbing stayed primarily a gentlemen's sport until the

1930s, when newcomers brought new, daring techniques. In the 1950s rock climbers from all walks of life began to arrive by motorbike, and the names of new routes changed to reflect that. While early routes usually had names like 'Great Gully', 'Central Buttress' and 'Overhanging Wall', the 1950s, 60s and 70s brought 'Communist Convert', 'Gandalf's Groove' and 'Lost Colonies'.

From the 1970s, on there was another step change in climbing among the elite climbers, with hugely demanding and technical climbs pioneered by climbers seen as 'ruthless' in their techniques; just across the valley from Richard and me was Pete Livesey's 'Footless Crow' on Goat Crag, where apparently even a crow could not find a foothold.

Most climbers are not in that elite bracket of course, and are there for the fun of it. As a youngster in the early 1970s, I remember my older brothers setting off from Wiltshire for the Lake District or North Wales in my mother's Austin A35. The tiny car would be completely full of bodies and climbing gear, every nook and cranny stuffed with ropes, rucksacks and helmets. They would pull away slowly from outside the house, the engine and suspension in no way designed for the purpose, and a week or so later reappear with a car-full of smelly clothes. Their faces would look fulfilled, but they were mostly silent to their mother, father and younger brother on the full extent of their adventures.

The road came out of the woodland at the lovely bridge over the River Derwent that leads into Grange. With its double-humped span over the river, and narrow road over it, drivers often show a deal of nervousness in crossing.

It was fine for bikes.

Grange had belonged to Furness Abbey, like so much else in Lakeland before Henry VIII. It was the centre for their sheep-walks locally, but they also grew grain in the valley.

The bridge is not quite as old, but still 17th century, and therefore built once the monastery lands were in the hands of the local yeoman farmers, who in time were able to build their own houses in stone and presumably to help finance a bridge. Honister Slate Mine's records also begin in the 17th century, and no doubt that is where some of the slate came from for older cottages in Grange.

From a choice of two tea shops, we chose the one with the riverside garden. The day was still sunny and warm, and the garden with its neat grass and flower beds overlooked the bridge and river, and made a great stop for tea. Well, tea and scones.

Even apart from 2009's floods, Borrowdale is legendary for its rain. But Grange, though still in Borrowdale, has much less rainfall than further up the valley. The Met Office says that the highest rainfall in England falls near Sprinkling Tarn above Seatoller – an average of 185 inches a year. Seathwaite has 131 inches, Rosthwaite 100 inches, and Grange 90 inches, less than half that of the fells just a few miles to the south. Further down the valley again, Keswick has 57 inches and just beyond the mountains, Cockermouth has 40 inches. It makes a difference.

We asked if the owner would fill our waterbottles, and for a small fee in the Mountain Rescue box, he was pleased to.

We didn't stop for long, tempting though it was by the river in the sun. We were on a deadline.

We thought about cycling up the west side of Derwentwater from Grange, another candidate for best cycling road in the Lake District, but there was still the idea of cycling up to Ashness Bridge on the east side of the lake, plus a canter through Keswick. So we headed north again on the main Keswick road, the valley widening as we approached the lake, and the fields on our left began to turn to marsh.

We were passing some of the most renowned hotels of the area, like the Lodore Falls and the Borrowdale Hotel, with views across to the long ridge of Maiden Moor and Catbells. Behind the hotels, woodland spread up the fellside, and I knew that beyond the woodland was the valley leading to Ashness Bridge, Surprise View and Watendlath. I was still in two minds about how much time we had.

We came to the lake, with signs for kayak hire, and there on the lake were a group of youngsters being taught their kayaking skills. I had accompanied each of my children on similar courses on the lakes. None of us took to the deliberate capsize in order to right the kayak safely. I remember it well, the cold suddenly hitting you and the immediate feeling of panic underwater, your legs stretched out inside the kayak and seeming to need to bend backwards at the knee to escape. These days when I hire a kayak, I go for a sit-on-top version with nothing to get caught up inside.

We cycled through another patch of woodland, with moss-encrusted dry-stone walls on each side, and then back on the lakeshore itself. I don't think either of us were really concentrating on road signs, with Derwentwater just a couple of paces away, and with a view across the lake to the ridge of Catbells and up the lake to little, wooded St Herbert's Island and beyond that, Skiddaw.

So the sign for Ashness Bridge and Watendlath came as a surprise.

"Turning right!" I shouted behind, and Richard very nearly piled into the back of me. "Sorry!" I said. "Should have given you some advance warning."

"Almost got you there," he said.

We turned up the narrow lane. It was reasonably steep, though not like Honister Pass. It didn't appear in '100 Greatest Cycling Climbs'.

Even so, it got the legs, lungs and heart pumping again as we climbed through woodland of beech and oaks on a narrow lane. A family walking up moved out of our way, and then we moved out of the way of a car coming behind us. The road was too narrow for the car to overtake, so we pulled into the side.

The woodland thinned, and we could see people milling around a stone bridge over a beck: Ashness Bridge, another of the images that adorns many a Lake District calendar.

We pedalled past a photographer standing on the bridge, locked our bikes together, and pottered back. There must have been twenty people there, each trying to find space for the iconic photograph of the little packhorse bridge in the foreground, and beyond, above the line of trees we had cycled through, a glimpse of Derwentwater and behind that the mass of Skiddaw.

Upstream, the beck bubbled over and around rocks and boulders, with couples and families sitting and taking in the view and the sound of the rushing stream.

In a car park hidden in woodland a Mountain Goat bus was parked, explaining the numbers of people at the bridge. We climbed again, and the woods were wonderful - beech, silver birch, sycamore, oak. All sorts. Really ancient woodland, I guessed.

The road opened up, with fields on either side, and then there were more woods, and these were damper, with moss-covered rocks and walls. And through on the right, beyond the trees, was not just a view but possibly The View. Well, Surprise View, anyway.

From a ledge (with no fence or wall of any kind) Derwentwater opened up way below. The Lodore Hotel was almost immediately underneath, and opposite were the fells Maiden Moor and Catbells, while northwards stretched the length of Derwentwater and beyond that Bassenthwaite Lake. Skiddaw stood proud on the right above Keswick, with Whinlatter Forest, Lord's Seat and Barf above the lake on the left.

Bassenthwaite Lake and Derwentwater seem to occupy separate valleys, but from here you could see that from Borrowdale right through to the far end of Bassenthwaite Lake was really one long valley, presumably once occupied by a glacier fed from the fells behind.

We could see Derwentwater's islands like floating green seaweed in the lake. In the centre of the lake was St Herbert's Island, the 7th century home of a hermit who devoted his life to prayer, and more recently the inspiration for Owl Island in Beatrix Potter's Tale of Squirrel Nutkin. Across to the right was Lord's Island, which had been the home of the Lords of Derwentwater, complete with a drawbridge to the shore, until the last Earl sided with the Jacobites against the King and was beheaded. And towards Keswick, Derwent Island with its grand 18th century Derwent Island House, owned by the National Trust but leased out as a home; running out of milk must be a bit of a trial, I imagine.

We didn't go on up to Watendlath. Time did not allow if we were to see Eddie for lunch. We had already spent too long on a side route.

If you go to the end of the valley, Watendlath is a clutch of farm buildings by Watendlath Tarn. The road there goes up and up again, not steep, but continuous, still under old woods, still on the narrowest of lanes, until the trees end, and the road levels in an upland valley. Dry-stone walls run alongside the road, with boulders and bracken all around and rocky buttresses above.

It seems a surprising distance along the valley, with Herdwick-studded fields in what must once have been a hidden valley. Watendlath consists of stone-built houses and barns, and the white-washed Caffle House Tearoom in the 17th century farmhouse.

It can be busy there, and busy on the single-track road, no doubt mostly because it is a beautiful valley, but perhaps also because of the associations with Hugh Walpole's Rogue Herries novels. Written in the 1930s, they are historical romances based in the 18th century, and Watendlath was the fictional home of heroine Judith Paris. The Rogue Herries books were hugely popular when they were published and have a good following eighty years later.

On the far side of the café, little Watendlath Tarn has another stone packhorse bridge over the outlet stream, and low ridges around it. For such a high valley, it seems surprising that none of the highest fells are visible, but the tarn gives the valley great charm.

Richard and I coasted back down through the woods, over Ashness Bridge, still with visitors taking in the sights. Just beyond, hovering above the fellside, was a bird of prey, its wings fluttering fast. I stopped to look, and saw it drop, and pull out again as its prey must have found cover, before the bird soared upwards. It was a kestrel, with a chestnut body, and a bar of black along its tail.

What I was really hoping for was a peregrine.

Once back on the main road, up to our right was Falcon Crag, which this year had nesting peregrine falcons, according to the website of the Fell and Rock Climbing Club .

Persecuted by game-keepers and egg-collectors for decades, then affected by pesticides, numbers dropped hugely until 50 years ago. Since then, they've recovered, with the Lake District a prime area, having around 65 breeding pairs.

The adults have a bluish grey back, their chests with black and white feathers intermixed. They are about two feet tall, but with a wing span of over three foot, so not quite as big as buzzards, which are far more common, soaring above the valleys on the lookout for rabbits and for dead animals.

Peregrines have different food. They drop down on to prey - grouse, small birds and mammals - at speeds of 100 to 200 miles an hour, killing with a powerful beak. Now that would be an awesome sight.

The Lake District's climbing community keep an eye out for the peregrines. Their website suggests reporting 'suspicious characters near peregrine nest sites'. It's hard to believe that people will still steal eggs from these wonderful birds, but it seems to be true.

The website also tells climbers which crags are closed during the nesting season, so as not to disturb breeding pairs, and Upper Falcon Crag was closed because of the nesting peregrines.

"Tell me if you see any peregrines, Rich."

It seemed unlikely.

We were very quickly into Keswick after that, the road too busy for sightseeing. Also, a sign said 'BEWARE OF THE BADGERS' and the thought of being leapt on by killer badgers spurred us on.

At a roundabout we took a swing left and passed the turn for Keswick's 'Theatre By The Lake', a fantastic venue, built from scratch in 1999 to replace the old 'Blue Box', as the Century Theatre was known. The original 'Blue Box' was a travelling theatre, made up of sections that were transported around the country and put up in different towns. It broke down in Keswick in 1975, and that's where it stayed for the next couple of decades or so, up on stilts. I remember the rain drumming on the roof and then running down through the inside gutters of the theatre; it was a little difficult to hear the actors, but quite an experience.

The new building of stone and glass, right by the lake, is magnificent, and is hard by another of the grandest views of Lakeland: from Friars Crag along the length of Derwentwater to Castle Crag in the Jaws of Borrowdale. Another one for the calendar.

We mooched into Keswick, past 'George Fisher', the almost legendary outdoor clothing and gear supplier, whose building is the former studio of the Abrahams brothers, early rock climbers and photographers of rock climbers. The road from there into the town centre is pedestrianised, and we wandered into the main square, with the tall Moot Hall in the centre. Keswick had its usual buzz of people, either shopping, or drinking teas and coffees, or just taking in the atmosphere.

After all, the town is now a mecca for tourists, especially

walkers and other outdoor enthusiasts, though it has not always been that. Keswick was the smelting centre for the mines in the area. At one time there were six furnaces in town burning local charcoal from the woods and peat from the fells to smelt the ores brought in by packhorse from the sides of Catbells, the Newlands valley, Threlkeld, Borrowdale and around. Copper was originally mined with the help of German miners brought over in the 16th century and so unpopular with the locals that they had to be housed on one of the islands. The locally-mined graphite was the origin of pencil-making here. Keswick was an industrial town.

The town's first tourists followed the poets here, such as Samuel Taylor Coleridge and Robert Southey, contemporaries of Wordsworth. Even more came when war made it difficult for the wealthy to take their Grand Tour of Europe. Then the railway brought a huge influx of tourists in the 19th century. The larger hotels and the guest houses followed, and Keswick became the bustling little town it is today.

For our own Grand Tour, we cycled north out of town, past the Pencil Museum. The company had moved pencil production elsewhere within the last few years, but the museum attracts 80,000 visitors a year. For a town with only 5,000 inhabitants, that's a lot of tourists.

We turned left for the narrow footbridge that leads over the River Derwent on its way towards Bassenthwaite Lake, and pedalled through the little village of Portinscale, now heading south west towards the Newlands valley.

The road ran through woodland and when we emerged, we were looking up at the end of the Catbells ridge. Catbells must be one of the most walked fells in the Lake District. There is generally a trail of people walking up the ridge, and today was no different. There's a good reason for it. The view from the ridge over Derwentwater is sensational, and the walk itself reasonably easy. We once took a friend of ours up there, who was not as fit as she might have been. We were surprised by how fast she took the final two hundred metres or so, breathing really fast, until she pointed out that otherwise she would have been overtaken by the toddler behind us.

We took the turn for Swinside, passed the pub and dropped down to the bridge over Newlands Beck right by the Adventure Centre.

"This is where I got my taste for the Lake District," I said to Richard. "I had been to the Lakes before that with my parents, but I came here with the school twice, once aged sixteen, once aged seventeen. I still remember being scared rigid in cloud and rain on Sharp Edge, and I guess that health-and-safety rules didn't apply in quite the same way they do now. But really it was great fun."

There was a short sharp hill up to the Newlands Pass road from the handful of houses that make up Stair. Richard was waiting for me at the top.

The road contoured around the base of Causey Pike above Newlands valley below us. We could see across to Little Town, really quite little, and not really a town, which was the home of Mrs Tiggy-winkle in the Beatrix Potter story.

The road did a little twist where a beck comes down out of the fells, and we stopped to look at the house that had recently been built. Just on this point had been a three-storey wooden building put up in 1881 as the Newlands Hotel. From the 1960s the house was owned by a sculptor who rented out rooms to the actors playing at the Blue Box in Keswick. The sculptor painted the whole house a very dashing shade of purple, and if ever there was a local landmark, it was the The Purple House on the hillside looking down over Newlands Valley. Just a few years ago it was standing empty and pretty well falling down. Then it burnt down.

I had been past the new build once or twice during construction, and although a modern building, it makes tremendous use of slate and glass. It has a rounded slate roof and two tall round chimneys, also of slate, plus a glass wall giving a view up the valley. The house is a great blend of local materials and modern design. Compared with The Purple House, it is maybe just not quite so, well, decorative.

Now we were heading up the long, gently sloping valley leading to the Newlands Pass and from there over to Buttermere. The road was part way up the slope on the right hand side. At first there was a patchwork of fields strung across valley. Below us was a field of Herdwicks, with a stream at the bottom. On the far side of the stream, the land rose beyond the fields to long ridges that made their way up to Hindscarth and Robinson, the fells that look down on Honister and Buttermere on the far side.

I was concerned about time, and the state of my legs. Not necessarily in that order. I was tired and I was slowing down considerably. Richard was having to go slowly to wait for me. At this rate, we would be late for Eddie.

"Rich, how about you carry on and at least you'll be in time to see Eddie. Otherwise he might think we're not coming."

He looked at his watch. "I think we're OK at the moment."

"Yes, but I can really feel I'm slowing. One of us ought to be there at least."

"Well, let's give it another fifteen minutes and see how far we've got to."

The land grew rougher as we continued to climb. The incline was still just that; we had not reached the pass yet.

There was a sudden very steep double bend in the road as we went through a farm. My legs were definitely complaining.

Richard said, "The farm dogs here have chased me once before. I had to really leg it up the hill."

"I don't think I'd be able to leg it," I said, but there were no dogs today.

The road was quite high now, and the fenced fields of the valley disappeared to be replaced by rough, marshy-looking ground, while above us on the right, bright green bracken led up to a barely visible ridge-line. Two Herdwicks looked blearily at us from the side of the road as we went past.

"Rich, I really think you should go on now. I'll be fine. I might just have to do this at my own pace."

"Are you sure?"

"I'm sure."

So he pedalled away and in no time was around a bend and out of sight. I suspect my speed dropped another notch at that point. This wasn't, I thought, going as well as it could.

The road flattened, but then started to rise again, and this time was the real thing. Steep, very steep, and I managed to keep going for some way, my legs pushing on the pedals and my hands pulling on the handlebars. I began to zigzag across the road, but it wasn't enough. I had no choice, and stopped.

"Rubbish!" I shouted.

A sheep looked up.

"Not... you."

Through gasping breaths I was aware that the road was heading for a lower point in the fells ahead of me, where the two ridges from either side met.

Setting off again was a challenge, heading across the road to give enough time to get my feet back in the pedal straps, and then straight into the hill again. I stopped one more time before the top, again with that tricky start, which I didn't get right the first time, and had to re-start.

The hill started to ease, and there I was - the top. Four down. Two to go.

There was a small car park with a couple of cars parked, and a man putting picnic things back into the boot of his car.

"Where you off to?" he asked.

Deep breaths. "Cockermouth."

"Ah, the place with the floods. All well there again now?"

"More or less."

"Good. Would be a crying shame not to have Jennings Brewery." He had finished loading. "Safe journey down."

I sat down to take in the view. Up to the left was a white ribbon of water breaking over the rocky top of the ridge and tumbling down a gulley through the bracken. On the north side, a gentler ridge rose towards the summit of Knott Rigg.

The ground was too flat at the col to see down the valley ahead, so I got back on my bike and began to coast down, the road clinging to the south side of the valley, a stream well below and the fellside of Whiteless Pike steep on the far side.

With a bend coming up, a 25% gradient sign appeared and I was going fast now, though not too fast, the brakes slowing me.

Two cars came up the other way and I squeezed past them. The road straightened, a slice down the wall of the valley, with a view a long, long way down to the bottom. It was fantastic.

A flatter section, and then down again, with the floor of the Buttermere valley appearing ahead of me. Cars were parked by the road, and then I was speeding in to the village itself.

'BUTTERMERE' the sign said, 'DRIVE SLOWLY'.

Brakes applied, I dropped past the church, past the tea shop and The Bridge Hotel, over the cattle grid and into the car park of The Fish.

I stopped, feet astride the bike. I was quite pleased to be here.

Richard and Eddie were talking about school days when I joined them at a table.

It was good to see Eddie. When he had come to play at our house as a youngster, I had liked him, but we had not spoken for years.

At twenty years old, the youngest farmer in the area was looking well - the cheery face I remembered. It looked as though farming suited him.

"So you and your dad and granddad each have a farm in the valley?"

"I mostly work on my granddad's farm," he said. "About sixty hours a week. I really only work my own farm in my spare time."

"Sixty hours a week? That's not a lot of spare time."

He smiled. "I've fourteen lights on the front of the tractor so I can work in the dark."

The farms, he said, don't just cover the valley floor, but stretch right up into the fells.

"How do you get up there?" I asked. "Quad bike?"

"Walk, mostly."

No wonder he was looking so fit and well.

They had four breeds of sheep, mostly Herdwicks and Swaledales up on the fell.

"The farmers have to cooperate," he said. "When we bring the sheep down for dipping, my granddad goes to one spot, and the others drive the sheep towards him, then we bring them down together."

"How many do you have?" I asked.

"I've got 750."

"That's a lot."

"Not really. My granddad has a lot more than that. We never know exactly how many. You can never count them all. You always miss some. They can stray right over to Braithwaite."

At lambing time, he said, they worked all hours. "I'm shearing at the moment, though it's barely worth it. I can do one every two minutes. Maybe not very neatly, but it seems to work."

He had cattle as well, Belted Galloways. "There's finance for indigenous breeds. Like there is for wild flowers and the like."

I asked about his granddad. Did the family go back generations in the area? I was expecting a 'yes'.

"No. My granddad was from Sheffield. Left school at fourteen, packed a suitcase and set off for the Lake District. Got a job on a farm and has been here ever since. He's still got the suitcase."

"Do you get away at all?"

"Not really. Don't need to though." He gestured out the window. "This is not really like a job."

A good guy, Eddie.

We cycled back on the same wonderful road alongside Crummock Water, retracing our route up to Lanthwaite Green beneath Grassmoor, back down past the fields of the Lorton valley and for a second time on into the town of Cockermouth.

Distance for the day: 43 miles / 69 Km
Height gained: 5,406 feet / 1,648 metres
Hardest hill: Honister Pass 784 feet / 239 metres
Average speed: 10.0 mph / 16.0 Kmph
Fastest speed: 27.4 mph / 43.8 Kmph
Total distance: 276 miles / 442 Km

Buttermere, I thought. There were worse places to work than the Buttermere valley. It was a beautiful place in the sunshine. Mind you, I wasn't so sure about being out in all hours in the worst of the weather that the Lake District could throw at you. That would take dedication.

And I wasn't sure about the forecast on the television that evening: there was heavy rain coming through in the next few days.

With the possibility of floods.

DAY SEVEN - LETHERA

THE RUGGED WEST

Cockermouth – Lorton – Loweswater – Fangs Brow
Ennerdale Water – Ennerdale Bridge – Gosforth
Wastwater – Wasdale Head – Wasdale YHA

44 miles

www.lakedistrictgrandtour.co.uk/day/seven

169

Today would be a day for three of the quieter lakes. Lowesater, Ennerdale Water and Wastwater, the final lake of my sixteen. All we needed was some nice sunny summer weather and the rugged west of the Lake District would be absolutely stunning.

I wheeled my bike outside, and a spot of rain fell on my forehead.

A mile from Cockermouth we reached the start of the hill that drops down into the Lorton Valley, and the bases of the fells were just about visible. The tops were not. They were swathed in a blanket of dark cloud. And I had to wipe the rain off my cycling glasses to see even that.

We pedalled in silence through Lorton and out past the turn-off for Buttermere, heading for Loweswater. After the fields of the Lorton valley, there was a climb to take us over to the other off-shoot of Buttermere and Crummock Water's valley, Loweswater. It was not a long climb, nothing compared with yesterday's hills, but my legs seemed to have no energy, and even though Richard went on ahead, he did not seem to have much zip either. He was not waiting for me long at the top.

There was a sign, which I usually enjoy:

RED SQUIRRELS PLEASE DRIVE SLOWLY

but in the rain, I was not so sure. Perhaps if the sign had said:

TEK CARE - SQUIRRELS ONT ROAD

it might have worked better.

We coasted down the steeper far side, the lovely Lanthwaite Woods off to our left, and crossed over the River Cocker on its way from Crummock Water to Cockermouth.

Richard was still quiet, but then so was I.

I pulled alongside him and we cycled together for a few minutes.

"Am I being miserable?" Richard said.

"Yes."

"Sorry."

We pedalled on.

He said, "I'm going to stop being miserable."

"Generally, or for the day?"

"Probably just for the day. Still deciding."

We took a left into Loweswater village, off towards the pub. We weren't stopping, but it felt wrong to cycle past Loweswater and not go past The Kirkstile Inn.

The pub is not special from the front; some sort of shed blocks the view. But inside, you step back in time with bench seats and oak tables, and the satisfying smells of open log fires and real Cumbrian ales.

It is an old inn, and the stuffed fox in a glass case inside the front door, courtesy of the Melbreak Foxhounds, is a bit of a clue to part of its history. They did brew on the premises, but the brewery moved to near Hawkshead, which is odd, with Hawkshead Brewery now in Staveley. Still, I can recommend Loweswater Gold.

And then there is the view from the back garden. Melbreak roars up skywards, a slate cliff promising hardly a foothold on its loose front. In fact, there is a path up the ridge, though one or two sections are loose and shaley, where a head for heights is needed. What a round trip it makes though, climbing up to the top, then sloping down to a grassy, marshy saddle before sliding off down steep slopes to a path and lane which lead you right back to The Kirkstile.

There was a short, sharp hill from the pub, and then we dropped towards Loweswater lake. That's when the rain started properly.

"Rich," I said, "this is rubbish weather. And my bike shirt is feeling pretty wet. I don't know if it's come through my bike jacket or down my neck, but it doesn't feel good."

Our road was just above the lake, a screen of trees most of the way along, but with plenty of glimpses through. One of the smaller lakes, with the fell on the far side reaching almost to the lakeshore and draped in woodland, it is always very pretty. For some, the prettiest of Lakeland's lakes.

We weren't in the mood. Well, I wasn't anyway. Richard might not be miserable any more, but I hadn't quite made that decision yet. The jury was out.

At the far end of the lake, we were at what must be one of the best named of hills, Fangs Brow. We were just starting into it, when five cyclists appeared coming the other way. They were spread across the road, and one had to take emergency action when he saw us.

"There's twenty more behind us," he shouted before he had

disappeared.

"C2Cers?" I said to Rich.

Our road was reversing the C2C route for a few miles.

"Must be."

Richard and I kept together as another group of cyclists appeared, going fast downhill. There was a sequence of 'Hello's and 'Alright?'s from them and us, as they flashed past. Cyclists, like walkers on the fells, are generally a friendly bunch.

Fangs Brow was slow, but the morning misery seemed to be dissipating a little, and I had six days of cycling in my legs by now, including Honister and Newlands the day before. I wasn't exactly quick, but it occurred to me that I was going up quicker than I would have a week before.

Another small group came the other way, and then we were at the top. We turned left at the C2C sign, and passed a lay-by with a view across rough fields to the backs of the fells above the lake, though it was too wet and cloudy to see far. The road began to drop, and another part of the C2C group came up the hill towards us. These were going fairly slowly, but they were cheerful, saying hello. They had no panniers, and some had no waterproof jackets on. They would be cold as well as wet cycling down Fangs Brow. Still, if they had no panniers, they must be on one of the many supported C2C tours, so could presumably get a change of clothes and a jacket at the next rendezvous with their van.

The road dropped away ahead of us, and what turned out to be the back-markers were struggling up the hill. One of them, wearing just a soaking-wet charity T-shirt on his top half, weaved across the road almost into Richard. It didn't bode well for Whinlatter ahead of them, and even less so for the C2C's big hills in the Pennines on the second day.

The C2C is an excellent long-distance cycle route to do, and there is a camaraderie amongst those doing the C2C: you do tend to meet the same people at different stops, and you have all conquered the same hills. I just hoped the young guy in the soaking T-shirt was going to make it.

"Good luck," I called, and I got a wave back.

Opposite the church at Lamplugh we passed a stone archway to

172

what used to be Lamplugh Hall, the home over centuries of the Lamplugh family, though pulled down in the 19th century and now a farm. It was a good archway though, complete with the coat of arms of the Lamplugh family and the date 1595.

Two more cyclists came towards us, these two with panniers and more appropriate cycle gear. They were pushing on fast and riding quick-looking bikes. Not part of the group, these were going to be overtaking the others very shortly, and it was just a quick 'Hello' before they were gone.

We passed a right turn where the C2C route went off towards its usual start point at the coast in Whitehaven, and almost instantly were on the long sweeping downhill of Cauda Brow with streams of rainwater flooding across it.

Ennerdale Water lay ahead of us in the valley. It looked as grey as the clouds that sat on the line of dark fells on the far side. At the far end the high fells had low cloud concealing their tops, but they must have been Pillar and Steeple, favoured haunts for rock climbers who don't mind a long walk in.

We were going down at a bit of a rate, and the sharp twists in the road almost took me by surprise, but we rounded them, still going down.

Ennerdale Water is by no means as 'pretty' as Loweswater, Derwentwater or Windermere, but it is ruggedly beautiful and, even though it is Ennerdale Water that is the reservoir, the others feel tame by comparison. Especially on a day like this.

Mind you, Bill Clinton proposed to Hilary on the shores of Ennerdale Water in 1973, so there must be some romance there as well.

It is certainly the loneliest of the lakes. The lake is well away from the tourist hotspots and from access to the motorway. The roads in are narrow and twisty and do not run along the lakeshore, and it also has no buildings on the shore at all.

The Angler's Hotel used to sit at the bottom end of the lake, and must have had one of the most dramatic views of Lakeland, looking along the steep southern rocky shoreline of Angler's Crag to the promontory of Robin Hood's Chair. But when the water level was raised as part of a scheme to use more of its water in 1961, the hotel was demolished.

173

The Ennerdale valley has not had a good reputation in terms of nature and wildlife. The whole of the top part of the valley was densely covered with forestry from the 1920s to the 1950s, much of it planted in absolutely straight lines, and Wainwright was scathing. When describing the climb to Pillar in his Western Fells book in 1966, he called the forest a "funereal shroud". What the authorities had done to the valley, he considered unforgiveable.

Things are changing. There is now a plan to help the natural flora and fauna to re-develop, and that is made easier by the lake being the loneliest in the Lake District. Under the Wild Ennerdale scheme, the forestry is being reduced, replaced by heath land, native woodland and marshland. 10,000 oak and birch saplings are being planted, fences removed and cattle introduced to roam almost wild so as to create a more diverse habitat.

Red squirrels are being encouraged, and encroaching grey squirrels dealt with. Marsh fritillary butterfly larvae have been introduced, and the reduced numbers of arctic charr fish restocked in the lake. There is a herd of roe deer and a smaller number of red deer, a peregrine nest and, I was pleased to read, ring ouzels.

It is a fantastic plan to take the valley back to a more natural state.

We would come back on foot some time and look for deer and pine marten and peregrines and red squirrels and marsh fritillaries and ring ouzels. And no doubt we wouldn't see any of them, though perhaps they would see us.

At the bottom of the long hill we came to the hamlet of Croasdale. Just along the way was another of Cumbria's small breweries, the Ennerdale Brewery which uses spring water from the fell behind. It was amazing how many breweries there were in the Lake District, but then I guess walkers, climbers, cyclists and visitors generally can be thirsty people, and somehow real ale goes better with the Lake District than, say, a glass of wine or a gin and tonic.

We turned right - away from the lane that would lead down to the lakeshore - and headed for the village of Ennerdale Bridge. It was a narrow country lane, fortunately quiet because there were not many passing places even for a bike if a car came the other way.

We did stop at a gate to look across the fields back up Ennerdale Water. Beyond Angler's Crag the fells were a dark grey, impossible to tell one from the other, but we were looking into the heart of Lakeland, and we would be even closer to the biggest of the fells when we were at the top end of Wastwater later that day.

First though, we had to get there. The rain was easing and, since we were heading for Ennerdale Bridge with its two pubs, I thought I might see just how wet my bike shirt was under my jacket, and change it for a dry one. Also, I was in need of coffee.

The road was surprisingly flat and ran through hedged fields, so that the contrast with the remote, dark valley behind us was considerable. It was a lovely little village, with a primary school in the middle of the village, and we cycled past it to The Shepherd's Arms Hotel, a traditional-looking inn.

We leant our bikes against a wall at the side. I looked at my watch. 10.45. It was a funny time to be arriving at a pub, and it didn't look very open.

"I'll go and see if they are doing coffees."

Inside the front door were piles of suitcases and rucksacks. Otherwise, all was quiet.

"Hello," I called.

No response.

I went through to the empty bar.

"Hello?"

This time there was a reply from behind the bar. "Sorry, can I help you?"

"Are you serving coffees?"

"I don't know, sorry. I'll find out."

She disappeared into the kitchen and I heard a 'yes' from there. I called Richard through and we sat at a table. A man appeared and came over with a friendly smile. We both asked for coffees, and when he brought them, I asked, "How's business? Are you quiet what with the rain and so on?"

"Well, a lot of our trade is coast to coast walkers, and they book a long time in advance. Ennerdale Bridge is usually the first stop. So we're always busy at weekends through the summer."

"Ah, hence the suitcases and rucksacks in the doorway."

"Yes, those will be picked up and taken on to the next stop, along with the people who don't want to walk today."

"It is a bit wet."

"Yes, it won't be nice on the tops, so there are definitely some who will be on the minibus."

Most walkers would have been here in a day from St Bees on the coast. From the village they then walk up Ennerdale past the lake, through the forest, passing the YHA's Black Sail hostel at the very top of the valley, and then over the fells to drop down into Borrowdale for the night. From there, the route goes to Grasmere, Patterdale and Shap - where we had seen the damp coast-to-coasters on our second day - with some quite high level walking. The route was designed by Wainwright, another of his achievements.

Ennerdale Bridge used to be part of a different route. The village is just a handful of miles from the former mining towns of West Cumbria and beyond them, the coast. When Whitehaven was one of the busiest ports of England - before the railways - a packhorse route from Whitehaven led through Ennerdale Bridge, up the Ennerdale valley, over Black Sail Pass to Wasdale Head, where there might be a change of horses, and then over Sty Head Pass to Langdale and out of the mountains from there.

I went through to the gents to check on my bike shirt. It was soaked, and I changed my shirt for a dry one. I was sort of convinced that it was my fault for not having the neck of my jacket tight enough at my neck. I hoped that was the problem anyway.

Still, with hot coffee inside me, a dry bike shirt, and no rain, the misery had disappeared. Mostly.

As we cycled out of town we passed the village's other pub. The last time I had been past the Fox and Hounds, it was closed. This time there was a sign outside: it was now a community pub, with the lease owned by a not-for-profit company, and the shares held by local people. With the village shop also having closed, they have plans for a shop and a tourist information centre as well. Wow, I thought.

We turned off the road to the coast to head over the fells again. At first the road rose relatively gently. No problem, I thought, taking in the view back up the Ennerdale valley in the distance. But the hill just seemed to go on and on.

We came to forestry, and then still climbing, we came out on to the tops – Blakeley Raise on the left, Flat Fell (surely a contradiction in terms) on our right. It was open rough moorland, peppered with Herdwick sheep. The land rose gently to our left, with more forest in the distance, and close to, a stone circle. There were a dozen or so boulders on the fellside in a rough ring, looking down over the flatter lands of West Cumbria and the sea. Maybe not as romantic as Castlerigg Stone Circle, but it would be quite a good spot on a dry and sunny day.

There were horses loose on the fell, but these ones were clearly not wild, and a sign said: "Stay, Ride, Relax".

There were some inclines on the road after that, but generally it contoured around the fells, sometimes with views down over the coast, at other times with forestry around. A speed camera was a little incongruous, but this was a short cut from northern Cumbria to the Sellafield Nuclear Reprocessing site, and the 40mph speed limit apparently needed enforcing. Fortunately, we were not cycling the route at shift-change time; there was just the odd car, and not speeding.

A valley appeared on our left, with a couple of farms in it, the access seeming to be rough tracks from our road, which might be a challenge in the winter.

The road dipped to Friar's Well, and off down in the valley was Monk's Bridge. Clearly the monasteries had been active in the fells here. St Bees (named after the same St Bega as the church on the shores of Bassenthwaite Lake) had been a priory and was really not far away, and we were cycling towards Calder Bridge, where the ruins of Calder Abbey were the home of another of Furness Abbey's smaller colonies.

And then there was the little climb on to Cold Fell. 'Cold Fell', I thought. There was a reason it was called Cold Fell; this was the first major hill to face the winds off the sea. It must get biting here at times.

On the far side of Cold Fell, the road started to fall, and here was another incongruity. Up on our left, rough moorland, down on our right, green fields studded with sheep, with a grey sea beyond, and there ahead, getting closer as we pedalled, the nuclear facility of Sellafield.

At first it was the chimneys that we could see, but as we got closer we could make out more of the site. Though still a fair way off, it was clearly a big site. I counted four cooling towers, one large chimney and quite a few smaller ones, plus lots of big blocks of buildings. But then it employed thousands of people, and the wage rates were a draw for the people of West Cumbria, now that the mines, the steel industry and the chemical industry were gone.

It's only in recent years that the 1957 accident has become better known about. Eleven tonnes of uranium were ablaze, with a distinct possibility of having deadly nuclear material spread across West Cumbria and the Lake District. That it was contained was thanks to the courage of individuals placing themselves in danger to deal with it, but the secrecy from those nuclear-weapons days has left a bit of a legacy.

It doesn't help that after the Chernobyl disaster in 1986, a plume of radiation blew across Britain. The rain brought it down on to the uplands of Wales, Scotland and the Lake District. Peaty soils in many areas absorbed the radiation, so that grass was contaminated. That left the sheep feeding on the grass open to contamination. Across Britain 327 farms were placed under restrictions, including a good few in Lakeland. It is only in 2012 that the last eight of Lakeland's farms have been given the complete all-clear.

For those who work at Sellafield, or have friends and relatives there, the site is a godsend, providing well-paid jobs in an area that desperately needs them. For those who fear nuclear power, there are new things to worry about; there is the possibility of a new nuclear power plant for Sellafield, just down the hill from Richard and me up on Cold Fell, and only a closely contested council vote ended investigations for an underground nuclear dump under a re-wilded and beautiful Ennerdale.

Our road crossed a cattle grid and the road fell away, with fields either side. It was a long descent, the sort that makes you realise how long you must have climbed for. It got steeper as we approached the village of Calder Bridge, and a car appeared round a corner. I must have pulled on the brakes too hard. The back wheel skidded, but righted itself.

"Almost lost it there," I said to Richard.

"You OK?"

"Fine."

The road from Calder Bridge to Gosforth wasn't fine. Not for bikes. It was busy with cars and lorries, each trying to squeeze past two bikes loaded with panniers that weren't going awfully fast. Unfortunately we had no option. There was no other road or cycleway from Calder Bridge and Sellafield southwards. It felt daft, with on our left-hand side the western boundary of the Lake District National Park, and on our right pleasant farm land, yet we were stuck on a frankly dangerous road. Somewhere, as a country, we had gone wrong over the years with providing safe routes for people not in cars. I was very pleased when we were able to get off the road, and coast down into Gosforth.

And I was hungry. We had cycled 26 miles, and I needed food.

The village had solid, sensible houses, some in sandstone, some rendered and whitewashed. There were pretty gardens in front of houses, and woods behind. It was a proper, traditional village, with a library, church and bank. There was plenty of choice for food as well. Gosforth had pubs and a shop, and it also had The Hungry Parrot café. With a name like that, we had to give it a go. Through the shop and up the stairs, past, yes, a parrot in a cage.

The café was in the roof of what would have been a mill building, with great wooden beams and a pulley. It was busy in there, with locals stopping by for lunch. The young waitress was friendly, and we ordered baguettes.

"I could do chips as well," Richard said.

"Chips? Yes, why not? Two lots of chips as well please."

She wrote the order down and I said, "By the way, does the parrot talk?"

"Not if you go up to him and try and make him talk. I've been trying to make friends with him for ages and not managed yet."

By the time we had eaten quite large baguettes and a plate of chips each, we were quite full.

"Those chips might have been a mistake," Richard said.

"See those beams up there. They could hang hammocks from

them for over-full customers to sleep off their chips."

"Now that's a plan."

Outside, we sorted out food from the shop into our panniers - pasta ready meals. I am not a fast learner.

I said, "Rich, I've got a cross to show you."

"A cross?"

"It's in the churchyard somewhere. Come on."

We coasted along the road to the churchyard surrounding the sandstone church. Tall trees overhung both the road and the older part of the cemetery, with its grand 18th and 19th century gravestones commemorating those passed away in the village. We left our bikes and walked into the cemetery. There it was - a narrow, fourteen foot high Viking cross standing tall above the others, dark red sandstone, weathered by over a thousand years, and placed here by the ancestors - probably - of families still living and farming in the Lake District.

It was round at the base, but changed to a four-sided column part way up, with carvings on each side. Close up, the images on the sides were not easy to interpret. We guessed at a Viking longboat, and there were clearly men on horses and curly snake designs - Norse gods, I had read. And then there was what looked like a crucifixion scene, while at the top of the column was a very clear Christian cross, Celtic-looking to my un-tutored eyes.

After all, the Norse folk who had carved this cross had probably come here by way of the Isle of Man and Ireland, where they had been living for a couple of generations since Viking raids had turned into settlement. By the time they fled their homes there in the face of more raids from Scandinavia and arrived here as refugees and emigrants, many were already Christian and inter-married with the Celtic population of Ireland.

"Guess they were covering all their options," I said. "We can probably find out more inside."

The church was by no means ancient, but Victorian re-builders had set Mediaeval stone coffin covers into the walls of the porch, and inside were more signs of the Vikings - a light switch lit up two 'hogback' tombs: elongated stone triangles, again with carvings, one possibly commemorating a battle in which the Anglo-Saxons

180

of Ethelred the Unready were roundly defeated somewhere near Ravenglass. And a sign led us to the 'fishing stone' set in the wall of the church, again a carved stone, and this one clearly a boat. Hence, the fishing stone.

I picked up a leaflet which suggested a more complex theory than 'covering all their options'. The Viking carvings were apparently from the Norse legend of the End of the World. Thor battles with a monstrous snake - the World Serpent. Odin fights a fire-giant. The sun is swallowed by a double-headed wolf-serpent. And so on.

And with the end of that world comes Christianity - Christ on the cross, defeating the Norse 'End of the World', which makes the Gosforth cross a fairly significant item for Lakeland and England generally.

"What do you reckon?" I asked.

"I was wondering if the Dacre bears were Viking?" Richard pondered. "They looked more like these Viking carvings than Roman lions."

I scanned the leaflets as we walked back to the bikes.

"Well, listen to this," I said, reading from a leaflet: 'Very often a hogback roof is gripped at each gable end by an animal, usually a muzzled bear. Perhaps this relates to a Viking burial tradition, not yet replaced by Christian rites.'

"Wow. Could be then."

"Rich, we might have just solved the riddle of the Dacre bears." I swung on to my bike. "Makes you kinda proud," I said.

We could see through to the wonderful 17th century Gosforth Hall Hotel. Room 11 has a priest hole with hidden steps down to the fireplace in the bar, so this must have been a Catholic household when that might have cost you your life. And perhaps it did; guests in Room 11 have reported the ghostly figure of a monk sitting by the priest's hole.

"On to Wastwater?"

Number sixteen of sixteen.

"Go for it."

Outside Gosforth, the road wasn't flat, and not much of it was downhill. We both became aware that the wind had got up and was fairly strong. Then it started raining again. At least one of us was thinking about a sleep in one of those imaginary hammocks instead, and it might have been me.

Richard had a different point of view. He said, "I might start feeling miserable again. Not sure. Just warning you."

The country on either side became more rugged, with rocks breaking through hillsides on either hand, and small woods overhanging the road.

Then we were dropping towards Wastwater and the village of Nether Wasdale. It was a handsome village, with two whitewashed inns facing each other across a small green with a maypole. The fourteen foot high cast iron maypole was put up in 1897 to mark Queen Victoria's Jubilee, and the children still dance around it every Mayday as part of the village festival. Which is of course wonderful.

From the village we could see the screes, the great bank of loose slate on the far side of Wastwater. We cycled down the hill, having to pedal against the wind and rain by now, and turned towards the lake. Despite the weather, it was a lovely cycling road, the fields on either side with mature trees dotted in them, plus small copses, and now there were glimpses of the fells on both sides of the lake, each side rocky and wild.

We passed a farm with a sign for home-made cheese, including ewe's cheese. Sounded good, I thought, but not for today.

We were staying the night at the YHA hostel, and we came on it suddenly as we cycled through woodland.

I slowed. "Rich," I said. "Are you too wet, full and miserable to cycle on to the end of the lake before we come back here?"

"Me? Miserable?"

So we pushed on past, up a gentle hill through the wood, and as we came out at the top, the gale hit us, pretty much bringing us to a standstill, rain and wind battering us.

"You sure?"

"Are you going?"

"Yes."

"Come on then," and he pushed off down the slope, the lake waters now ahead of us, a big rocky lump on our left, and the long fall of the screes on the far side of the water.

As we reached the shoreline, we came out of whatever shelter the great rocky lump had given us from the wind, and the gale was even stronger. We were pedalling hard now to make any progress at all. The road was flat, but it felt like we were cycling over a mountain pass.

Waves broke white on the rough surface of the water, and on the far side long stretches of loose scree seemed to flow down at an impossible angle from the buttresses above into Lakeland's deepest lake.

We could see right along the lake now, Yewbarrow dark on the left, looming over the valley. At the far end, grey and ominous, were Kirkfell, Great Gable and Lingmell, their summits cloaked in cloud. The only distinct colour was green - the grass and bracken on either side of the wet road was a bright green despite the weather, and the odd brave tree flopping and flailing in the wind was a dark green. Everything else was grey. It was another of the iconic calendar views of the Lake District. But not today. Even the odd disconsolate sheep was grey.

"I think it might be another clearing-up shower," I called to Richard.

The road bent and curved around rocks and hummocks, never more than a stone's throw from the lake. A couple of cars were parked, their owners staring out at the weather, and we pulled over several times for cars to overtake us.

Then something strange happened. The rain stopped. Vanished. Not the wind; we were still cycling into an extraordinary gale coming down the valley directly at us. But the rain had gone, and the ground was dry, as if there had been no rain for some time. I looked up, the dark clouds were gone, replaced by slightly less threatening ones.

"I knew it," I said to Richard.

A few more minutes of pedalling into the wind, making slow progress, and there was the suggestion of brightness in the sky. I couldn't say sunshine, but looking up to the end of the valley, the aspect had changed. The bright green of the bracken and grass by the road, had now spread up the fellsides. High up was still dark grey - the rocky outcrops just under their cloud coverings. But the valleys now had a grandeur, and it put strength into my pedal strokes.

We were directly opposite the screes, and they were even more impressive.

"There's a path of sorts across the screes," I said to Richard.

"Is there? Doesn't look like you could walk it."

"Wainwright advises against doing it in stiletto heels."

"I'll bear that in mind."

We came to a flatter part of the valley, with fields and a farmhouse off to the left, and trees acting as a windbreak along the shoreline. Then the road came out into the ruggedness again, hugging the shore as the slopes of Yewbarrow fell sharply into the lake. Going up a small slope, we were sheltered, only to crest the top and have the wind hit us all over again.

We were coming to the end of the lake now, and up to the right were the slopes of Scafell and Scafell Pike, their tops hidden in cloud. At 3,209 feet (978 metres) Scafell Pike is just a stone's throw higher than Scafell, but enough to make it the prime target for walkers looking to scale the highest mountain in England. The top is stony and barren, with a grand cairn, and on a good day, views over lesser siblings – Great Gable, Bowfell and so on, across to the Pennines and down to Furness.

Still hugging the base of Yewbarrow, we went past fields that are marked on the OS map as 'Down in the Dale', and crossed 'Down in the Dale Bridge', which were, I would say, accurate descriptions. The fields had the most wonderful walls, thick and high, curving and intersecting, and using up some of the vast amount of stones in the valley in great piles. They were almost certainly very old, perhaps Norse, such was the heritage of the valley; 'Wasdale' comes from the Norse 'vatnsdalr' - the dale with the lake, and the church building is very old, possibly dating back to those times, when maybe it was the centre of a village of wooden homes, long since gone.

The wind dropped. Not completely, but it was no longer quite the gale it was. That was good, because there were tents in the field off to our right, and a field on our left was being prepared for an event. There were portable toilets at one side and, the biggest clue, Pete Bland's mobile shop. Pete Bland runs the fell-running specialist shop in Kendal, and he attends almost every fell race of note in northern England.

A young-ish man was standing by a mini-tent on the other side of the wall. He was slim and wiry; a runner's build.

"Hi. What's the race?" I asked.

"It's the Saunders Lakeland Mountain Marathon tomorrow."

"And you're racing?"

"Well, I was hoping to, but it's a two-person event, and my partner has done his leg in. I thought I would come up on the off-chance and see if anybody else needs a partner."

"Where've you come from?"

"Southend."

"Ouch. Long way. Hope you find someone."

The SLMM is run over two days, with a number of different courses for different abilities. The pairs have to navigate to various waypoints over the high fells, and stay overnight at a designated campsite, so it is part of the rules that they carry full camping and emergency gear, including food. The only things they don't need to carry for the overnight stop are milk and beer. Though they might not necessarily drink them in that order.

I looked up the results later, and the leading pair on the highest grade course took six and a half hours on the Saturday, with four and a quarter on the Sunday. Another pair were nearly twelve hours on the fell on the first day and nearly seven on the second. That seems to me a very long time.

Mind you, this is the place for fell-runners if ever there was one. Joss Naylor, the legendary fell-runner, has lived and farmed in Wasdale all his life. A month before our visit here, he ran the bounds of the parish to celebrate the Golden Jubilee and to raise cash for Nether Wasdale Church and the community hall: 26 miles over Caw Fell, Haycock, Scoat Fell, Pillar, Kirk Fell, Great Gable, Great End, Scafell Pike, Scafell, Illgill Head and Whin Rigg above the screes. He told the local paper, "It's not as easy as when I was younger."

Joss's age: 76.

We carried on past a car park where more cars were decanting potential runners and their tents, and coasted to a halt at the shop in an old outbuilding selling outdoor gear and postcards. Across the yard was the Wasdale Head Inn. On another occasion we would definitely have gone in as a scientific investigation into what ales they had behind the bar, but we didn't. It was partly because our destination was just back the way down the lake, and partly because there seemed to be another event going on. The hotel and tiny St Olaf's Church up the lane were hosting a wedding.

There was a tent across the grass, and we watched as a couple came out of it, he in smart suit, she in lovely purple dress with matching fascinator, and made their way over to the inn. As they came off the grass, she leant on her partner to remove the plugs of grass from her high heels.

I learned later that this was the inn managers getting married.

The inn itself has a lot of stories to tell. The publican of the hotel at Wasdale Head in the 19th century, Will Ritson, was legendary for his tall tales, attracting audiences including Wordsworth and other notables of the time. These days, his legacy is continued in the World's Biggest Liar Competition at the Bridge Inn in Santon Bridge a few miles away. This year the trophy was won with a tale about badgers, "deadlier than cobras or crocodiles... the Romans sent Christians to the badgers..." Of course, Richard and I had seen the 'BEWARE OF THE BADGERS' sign outside Keswick. It was all starting to make sense.

Another part of the inn's heritage relates to climbing. Wasdale was the birthplace of rock climbing.

In 1881, Walter Parry Haskett-Smith started the sport of climbing routes up rock faces for the sake of the climb, rather than to reach the summit of a mountain. Wasdale Head began to attract other young Victorian gentlemen escaping from their narrow professional lives and wanting to try not just a new sport, but a new lifestyle.

Haskett-Smith's most famous ascent was of Napes Needle, which he did alone, leaving his handkerchief tied around a stone on the top as proof. His final ascent of Napes Needle was age 76 in 1936, this time with a full audience and applause.

Another of the young professionals was O.G.Jones, with a BSc in Experimental Physics, who created a 400 foot route up the face of Scafell Pinnacle in 1896. O.G.Jones teamed up with two photographer brothers in Keswick, George and Ashley Abrahams.

They were climbers as well, setting up new routes, including 'Keswick Brothers' on Scafell. They carried incredibly heavy and bulky photographic equipment to record climbs. With O.G.Jones, they published the very first book about climbing - 'Rock Climbing in The English Lake District' - in 1900, complete with action photos by the brothers. The book, of course, brought even more prospective rock climbers to Wasdale Head. It was the start of the 'Golden Age' of rock climbing.

The young men escaping from their professions didn't just climb in the fells either. They would climb around the inside of the rooms in the inn for a bet, including a trick climbing under the billiard table and up the other side without touching the floor. It wasn't popular with the landlord.

As we came away from the Inn, the runner was still by the wall, looking up at the fells he was hoping to navigate the following day.

"I hope your tent is OK in this wind," I said.

"Mine will be fine. I'm in the lee of this wall. It's that one I'd be worried about."

He gestured at a much larger tent, billowing in the gale.

"Mm, I see what you mean. Well, I hope you find a partner for tomorrow."

"Thanks. Where are you off to?"

"Just the YHA tonight."

"Ah, you'll find some runners there as well."

The ride back to the hostel at the other end of the lake was extraordinary. The gale was behind us now. Barely pedalling, my bike computer showed us going at 26 mph. Now that's cycling.

We were back in what seemed like moments.

The YHA hostel was quite a grand building from the outside, with what might have been centuries-old windows in heavy stone walls, and with a half-timbered wing. That probably meant that it had been built by a 19th century industrialist but, nevertheless, it was very imposing.

Then there was the view. As we pulled in at the front, we could see that it looked right down over the lake and across to the screes.

We were too early to check in, but found the kitchen and made coffees. We had been going to drink them in the lounge, but it was occupied at one end by an assessment panel for outdoor activities instructors. It all seemed a bit formal, and we moved into the dining room with long tables.

A young YHA lady came in with a breezy hello and a cheery smile. A YHA tradition, surely.

"Do you know the weather forecast for tomorrow by any chance?" I asked.

"Well, I heard a forecast this morning, and it wasn't at all good. They're predicting a month's worth of rain in twenty four hours."

"What?!"

"Yes. And flooding. It's a shame. I was hoping to go running tomorrow."

I said, "That's not ideal for cycling either."

I had decided that I didn't really like floods. Once was enough.

Also, Richard would be miserable.

We were able to check in at five, and we took our panniers upstairs to find our dormitory. It was big, and busy with people unpacking. There were six sets of bunk beds and we claimed one of the last pairs, next to a couple of slightly older guys sorting out their walking boots, and discussing classical music. Bruckner and Mahler, I think it was.

Geoffrey and Roger were frequent walkers in the Lake District, Geoffrey especially. "I come up about six times a year," he told us. "If you book a train in advance, it can be very cheap. Mind you, last time I came, the only cheap train was at night, and I had a six hour wait overnight at Crewe station."

"That sounds awful."

"Oh, it wasn't too bad. The waiting room had a long curved window seat, and I curled up in that. It was absolutely fine."

"And you always stay in hostels?"

"Oh yes. It's much the friendliest way."

Richard and I cleaned ourselves up and took our wet clothes to hang in the drying room. On our return, Geoffrey was still sorting his gear.

"You must have walked pretty well every Lake District mountain by now?" I said.

"Pretty much, but that won't stop me coming back. What about you? Where are you cycling to tomorrow?"

"We're doing a big loop south and then coming back north to Eskdale Youth Hostel."

"Oh, we're walking to Eskdale Youth Hostel, so we'll see you tomorrow night as well. By the way, the pub next door does a tremendous steak and kidney pie. And it's enormous."

That was a mouth-watering thought, but today was to be a cheap eating day, so we ate our pasta ready meals in the kitchen/dining area of the hostel, whilst savouring the aromas from the couple cooking their own pasta meals, complete with crushed garlic and parmesan cheese. Ours was, in fact, rubbish.

Afterwards we found our way to the big and comfortable lounge, where we chatted with various runners in the Mountain Marathon. Our weather news was a surprise to them.

"We'd heard it's going to be warm and sunny tomorrow," said one.

"I'd heard showery," said another.

In fact, we had the complete range of forecasts from 'warm and sunny' through to the sort of rain that used to be referred to as 'of biblical proportions'. I didn't fancy being in that sort of rain and floods, but I loved the phrase 'of biblical proportions'. In fact I decided that I really should use it.

I had a thought. Richard and I had been tempted by 'hearty' on a menu before. We had been in New Zealand on a cycle trip (a different story...), had had a hard day, and had arrived at a pub which had on its menu 'HEARTY VENISON CASSEROLE'. We had got no further down the menu. Just the word 'HEARTY' sold it to us.

What if we were to arrive at the pub tonight and on the menu was 'Steak and Kidney Pie OF BIBLICAL PROPORTIONS'? Well, we and virtually every walker, fell runner, climber and cyclist would find it very hard to go past it.

Word would get around the sporting communities. "You have to eat at such and such pub - the Steak and Kidney Pie is OF BIBLICAL PROPORTIONS."

I wasn't sure if it would work for vegetarians. I just couldn't quite imagine a menu with 'Spinach and Feta Cannelloni OF BIBLICAL PROPORTIONS.'

Puddings would be good though. 'Sticky Toffee Pudding OF BIBLICAL PROPORTIONS' could be VERY popular.

Distance for the day: 44 miles / 70 Km
Height gained: 3,848 feet / 1,173 metres
Hardest hill: Blakeley Raise 627 feet / 191 metres
Average speed: 10.7 mph / 17.1 Kmph
Fastest speed: 32.8 mph / 52.5 Kmph
Total distance: 320 miles / 512 Km

The lounge gradually emptied and we were left, by 10.15, with just half a dozen runners. These were not the elite runners, but even so there were some fit young athletes here.

I confessed to them that I had run the London Marathon in younger years, but that my time was over four hours, and I had been overtaken in the last mile by a pantomime horse.

This led one of the young runners to his own confession - being overtaken by the Easter Bunny in a half-marathon. "I did hear afterwards," he said over the laughter of his friends, "that he had been a professional runner..."

More laughter.

"... doing it in costume for a bet."

Sometimes it's best to quit when you're ahead.

DAY EIGHT - HOVERA

SEA AND SAUSAGES

Wasdale YHA – Ravenglass – Waberthwaite
Silecroft – Millom – Broughton-in-Furness
Ulpha – Eskdale Green – Boot – Eskdale YHA

49 miles

www.lakedistrictgrandtour.co.uk/day/eight

193

I woke up to the sun shining in through an open window, and an alarm bleeping on the other side of the dormitory. I looked at my watch. 5.55am. Not good.

One of the runners was rousing himself. He must have had an early timed start. He wasn't quiet.

I turned over and closed my eyes.

The next alarm went off at 6.15, with more clattering of running shoes and gear.

The next at 6.30. More clattering. And some too-loud talking.

I gave up at 6.45.

Still, I thought, it looks more like being 'warm and sunny' than floods 'of biblical proportions', and that cheered me up.

Richard was sound asleep, and we'd agreed to get up at 7.30, so I went down to the drying room to collect yesterday's damp clothing, now dry. When I got back, everyone was awake and stirring except Richard. I packed up my own gear and at 7.30, woke him.

"Errgghhh."

"Sun's shining."

He propped himself up on one arm and looked around at the noisy runners and walkers. "Am I the last up?"

"Yup. And breakfast is at eight."

He raised himself and sat on the bed. "You snored."

"Did I?"

"The bunk shook. I almost threw something at you."

"Ah. Sorry."

"There was quite a lot of snoring in here, but you were easily the loudest," he said. "You weren't the funniest though. That was the guy with the comedy whistle as part of the snoring."

"I didn't hear anything."

"There's a reason for that," he said.

We went down for breakfast, but found the sun shining through the open front door, so went out into a morning that definitely looked as though it would turn into 'warm and sunny' rather than floods. We could see down to the lake through trees, and the surface of the water looked absolutely still. Floods! Pah!

We had paid in advance for a cooked breakfast, so it was with a stomach groaning at the additional volume that I retrieved our bikes from the bike shed and then walked down to the lakeshore in the sunshine. There was no breath of wind in the air.

With the sun behind the ridge, the screes were in deep shadow, but looking up the lake, I could see past shoreline trees the whole length of Wastwater to green, sunlit mountains beyond. The water had the merest suggestion of ripples, making a masterpiece of alternating reflections of dark screes and bright blue sky. It was another candidate for a Lake District calendar. It was absolutely glorious.

When we left at nine, the day was already warm and the suggestion of heavy rain from the day before seemed ludicrous. A good day to head towards the sea.

The plan was to cycle south west to the coast, then turn directly south, looping around the most southern of the Lake District's fells, before turning back north again for the big hill of the day: the climb over to Eskdale, finishing at Boot. Fifty-odd miles.

As we left Wasdale we passed grazing fields and oak woods, and the cycling was lovely, even though my legs felt tired from the day before and the small hills were not feeling easy. A longer downhill took us into Santon Bridge. There were more ups and downs through woodland, and then the road straightened and flattened in a very un-Lakeland way towards the coast. For almost a mile we built up speed, by the end steaming along, until we came to a halt at the main road, the same one that had been so dreadful the other side of Gosforth, north of us.

Today, it wasn't dreadful, and we turned south, with just the odd car and lorry feeling its way carefully past us. We had farmland all around, the grass looking lush, and away to the east the mountains of Lakeland still, though seemingly far off and of no relevance to the coastal plain. I checked the map. I had it right, we were still inside the Lake District National Park, and would be along the coastline itself.

At a long curve in the road we saw for the first time the line of La'al Ratty, more formally, the Ravenglass and Eskdale Steam Railway. The narrow-gauge railway runs from the coast at Ravenglass up the Eskdale valley, just a single track with turntables at each end to turn the engine around.

We were heading for Ravenglass now, and the road took us up the side of a ridge with woods on our left, before we turned off the main road, and dropped into the village – the only coastal village in the National Park.

By a bridge over the road, a sign pointed towards Ravenglass Station. We had just missed a train, and the platforms were quiet, but it was still an atmospheric place, with the feel of an enthusiasm brought to life. I had expected the station to be like a cross between a Thomas the Tank Engine book and Platform 9$^{3/4}$ at King's Cross Station in the Harry Potter series, with pint-sized trains in red, green or black livery arriving at the platform, steam billowing from their funnels, while families with children waited cheerily by tubs of colourful flowers.

The tubs of flowers were there, but the families had already left in little carriages behind a steam engine on its way to Dalegarth Station, not far short of the village of Boot. Richard and I were cycling to Boot, though our route would be a little more circuitous.

We cycled out of the car park, under the rail bridge carrying the main line, and past a grassy foreshore with blue-painted benches looking out over the empty estuary. It was pretty, the sun shining on the far side of the estuary, beyond ribbons of blue finding their way westwards towards the sea through pinky silt, with a handful of sail boats marooned until next high tide.

The road led into a village of whitewashed cottages and houses. The entrance was narrow at first then curving out on each side to form what would have been the market, and curving back with a narrow exit to a slipway at the far end. We stopped at the slipway, leaning our bikes by a pile of lobster pots, and looked down across the stony, silty bed of the estuary. Off to the left, the long dark ridge of Corney Fell strode away southwards. Away to the west the sands stretched into the distance towards the Irish Sea. Behind us, the village was quiet and peaceful.

In Roman times this was a major port, the southern end of the fortifications dividing the British Isles into Roman and barbarian. From Carlisle eastwards those fortifications were Hadrian's Wall. West of Carlisle was a chain of forts and look-out stations all down the coast as far as the fort and harbour at Glannoventa, modern

Ravenglass.

The harbour was also the western end of the supply route across Lakeland. A Roman road ran east from here up the Esk valley, over Hardknott Pass, on over Wrynose Pass and down Langdale to the fort at Ambleside.

For over three hundred years this was an important and busy town. With the end of the Roman empire, the purpose was gone. The estuary silted up and the fort decayed; the only remains are 'Walls Castle', actually the former bathhouse.

We followed a sign for them through a car park, over a footbridge and into a little lane, where there was no other signpost.

"Where now?"

"No idea."

We pedalled up the lane a little, but there was still no sign.

Richard said, "Does this rank alongside our success in spotting golden eagles and ospreys?"

"No," I said.

We pedalled back up out of the village to the main road, up through woods with steep little stretches where passing lorries made a wobbly cyclist feel a touch vulnerable, and passed the entrance to Muncaster Castle.

The castle had been home to the Pennington family for eight centuries, and the old pele tower defence against the Scots was an integral part of the stately home created in Victorian times.

I had been to the grounds of Muncaster Castle a few months before, at Easter. It was the scene of the 'Baby Easter Chicks Incident'.

We had walked in from the car park past surprisingly tall rhododendron trees covered in giant red, pink and purple flowers, then round past the side of the castle. There were three storeys of stone, with windows looking across the valley to a ridge opposite of scrub and fern, and up the valley towards high mountains silhouetted against the sky.

All seemed quiet until we came round the back to the owl display, which filled very quickly with families and children. Owls were on display from the World Owl Trust, flying from roost to roost or gloved hand to gloved hand, then being held for photos.

Along the garden terraces there were views over the yew and box hedge down the valley with, on the left rhododendrons and other plants collected from China, India and elsewhere. It was fantastic.

Then back to the owl cages to see eagle owls, barn owls and other owls from the far corners of Europe and Africa. In each cage was a tree post, and on top of each tree post lay their food: a small pile of pale yellow baby chicks.

"Eurghh," said my vegetarian daughter. "That's gross."

"Baby chicks are really quite traditional at Easter," I said.

"That's disgusting."

Then there was the cage with an eagle owl chewing the head of a rat held in its claw. It was clearly tea-time for the owls.

"Eeuurrgghh."

So, the 'Baby Easter Chicks Incident'.

Not to mention 'The Rat Incident'.

Good place though. And I think the owls enjoyed their tea.

We stopped at a bridge to look back up the valley of the River Esk across flat, marshy fields and into the heart of Lakeland. We were in bright sunshine still, though clouds were beginning to gather over the fells in the distance where the runners would even now be on the peaks. Some would no doubt wish for dry weather, some for cool weather. Richard and I, cycling in shorts and bike shirts, were happy with warm and sunny.

The road climbed up the side of a hill and then dropped again, one of those unexplainable roads where you think, 'why does it not contour around?' Then we came to our turn-off from the main road so as to loop around on the Lake District's shoreline, rather than stay on the main road. We dropped into the hamlet of Waberthwaite, a name almost legendary in the world of Cumberland Sausage.

This had been the home of 'Richard Woodall Butchers' for over 180 years and eight generations of the Woodall family. At their peak they had supplied Harrods, Fortnum and Masons, west end hotels, airlines and the large supermarket chains, and once a fortnight they had sent off an order of sausage, ham and bacon to Buckingham Palace, by appointment to the Queen.

I had read that it had closed and been disappointed. But here was a shop, clearly open, and with hams hanging in the window. On the wall was an old but still fine of coat of arms: the lion and the unicorn, Dieu Et Mon Droit, and underneath that:

BY APPOINTMENT TO
HER MAJESTY QUEEN ELIZABETH II
SUPPLIERS OF
TRADITIONAL CUMBERLAND SAUSAGE
RICHARD WOODALL
WABERTHWAITE CUMBRIA

I had a vision of the Queen sitting down with Prince Philip to a plate of Cumberland sausage and chips, followed by a Sticky Toffee Pudding of Biblical Proportions. (I was wrong; according to the local paper, the sausage was for the royal breakfast).

Inside was a small village shop, but through in the back room I could see the meats section – hams and sausages and bacon, and it all looked wonderful.

The lady by the counter had a young helper, but the toddler was too shy to come out from behind her legs.

"Hi," I said to her. "I had read that you were closed."

"Yes, the company, Richard Woodall's, had to be sold due to ill health, but we thought the village still needed a shop and a post office, and it's a family tradition with the hams, the bacon and sausages. So my aunt and I did some refurbishments and re-opened the shop a fortnight later. We're now R B Woodall (Waberthwaite) Ltd, and we're producing all of the same products as before."

"That's wonderful."

"There were twenty five people working here, and we are just five now, but we are back selling to local hotels and businesses. We still use the old family recipes."

"I'm really pleased. Do you mind if we look through?" I said, gesturing through to the back, where the cured hams and thick rings of Cumberland sausage looked magnificent.

"No, of course not."

The lady's son came through with her, still clinging to her and peering round her legs at us. "Oh, Richard," she said indulgently.

199

"A Richard? You're keeping the family name going?"

"Yes, we are that."

"Well, my son's a Richard as well, and I'm Mike."

"Joyce", she said.

I looked at the sausage. "Rich," I said, "it's not really practical to take it with us in a pannier, is it?"

"Not really. Shame that."

Joyce was joined by her aunt and husband, both with a hello for us. A proper family business.

"Do you," I asked, "do mail order?"

"Yes, we do. You can find a list on our website, and we can send out by courier with an ice pack."

"Fantastic. You shall hear from me."

She did, a few weeks later. I ordered two packs of Cumberland sausage, which arrived in a cardboard container complete with an ice pack. They were truly wonderful. Fit, I would say, for a Queen.

The road carried on to the estuary of the Esk, went under the railway line, and took a sharp turn south towards the sun.

There was a red triangle sign with an exclamation mark in the middle, and underneath that the word GUNFIRE. In fact, the day could not have been more peaceful. On our left, flat grassy fields disappeared away, with in the distance a line of green hills. On our right was a Ministry of Defence firing range, a high fence blocking off part of the coastline, presumably with the military able to practise firing out to sea. More signs warned us not to pick up any ammunition found on the beach, which seemed sound advice.

Beyond the firing range we came to the beach proper, long, sandy and pebbly. The concrete blocks of a beach wall provided us with a seat to munch biscuits and to look out over damp sand to the sea.

A car pulled up, and a couple got out with two greyhounds, taking them past us towards the beach.

"Good place to exercise them," I said.

"They'd run forever here," the lady answered.

They took the dogs down on to the wide wet sands and let them go free, the hounds loosening their limbs and running.

"It's hard to think of anywhere that you would less expect to be in the Lake District National Park," I said to Richard. "It makes you wonder how they chose the boundaries, to include the sea here, but to miss out the Greystoke area, and the fells the other side of Shap."

"All this is in the National Park? The firing range as well?"

"Certainly is."

The road turned inland past neat bungalows into quiet Hycemoor, and on again to Bootle, back on the main road, where a scarecrow robber was trying to escape a scarecrow policeman, and scarecrow footballers were getting ready for a game. So were a group of real footballers setting off for their Saturday afternoon match.

We had no choice but to use the main road again, but it was wide with good sight lines, and not too much traffic. Black Combe marched alongside us, surprisingly high for a distant outlier of the fells, while away to our right, fields led down to the sea.

We came to the village of Silecroft at the south-west corner of the Lake District and had a choice. The main road turned sharply north-west here, heading for Broughton in Furness. A smaller road headed straight on, out of the National Park to Millom. I had never been there, and knew it only as the home of a poet.

If Wordsworth was the poet of the Lake District for the 19th century, arguably the accolade for the poet of the Lake District for the 20th century would go to Norman Nicholson. Try this:

The Wall, by Norman Nicholson

The wall walks the fell -
Grey millipede on slow
Stone hooves;
Its slack back hollowed
At gulleys and grooves,
Or shouldered over
Old boulders
Too big to be rolled away.
Fallen fragments
Of the high crags
Crawl in the walk of the wall.

Which is, I think, brilliant.

He wrote about the town, the mines, the quarries, the people, the sea and the mountains. He first published his work in the 1930s, and wrote until his death in 1987. He described 'cubist fells' and mountains 'like gilded galleons'. He wrote as a local man, but with a real gift.

Nicholson lived almost his whole life in Millom. So we cycled to Millom.

The road was busy and twisting, with sharp little hills and unforgiving traffic.

"Rich, I think this was a mistake," I called after one close call with a car.

Iron ore was discovered nearby in the 1850s. Until then, there was no town here. Furnaces were built, and the new iron and steel industries, as well as the haematite mines, brought in those in need of jobs, even if the 19th and early 20th century working conditions were notoriously bad.

The mines and ironworks are long gone now and, as we cycled into the town, it became clear that a town square that was once reasonably grand was that no longer. Millom seemed to have more in common with the towns of West Cumbria that have lost their iron and coal industries, and with Barrow, than Lakeland.

We pulled up in the square by a memorial sculpture to Millom's greatest son. It was of a 'scutcher' whose work was to halt heavy iron tubs by forcing an iron bar through its wheels. On the side it said, Norman Nicholson, Poet, 1914 - 1987.

I suppose we should have gone to the exhibition on Nicholson or down to the nature reserve at the old iron mines, but, well, this was a tour of Lakeland, and I felt we had strayed too far outside.

"Let's head back to Broughton in Furness," I said.

Richard didn't argue and we bought sandwiches and pedalled out of town to find somewhere to sit and eat lunch.

Just outside Millom we found some benches bathed in warm sunshine by a church hall and next to the remains of a castle. Great strong walls were now ruins, and a farm occupied the site. We stretched our legs out for a while. We had cycled 25 miles, and I needed a break.

The road from Millom back towards the fells was easier for that rest, even if not flat. It was a climb up to a junction and then another climb after that but from the top we could see up to the first of the fells, Black Combe and White Combe, and to the right the land falling away to the estuary of the River Duddon, with the low Furness peninsula beyond.

We seemed to ease upwards more and more, until we came to a 10% gradient sign - downhill. It just seemed to go on and on, reasonably straight, and with a gradient where you can just go effortlessly faster and faster. We piled on the speed. Water was running across the road from the woods to our left. I could feel the spray on my legs, and gathered from Richard behind me that he was in my wake.

"Hey, you're soaking me!"

When the road finally levelled out, our momentum carried us on at speed, and we pedalled hard until the traffic was stalled at traffic lights for the bridge over the River Duddon. I checked my bike computer.

"We've just done 36.9 miles an hour," I said. "Fastest we've done. Well, fastest for me."

I looked at him. He was very wet, his bike shirt and face speckled with dirty water.

"Do you know," he said, "you produce a lot of spray at 36.9 miles an hour?"

"Yes," I said, "I can see that."

Two roads went off up the Duddon valley from the bridge, one on each side of the river. We were due to take the second, but first I wanted to go into Broughton in Furness. It was only a mile ahead, though I had forgotten the golden rule that what goes down, must cycle back up. So we cycled back up much of the height we had lost, and then we dropped down again into Broughton, 'Village of the Year 2002'.

I liked the town very much, with its mix of Georgian houses and tiny cottages, pubs and local shops. There was somehow a quiet assuredness about the village. The stocks in the square, I reckoned, were probably not needed too often.

A cyclist pedalled over to where we were stopped.

He pulled over. "Beautiful day. You going far?" he asked, his accent Irish.

"We've come from Wasdale," I said, "and we're heading back north to Eskdale. You?"

"I've come across from Windermere, and I'm going home up the Duddon valley and back over Wrynose Pass."

"Wonderful day for it," I said. "You live in Windermere?"

"Not far. Twenty five years I've lived there now, and I love it. It's the people," he said. "So welcoming and friendly."

He was right, I thought.

We reversed our route out of town, and back down to Duddon Bridge, turning right alongside the river. There was a little flat stretch, perfect to lull me into a false sense of security, and then we hit a hill. Quite a steep little one too. Richard was gone even as I was changing gear and getting sorted for the climb. At the top of the steep first section, I was panting and feeling my legs. Really, this was ridiculous. It was our eighth day. I should be easing up hills like this.

I pulled over to get my breath and then headed on up again, the narrow road not as steep now, but long, up through woods and past fields, twisting and turning.

Richard was waiting for me at the top, looking fresh.

"Quite a view," he said.

And it was. We were in a different world. Back in Lakeland.

The road was part way up the side of the Dunnerdale valley, the River Duddon way below us amongst trees and pasture, while ahead of us the higher fells were appearing.

We cycled on, climbing gradually, the fells ahead of us getting closer, and the land on either side losing its pasture and becoming wilder, with rocky outcrops and lone trees amongst long bog grass or tufted hill grass, just right for the Herdwicks wandering across the lane.

The road dropped down through bracken and ran alongside the fast-flowing river scurrying around the rocks littering the river bed. A hillock of distinctive boulders emerged from grass near the side of the road.

"I recognise this," I said. "You should as well."

"I should?"

"Yes, I picked you and your friends up here when you did your Duke of Edinburgh expedition."

"Really? I don't recognise it."

It was a lovely place, a gentle green valley with woods on the far bank of the river, and on this side those boulders that any child should climb. King of the castle boulders.

"You came down there." I pointed up the slope through the bracken to a rocky ridge line. "If I'm right, we'll pass a shop somewhere along here."

We pedalled on, rising over the end of a ridge and then following on up the valley, with sheep-filled fields on our left, green bracken-covered fell on the right.

A stone bridge arched over the river, just where Dunnerdale took a right turn, and there were a handful of houses on each side. We were in Ulpha, Norse for 'hill frequented by wolves'.

There was no shop, and I was doubting my memory, but then there was a little climb past a whitewashed ancient church, and ahead of us Ulpha Post Office.

"I knew it."

"OK. Yep."

"And now," I said, "I need a stop and a drink. We've a steep bit coming up."

If there had been a café at Ulpha Post Office, they would have had two customers for cappuccinos and scones. As it was, we made do with Mars Bars (other chocolate bars are available) and sports drinks from the tiny shop, and sat on the sun-warmed wall opposite.

I was surprised by how many cars pulled in, some clearly local, others obviously tourists. It was a busy spot for the lady and her family in the shop.

We turned to face northwards, looking up the Dunnerdale valley, our legs dangling over the wall on the other side. Close by was what looked like almshouses in a row across the valley, with beyond that a mix of woods on the lower slopes of the fells, and fields in the flat valley bottom. Ridges and peaks in the distance made the skyline.

Not on a through route to anywhere, and with no lake to draw the tourists, just the Duddon meandering from one side to the other in its progress down to Duddon Bridge and the sea, there was a peaceful feeling to sunny Dunnerdale.

"This is nice, Rich," I said.

We looked at the map, which appeared to show a double arrow on a hill just along the way, going up over the ridge to Eskdale.

"It can't be that bad," I said. "Look, it doesn't even have a name."

Richard looked at me.

"They're probably exaggerating," I said.

We got back on our bikes and pedalled to the turn that would take us out of Dunnerdale.

It was massively steep.

It felt very unfair.

The road bent and twisted up through woods.

Steep, steep.

Legs. Aargghh.

Richard did his usual trick.

I did mine.

He was waiting for me at the top by a sign that showed we had just come up a 25% gradient.

"25%!" I said. "Bloomin' 'eck. No wonder that was hard."

Down a lane, a white farmhouse stood out against a backdrop of green fells close to, and darker, higher peaks beyond, the one a conical volcano shape. There was also what looked distinctly like a stone circle, or rather, a double circle of stones. One larger stone was up on end, the others prone, like sheep on one of their lazier days.

There are about fifty stone circles in Cumbria - fifty that are recorded anyway and have not been destroyed during various purges of the pagan over the centuries. Fifty is a lot of stone circles for a relatively small area, but then, I suppose, Cumbria has a lot of stone to play with.

Clouds were beginning to gather over the tops, some of them distinctly darker than others. We had missed the forecast rain, so far at least. If it started now, well, we'd get wet, but we were nearly there.

The narrow road ran through dry stone walls to reach a plateau, with red-marked, black-faced sheep in ridiculously emerald fields on one side, and a boggy, gently-sloping hill on the other. At a kink in the road, a beautiful arched stone bridge took us over a little beck with Herdwicks chewing the grass nearby. The road rose again, not steeply at all; this was gorgeous cycling now, with high hills in the distance almost every way we looked.

The walls disappeared from beside the road, with just tufted hill grass stretching away from us as the road took Richard and me higher, still ever so gently, and then the view opened up north and east. We were above Eskdale, with little rocky summits projecting from grassy slopes, and larger fells beyond.

Now the road began contouring, and an almost flat ride led in sweeping curves to a crossroads with, oddly, a real old council signpost, with black and white hoops painted round a cast iron post, as incongruous as a lamppost in Narnia. Eskdale, the signpost told us, was just three miles. To the left, a track led up to the little tarn of Devoke Water, while to the right a track led to a farmhouse. We had already passed another farm right up here.

"It must be some of the most difficult country to farm," I said.

"It's high, isn't it? Must be just sheep."

"And these hills in winter. Imagine this with snow and ice for weeks."

Each new curve of the road opened up the view more, until we came to where the road began to drop. Four cyclists, probably in their thirties, were pulled in. They looked a bit like I felt. Three of them anyway. Red, sweaty faces. Slightly haggard look. The fourth didn't. He just looked like he had come out for a little jaunt.

"How far have you come?" I asked him.

"From Ambleside."

"Over Wrynose and Hardknott?"

"Yes. Well, after a fashion."

"And then up here?"

"That's it."

"We're doing Hardknott and Wrynose tomorrow. Richard will cycle over anyway. I had to walk some of them last time."

"Hey," Richard said. "Wait and see."

The cyclist turned to his slightly bedraggled companions. "OK? Better get on."

The other three put feet to pedals and headed away, but he turned back to us. "Make sure you don't go too fast up Hardknott," he said. "You could easily launch yourselves into the air on the far side."

"Thanks," I said. "I'll try not to."

The road down into Eskdale was fantastic: long, gentle bends as we came off the plateau, then into a small, bracken-filled valley above a rocky gorge, still with these wide turns. Finally the gorge opened up below us to reveal the valley of the Esk, with flat, stone-walled fields leading away into the distance.

The road straightened and we sped down into Eskdale, hills above us on our right, green fields on our left. It was flatter now and we eased back, a little hill taking us up and over the end of the ridge and back down to the flat valley floor. We passed the lane that would lead in two or three miles to Muncaster, crossed a stone bridge over the River Esk, and then pulled in at the junction with the lane that would lead back up to Wasdale.

"Amazing ride down," Richard said.

"We've definitely come the long way round."

"Been a great day, though."

"A contender for best day of the ride, I reckon."

He considered. "Yep, could be. Hard to say though. They've all been good in different ways."

"I thought this was going to be one of the easier days. Mostly flat. But that 25% was a bit much."

I looked down the road, and for the first time noticed two triangular road signs. The top triangle had an exclamation mark. Underneath that was another triangle with a 30% gradient sign.

"I think that sign says 30%. Does that sign say 30%? I'd forgotten that. I was thinking Hardknott was another 25% pass. I can't believe that. THIRTY PER CENT."

"Yep, and it's long as well."

"Thanks, Rich."

The road meandered past fields, with the rocky sides of the valley set back, and into lovely woodland. For a time the La'al Ratty railway line joined us, and then the Esk replaced it, burbling and bumbling over rocks on its way down to the sea at Ravenglass.

It was sobering to think that in the 1930s the Forestry Commission - if not for a public outcry - would have forested 2,000 acres here and in Dunnerdale, so that most of the western valleys of Lakeland would have been uniformly filled with industrial planting.

At Dalegarth, we stopped by the terminus for the railway, a cream-and-burgundy station under the crags behind. Families were waiting on the platform for the next train back to Ravenglass. The narrow-gauge line divided at the platform, allowing the half-size steam trains to de-couple, turn themselves round on the turntable by the road where we stood, and join up with the carriages again at the far end.

A few hundred yards on, a lane went off to the village of Boot, and its mix of whitewashed and stone cottages, with an arched bridge over the beck that comes down from Burnmoor Tarn at the back of The Screes by Wastwater. I liked to think that Nicholas Size was right in claiming that Boot was named after Earl Boethar's last resting place, but apparently Boot is Norse for a hut. Not half as romantic, that.

The fields below Dalegarth had been flatter and more pastoral, but now they became rougher, with the valley narrowing and the road rolling over small hills. Fells were appearing directly ahead of us as well, and somehow Hardknott Pass would have to make its way through them.

We passed the Woolpack Inn, a series of whitewashed buildings that had been formed into a pub and restaurant.

"Rich, that's the place that the walkers at Wasdale recommended for enormous steak and kidney pies."

"Brilliant."

Half a mile ahead, and we were pedalling up the drive to Eskdale Youth Hostel. It was a large stone building on a low hill looking down over the valley. We leaned our bikes against the wall and went through to the reception. The man at the counter was cheery and welcoming, and he showed us around the hostel - the large dining room with its view over the valley, the homely lounge and our neat dormitory, designed for six, but with only ourselves booked in.

Eskdale YHA was very different to Wasdale YHA. The building at Wasdale had originally been a grand private house converted into a hostel some time ago, and was perhaps in need of some money spending on it. Eskdale YHA had been purpose-built, and it showed. With the YHA's usual standard of friendly staff as well, it felt very homely.

We walked back through early evening sunshine to The Woolpack Inn. Geoffrey and Roger were walking the other way.

"Don't forget the steak and kidney pie," Geoffrey said.

There wasn't much chance of that.

At the bar a Dutchman was asking about the beers.

"Which is the local beer?"

"There's Harter Gold. It's our own lager. It's brewed at the Hesket Newmarket Brewery for us."

"Hesket...?"

"Newmarket."

We had the same. "And," I said to the lady at the bar, "we've been told that we have to have your steak and kidney pie."

"Oh, we've just sold the last of the pie. Sorry."

"Sold the last of the pie!"

"We've 'Tatie Pot'. I wasn't sure what it was when I first came here, but it's really good. It's local Herdwick as goes into it."

She was right. It was brilliant. And it was almost
OF BIBLICAL PROPORTIONS.

It was our last night, and we sat and talked and ate, with a couple of pints of the 'cask conditioned lager' that was the very nice Harter Gold. We spoke about him at uni, about me when I was his age, about what I had done, and what his plans were, about life really. We spoke some more through Richard's choice of home-made Apple Pie (of similar proportions to the Tatie Pot).

"You know," he said, "there are quite a few things that we'd never really spoken about, but now that I'm older, I suppose it's easier."

He was right, but there was also the opportunity here, he and I riding around the Lake District, taking, quite literally, the highs and lows together.

"Good day," I said.

"Yes. Good day."

*

Back at the hostel we found that a walker had moved into our dormitory as well. His rucksack had exploded around the bottom end of the room, including wet gear landing on the radiator, so there was a bit more of an odour to the room than before we had left.

He, Ben, was apologetic.

"Sorry about this. Got a bit wet today."

So there had been rain. We had missed it completely.

"Where did you go?" I asked.

"Up over Scafell and Scafell Pike."

The Eskdale route up them must, I thought, be one of the quietest ways up. The second highest and highest fells of the Lake District have their most popular routes from Wasdale Head and Borrowdale, but the River Esk is fed from the rocky tops of both, as well as from some of the other highest peaks in the central fells, such as Bow Fell, Great End and Crinkle Crags.

"Many people on the route?"

"Hardly any, except on top of Scafell Pike."

Lakeland's highest fell can sometimes be over-busy. Wasdale Mountain Rescue Team complain of the mess left by competitors completing Three Peaks challenges (Ben Nevis, Scafell Pike and Snowdon), with no regard to what they do or drop on the fell when all they are worrying about is the speed they are going at. It can apparently be unpleasant on occasion, which is a shame for one of the great fells of the Lake District. It is not, they say, the ordinary fell runners, nor the Mountain Marathon runners, nor the walkers, but almost solely the Three Peaks groups, which is food for thought.

Richard and I made our way down to the dining room, where I wrote out our vital statistics.

Distance for the day: 49 miles / 79 Km
Height gained: 4,287 feet / 1,307 metres
Hardest hill: Brown Rigg from Ulpha 528 feet / 161 metres
Average speed: 11.1 mph / 17.8 Kmph
Fastest speed: 36.9 mph / 59 Kmph
Total distance: 369 miles / 590 Km

"Do you realise," I asked, "that we have cycled 369 miles so far?"

"And only been lost three times."

"A triumph, I reckon."

Ben came down via the kitchen, bringing with him an enormous bowl of cooked pasta. I looked at it. It was just pasta. No sauce. It looked even worse than some of the meals Richard and I had had.

Ben wolfed it down.

In the dormitory later, when Richard and I were getting ready for bed, Ben had already got into his bunk. He seemed to be fiddling with his ears. "Sorry," he said. "I've got a thing about snoring. I'm sure you don't snore, but I put in earplugs at night because of other people's snoring."

Ah, I thought.

"Dad was the loudest snorer at Wasdale Youth Hostel last night," Richard said to him. "But he wasn't as bad as the guy with the comedy whistle as he snored."

"See, it can't be all bad," I said.

Ben looked from one of us to the other. "Oh, well, I'm sure I won't hear you anyway, because of the earplugs, but it does mean that I may not hear my alarm in the morning for some time."

"Right," I said. "Do we kick you or throw things at you to wake you up and switch your alarm off?"

DAY NINE - DOVERA

THE HARD BIT IN THE MIDDLE

Eskdale YHA – Hardknott Pass – Wrynose Pass
Hawkshead – Near Sawry – Far Sawry
Windermere – Bowness-on-Windermere

23 miles

www.lakedistrictgrandtour.co.uk/day/nine

215

Someone was about to make a speech at a wedding. It was the ding-ding-ding-ding of a spoon on a glass to get the attention of the guests.

Ding-ding-ding-ding.

I opened my eyes, looking at the bunk above me. I wasn't at a wedding.

Ding-ding-ding-ding.

I hadn't slept well. I kept waking up thinking that I was snoring and disturbing Ben.

Ben. Earplugs. Alarm.

Ding-ding-ding-ding.

Ben stirred in his bunk. A click. He had switched it off.

He got up and went out of the room towards the toilets, coming back a few minutes later, getting back into bed, and throwing the covers back over himself. Within seconds he appeared to be asleep again.

Which begged the question: what was the point of the alarm?!?!

Richard and I had been all around the Lake District, to the northern, southern, eastern and western extremities, cycling past all of the lakes in the process. We had crossed all of the mountain passes except two: Hardknott and Wrynose.

Today we would be back in the middle of the Lake District. The hard bit in the middle.

Hardknott would have a 30% gradient and a score of 10/10. Wrynose, well, we'd find out when we got there, and even if Wrynose's 10/10 in '100 Greatest Cycling Climbs' was actually for doing it from the other side, I expected it would still be a bit of a toughie on this side as well.

It was a short day to finish, though. A half day, Hardknott then down into Dunnerdale, Wrynose then down into Little Langdale. Then on into Hawkshead, crossing the route of our first day to get to the shore of Windermere, from where the ferry would take us across the lake. Then a loop around the town of Windermere, to coast down to Bowness and meet up with my wife at the steamer quay. First though, we had The Challenge.

10/10.

30%.

Bloomin' 'eck.

216

*

The breakfast room was busy with walkers and families eating cooked breakfasts from the kitchen. My plate was reasonably full, though actually I could still feel the effects of the Tatie Pot from last night. Richard went for the full works: two Weetabix and the Full English, including the black pudding, potato waffles and beans, plus toast.

"You're going to cycle over Hardknott after that?"

"It's for the protein."

Geoffrey and Roger sat on our table, finishing their talk on composers for the moment and discussing the day's plans. They were walking to Borrowdale, and from there by bus and train home.

A family were there with their small children. Having had an adventure of a train ride to the hostel, today seemed to be taking La'al Ratty back to Ravenglass and then visiting the owls at Muncaster Castle. I looked at my watch. Perhaps they would miss feeding time at the owls.

Ben came in with a new bowl of pasta - just pasta - for his breakfast. His plans were more ambitious, if still fluid. He'd be going high. At least he had done his pasta loading, and presumably slept well.

"Rich," I said, "did I snore last night?"

"No more than normal."

"Ah."

Richard pushed his plate aside, the Full English unfinished.

"I'm disappointed," I said.

"I'm pogged."

Geoffrey stood to go. "Good luck with Hardknott, young men," he said.

I liked him.

"You fit?" Richard asked, as we finished packing our bikes up outside the hostel.

"It's comparative," I said. "Compared to you, no. Compared to how I was nine days ago, yes, sort of."

"Fit enough for Hardknott?"

"There's the question."

217

We coasted down the drive from the hostel in sunshine, though dark clouds hung over the end of the valley. At the road, we turned east. High dry-stone walls hugged the narrow road as we climbed around the side of a ridge, the view over fields to woodland on the far side of the valley, with a low rock-topped ridge above that. It beggared belief that this might all have been a plantation of conifers, but for the public outcry.

A stone bridge took us over the Esk, and then the road crossed the valley floor to the ridge on the far side. There were hedges now, with tall foxgloves pink against the dark of the leaves. Behind the hedgerow, the land rose under the bright green of bracken, and was punctuated by darker green of lone trees. Fifty shades of green, I thought. Good title for a book.

Eskdale seemed to continue on for a way, but the road wasn't following the valley any further, it was going up and over.

There was another sign: the exclamation mark, the 30% sign, 'NARROW ROUTE WITH SEVERE BENDS' and a warning that the road was suitable only for cars and light vehicles, and not even for them in winter conditions.

"It doesn't mention bikes," I said.

"Should we turn back now?"

The sun had gone. The dark clouds were directly over us.

"That's one plan."

"What's the other?"

"Well," I said. "The big thing that you wanted to do was to cycle over Hardknott Pass without stopping. Now, if you wait for me part way up, you might feel you haven't done that, even if you could. So I think you should just set off and go for it. All 30% and 10/10 of it. That's the other plan."

"I'm a bit torn. I'd like to cycle up it with you to help you up it, but I also want to see if I can go over in one."

"Seriously, you have to do it. My aim is different. I know I'm going to have to stop, but as long as I have cycled all of it, and not pushed the bike at all, that's my aim. Also, I want to stop and look at the Roman fort on the way."

He smiled. "Fair enough. Well, good luck."

"See you at the top."

I watched him go, blue bike shirt going up and down as he

stood on the pedals to pull himself, his bike and the two black panniers on the back up the first instantly steep section.

"Good luck," I called.

He rounded a corner, and was gone.

I took a deep breath, pushed down on the pedals and began a slow, slow climb up through woods. They were probably gorgeous woods, but now I was concentrating on turning pedals and keeping moving without completely doing in my lungs before the pass had even really started. At a cattle grid, the woods finished, and I kept going. Just.

A zig. A zag. Each time the lungs busting that bit more as the road just kept going up and up. 25% corners, the author of '100 Greatest Cycling Climbs' says. And then lungs, heart and legs all gave out at once, and I fell over the handlebars gasping for breath, brakes on to stop me rolling backwards.

When I could focus on my surroundings, I found that the fellside was entirely bracken, the emerald green ferns carpeting the ground. Behind me, Eskdale stretched away into the distance, the flat valley floor broken into fields more regular than those we had seen in Wasdale, with woods and low ridges on either side.

My heart returned to somewhere approaching not exploding, and my lungs stopped sucking in air like a vacuum cleaner on full power. My legs, well, they'd have to do as they were told.

I eased over to the side of the road, careful not to gain any altitude while not pedalling. I was going to do this properly.

Deep breath, right foot in pedal strap, push down on pedal to go across road while vainly attempting to put the left foot into its strap. Failure. Turn into hill and just pedal, adding my own little zigzags to those of the road.

Lungs.

Heart.

Legs.

Keep going.

A car comes up behind me, and I have to give up my own zigging and zagging to allow him past. The manoeuvre fails, and I put a foot down. A rude word emerges.

I set off again across the road, again failing with the left foot, but make it to a sharp left corner just as I realise three cars are coming down the hill towards me. They are coming down what looks even steeper than the hills I have just done. This, I thought, needs a special effort. I need to steel myself. And there's no point trying to do it with cars coming the other way.

I pull into a passing place at the corner.

The three cars go past. From the back one, two children stare at me. Can't think why.

OK. Go for it. Dig deep.

I push off, left foot into strap. Yes. And up, criss-crossing the road, definitely the steepest part so far, heading up the straight section for a corner, where, surely, it will ease off.

Three quarters of the way up, the legs give in. "Come on, you …"

It was no good.

A brief break, no altitude from walking, and off again, round the corner and yes, less steep. I keep going, and going, and going, until a sign for Hardknott Roman Fort.

"OK legs," I said. "You get to stop here, but don't think I've finished with you."

There was a lay-by, and I leant my bike against a bank. For a moment I considered locking it, and then thought, "Who on earth would be here looking to steal a bike?"

Hardknott Roman Fort must have the most extraordinary position of any Roman remains in the country. On a small plateau, it looks right back down over Eskdale below, while the fells seem to crowd around it on the east. A thin ribbon of road trails over those fells, and is the reason for the fort. The Hardknott Pass was, amazingly, a Roman road.

I looked up to the ribbon of tarmac. A small blue object was making its way up a steep section, way ahead of me. I couldn't spend long, I thought, but, well, I had to see the fort now I had cycled to it.

I set off at a jog across the wet ground and hopped over the marshiest parts as far as the outer wall. Really quite a considerable wall, Herdwick-grey against the bracken, still about ten stones high and wide enough to stop a charging elephant should Hannibal appear with them over Hardknott Pass.

Piles of stones lay by the wall - it must have been much higher when the 500 men from the Fourth Cohort of Dalmatians were stationed here. Maybe it wasn't so bad on a summer's day, but it must have felt like the end of the world in the winter, compared with home on the Adriatic coast.

I worked my way along to the gate, from where I glanced back up towards where Richard must be, high above.

In the centre of the fort were the remains of low stone walls amongst the grass: the headquarters, a temple and a granary. Archaeologists say there is not much sign of barracks, and speculate that the soldiers may have been housed in leather tents. Brrrrr....

A bath house and parade ground were outside the main walls. Well, you'd have had to warm up somehow.

Richard would be waiting for me, I thought, and I jogged back towards the road.

There would have to be a very good reason to keep 500 men here. In fact, the fort was built and occupied, abandoned, and then re-occupied. Now why would you re-occupy a site like this unless the natives were restless? The Celts of Lakeland were perhaps never fully Romanised, which might be why afterwards the area reverted so quickly to Celtic culture, with almost all trace of Rome gone, apart from the crumbling remains of forts, and the routes of roads.

Nobody had stolen my bike. As I got on the saddle, a yellow-shirted cyclist went past. Road bike. No panniers. Making it look a bit easier than was absolutely necessary.

"Well done, mate," I called.

"See you at the top."

"Only if you're planning on stopping for half an hour."

He was gone.

A flatter section came next, and I took it gently. I reckoned I still had the 30% to come. The road headed towards a cleft in the rocky ridgeline, cutting up through bracken, with a gulley off to the right and buttresses all around. The slope increased, the road swinging a little. Steeper. Steeper again. Must be 25% now. Keep going. Come on.

Steeper again, and a sharp twist in the road, and ouch, this must be 30%. Push down on those pedals, heart thumping, breath in gasps, push, push. Anddddd….. stopppp.

Brakes on to stop rolling backwards. Feet down. Another rude word.

OK, on we go. Across the road and go for it, round another sharp corner, and it's not as steep. A car is waiting, the lady driver watching.

Keep… going…

I make it past the car, grimacing a thank you, and the road is less steep, less steep, less steep. I'm on the col, rough grass around, with a boulder field under a great rock buttress on the left. Breathing and heart beginning to approach acceptable levels as the road continues to flatten, and there ahead is Richard, his jacket on now while he waits. It must, I thought, be cold here, though cold was not what I was feeling. Over a cattle grid, and at the very, very top.

I have made it.

"Yehey! You did it!"

"I… did…" I took a breath. "You?"

"Yeh, I did."

"Fantastic."

"I thought you were doing alright. A guy on a bike passed and he asked if that was my dad down there. He said you were looking OK."

"I'd just stopped to see the Roman Fort. He didn't see me just before that, on the steep bit."

"What about that last bit, as well?"

"I had to stop a few times on those. I just didn't have the power."

"They were tough," he said.

"You made it though. Great. Bodes well for your next ride."

"Yeh, reckon it does. Hey, photo. Stand there."

It was cold and I slipped a jacket on as he raced over the road, set the timer on his camera and ran back. The camera clicked as we fell against each other, smiling, by the cairn.

"OK. Another."

He climbed up the fellside with the camera.

"Ready?" he shouted.

I held both arms aloft, and he took the photo.

"Brilliant," I said.

So it wasn't the Fred Whitton Challenge, it wasn't the Bob Graham Round, it wasn't a lot of things that maybe I could have trained for if other parts of my life didn't have a call on my time and energy, but it was one of the things that the ride was about.

Richard showed me the photo he had taken from the ridge, looking back down towards a figure in a red jacket, arms aloft, with the top end of the Duddon Valley behind me, the road a thin grey thread snaking across to the dark dip in the ridge where Wrynose Pass found its way into a gateway of black cloud and on down to Little Langdale.

We were definitely getting cold now, and black clouds were gathering all around. We both peeled off jackets to add a middle layer, then put jackets on again.

We straddled our bikes, waited for a couple of cars to come up from Dunnerdale, and then released the brakes. It was very, very steep down. 30% down as well as 30% up.

This was the way I had come up the one time I had tried to cycle over Hardknott before, and had failed, and pushed. Nine days cycling had done something for my fitness at least.

We dropped and dropped, brakes on, twisting round corners, avoiding the worst of a lumpy, bumpy road. There was high ground on our left up to Hard Knott, the land falling away from us on the right down to the grassy fields of Dunnerdale below, with the river Duddon meandering through. Down and down again, with a particularly sharp left bend, slowing, and round. A bridge over a beck, down again, then the road flattening and taking us through the wilderness of the valley bottom across and down again, a gentle dip to Cockley Bridge.

The highest bridge over the Duddon, here a fierce flow racing past rocks and boulders in its bed, led across to the highest farm in the valley, whitewashed and slate-roofed amongst the fells. To the right, the road would have led us back down to Ulpha and Broughton. We cycled straight on, the river swinging round to accompany us, great banks of rocks in and around the river, brought down by floods from the mountains around us.

The route was flat, but the ground too high, rocky and wet for fields. There was rough grass and bracken, while broken down dry-stone walls had been replaced by fences. Ahead of us, the fells on either side of the valley merged into a dip that was the Wrynose Pass, and we could make out the road shimmying up it as we drew closer. All the time the river ran next to us, flowing back down the valley. It was surprisingly wide at first, but as we passed tributaries adding their own waters, the river began to narrow. Now we had a smaller Duddon hard by us with the fells closing in - Cold Pike on the left, Hell Gill Pike on the right. Names to conjure with.

Our road rose towards the pass. Banks of stones climbed the fellsides, the tops disappearing into low grey cloud. Ahead it looked mighty steep.

Still the bed of the Duddon accompanied us, but now it was a beck in a channel through tussocky hill-grass, with a wall on the far side running parallel over dip and hillock like Norman Nicholson's 'grey millipede'. The occasional cars came down, and we moved to the edge of the road for them to squeeze past.

It was getting gradually steeper, and I sent Richard on ahead so as to take my slow time. Part of the beck disappeared away off to the left, and the Duddon became a tiny ripple of water breaking the ground by the road.

Steeper again, and again, and I could feel Hardknott in my legs. What looked like the top came into sight. Now it really was steep and I found that it helped to swear rhythmically with each stroke of the pedals, which was a bit of a revelation, if a little late in the scheme of things. Great heaving breaths were coming but I was somehow still going as the road began to flatten, and then Richard was there, cheering me up the last stretch. I was up.

That was all six of the Great Cycling Climbs, all the lakes, and north, south, east and west in the National park. I looked around us. No classic views, no iconic images of Lakeland, no dramatic scenery, just a handful of cars parked by the side of the road amongst rocks breaking cover from the sheep-cropped grass. Low cloud loomed over us.

I got my breath.

"Bit bleak, isn't it?" I said.

We pressed on, down past the Three Shires Stone, placed there in the 19th century to mark where the three counties of Lakeland had all met: Cumberland, Westmorland and Lancashire, before the first two, along with North Lancashire's Furness and some of Yorkshire were made into Cumbria in 1974.

A group of cars were following each other up the hill towards us, so we pulled over where there were some parking spaces, and from here the view had really become dramatic. Under a dark sky, lines of blue hills chased each other away into the distance, while the valley below had the mirror of Little Langdale Tarn to reflect a lighter sky beyond.

The road fell away more steeply now, but cars kept coming up, mostly allowing us space to squeeze through. Apart from one or two. I guess there are always one or two.

We dropped and dropped, and as the road cut through rocky outcrops and rounded low mounds, the tarn kept reappearing.

Wrynose on this side was much tougher than on the far side, a proper 10/10, but we were coming down, with the road now sliding across the fellside, over a stone bridge, and on down and down.

On stretches with no cars we were able to pick up speed, but more than any of the other passes, this one seemed to be busy, and I couldn't think why. In centuries gone past this was an important route, but surely not today.

As we came out of the hill, we passed on one side Castle How, a rocky little ridge that had been a hill fort, and on the other side Ting Mound. No more than a raise in the ground in a field to look at now, the Ting Mound was a man-made platform for meetings and gatherings, still used in Mediaeval times, but dating back to the Norse period (think Tynwald, the parliament of the Isle of Man, of Norse origin). And the road itself was following a Roman route.

The road twisted and passed the aptly named Fell Foot Farm on the flat of the valley floor, the ridges away eastwards on either side of Little Langdale declining in scale as we rode towards them. Immediately afterwards a road went off towards the end of Great Langdale - the road Richard and I had looked at as it snaked down the side of the valley.

Up and over a little hill, and now Little Langdale Tarn was just a sheep field away, with woods on the far side, and no sign of fells in front of us. We cycled into a settled Lakeland of whitewashed farms, little stone cottages, old dry-stone walls and National Trust woods. A pretty beck accompanied us but then set off towards Elterwater as Little Langdale merged into the bottom end of Great Langdale. It was all so different to the bleak top of Wrynose Pass just a short distance behind.

It occurred to me that we had seen so many sorts of dry-stone walls as we rode. Some curved and bent around fields; others - more recent - were dead straight, dividing valleys into oblongs, while others again set off up and over the fells. But they varied in other ways as well, like the stone that they were made from, such as the pale grey slate of the northern fells, full of splits and cracks. Or the green-grey slate often in squared-off blocks in central and western Lakeland. Elsewhere there were sandstone blocks, or rounded rocks with a layer of flatter stones to bind the wall together. Then there were the lichens: sulphur-yellow patches, or bright orange, or circular white blobs like a child drawing a chalk circle. Or the mosses where the walls ran under a canopy of woodland, as in Borrowdale's damp valley, with freeze-framed waterfalls of emerald almost completely obscuring the wall underneath.

A sharp uphill brought us out on the Coniston to Ambleside road, and we began to pick up speed down through woodland, until we flew past the lane I was looking for that would take us off the main road.

"Stopppp!" I shouted, and we turned in the road and pedalled back up. We were going to be back on little lanes. The sign said, 6' 6" EXCEPT FOR ACCESS. Perfect.

We were straight into a hill up through the woods of Brow Coppice, and it felt hard after our passes, and then out again with a view towards Loughrigg Fell and others of the Lake District's lower southern hills. Without a single car, this was a lovely road, as long as you didn't mind the constant ups and downs. Actually, more ups.

The road came out by The Drunken Duck Inn, with its Barngates Brewery yet another source of Lakeland-brewed ales. "Chesters Strong and Ugly" was particularly well named.

Legend has it that The Drunken Duck's own name derived from

a landlady plucking seemingly dead ducks for lunch, only to find that the ducks had drunk some dripping beer and passed out. In remorse, she knitted them waistcoats to keep them warm.

We crossed the crossroads on to another tiny lane, still having seen not a single car, which is probably why we were not really paying attention as a car came round the corner. 'Wait until you see the whites of their eyes' I seem to recall. Well, I saw the whites of the driver's eyes, and was just about to leap from the bike into a hedge, when all three of us came to a stop.

"That," I said to Richard, "was close."

We had had very few scrapes and near misses on the journey, but that was definitely one of them. It was a good job the car was going slowly.

We joined the Ambleside road, and it was a speedy ride south into Hawkshead, where we would cross part of Day One's route on our way to the ferry across Windermere.

Hawkshead was our first proper rest of the day. We had only cycled 14 miles, but with Hardknott and Wrynose, that was going to be me for a short while. There was a bench by a newsagents, so I parked myself there with a Mars Bar (I wonder if they do sponsorship deals?) and a drink. All around were Hawkshead's glorious buildings, whitewashed walls and slate roofs.

Tourists were few that Sunday morning, and perhaps Hawkshead was a gentle reintroduction to the Lake District as a tourist destination. Windermere and Bowness were still to come.

A gentle road took us south past Esthwaite Water, and at Hill Top in Near Sawry, Mr McGregor was still in his garden.

In Far Sawry we climbed the same hill as on our first day. Off to our left the land rose towards Claiffe Heights, a wooded hill that looks down over Windermere. Used today by mountain bikers and walkers, it's also the scene of one of the Lake District's better ghost stories.

In the days when the Windermere ferry was a man with a rowing boat based on the far side of the lake, the ferryman heard a call of 'Boat' from this side. Finding nobody waiting for the ferry, he walked up to Claiffe Heights to look for whoever had called him, where he was confronted by the ghost of a monk from Furness Abbey still wandering the hill in search of a secret, lost love. The ferryman returned to the far shore a broken man. After that the Crier of Claiffe was heard during storms over the lake calling 'Boat', until the ghost was finally exorcised. Well, that's one of the versions of the story, anyway.

On our first day we had turned off this road for a big loop round to Grizedale and Coniston. Today we coasted down the hill towards the ferry. With lakeshore on our right and woods on our left, it was a fabulous little ride.

There were just two cars waiting for the ferry, which was approaching the far side on its cable. Beyond it, the white masts of dozens of sailing boats made scissor-cuts through the dark green of the wooded shoreline. On our side of the lake, a small bay held its own share of sailing boats. A tiny island was close to, completely covered in trees, and on the far side of that, Belle Isle.

Almost dividing the lake in two, the half-mile long island has a three-storey circular house with a domed roof dating from 1774, part-hidden by its own woodland. Wordsworth had been scathing, calling it a pepper-pot. He hadn't even liked the whitewashing of traditional houses, so he must have been apoplectic about a classical Italian design in the heart of Windermere.

We eased off our bikes and leaned them against jetty posts.

A little girl got out of one of the cars.

"Which bike is yours? Are you his daddy? I'm going on the ferry. Which bike is yours?"

"This one is mine."

"We're going to see Peter Rabbit."

"That's great. You'll really enjoy that."

She chattered away to us until the ferry began approaching the slipway, and she was called back to the car.

The ferry's car area was open to the sky, with a cabin on the right for the crew and foot-passengers. The ramp was lowered on to the slipway, and a handful of cars were waved on. We took our bikes to one side, and as the ferry pulled away, one of the crew collected the fee.

It was a simple, flat crossing, over before we knew it, but then, with a fixed cable to cross on, I suppose it ought to be reasonably simple.

228

The cars drove off first, and a girl's face appeared in a back window. We waved, and she waved back. She would definitely enjoy the World of Beatrix Potter Attraction in Bowness. Years before, we had gone there as a family. Richard would have been a toddler, smaller than the figures of Peter Rabbit, Mrs Tiggy-Winkle and Jemima Puddleduck. I asked if he remembered going.

"Was I less than ten?"

"Much less."

"Definitely not then. I can't remember anything before the age of ten."

"I'm not sure there was much point taking you anywhere before your tenth birthday."

"Perhaps you didn't."

"Fair point."

We cycled away from the slipway past the marina and out on to the road. Our finish point was to be at the steamer quays further along the shore in Bowness, but first we were heading uphill into Windermere. So we forked right as the houses started, coming out at a busy roundabout in the centre of Bowness.

And it was certainly busy. An extraordinary contrast to Hardknott and Wrynose.

We pointed our bikes up the road, past full cafés, pubs, gift shops and outdoor clothing shops, the pavements packed, the road even busier. On up the hill we rode, and the shops finished, to be replaced by houses, many of them quite large and now working as guest houses or small hotels. Still the road rose, and the houses were set back now from the road. There was a church and a park, different again to the centre of Bowness just behind us, with the road now much quieter.

At some point we had cycled from Bowness into Windermere and here were the slate-fronted shops of a hundred and more years ago, brought up-to-date with coffee shops, estate agents, chemists and newsagents. A real little town, that seemed to have had a make-over. The pavements had been re-laid with stone slabs, some of the roads cobbled, and a sprinkling of benches, flower tubs and curvy cycle-parking stands added. There were too many cars using the only route into Bowness for it to be just what the town needed, but it was a bit of a surprise.

Until 160 years ago this had been a tiny hamlet called Birthwaite. There had been no town of Windermere. But then Birthwaite was selected as the terminus of the new 'Kendal and Windermere Railway'. Wordsworth protested:

'Speak, passing winds; ye torrents, with your strong

And constant voice, protest against the wrong.'

The protests against the wrong were ignored, and the first steam trains arrived half a mile from the peaceful shores of Windermere in 1847. The terminus was called 'Windermere', despite it not being on the lakeshore, and as houses and businesses developed around the railway station, the new town took the same name.

The trains opened the way into the Lake District. There were the wealthy mill owners of Lancashire building their houses around the lake, who even had their own 'Club Trains' to take them to and from Manchester without having to mix with the working classes coming from the mill towns in Lancashire in their 'wakes weeks'. Then there were the professional classes beginning their new sport of rock climbing, and the cyclists coming to cycle the roads and go 'pass-storming', and those who just came to walk the fells.

Buses to the new town of Windermere followed, and it was one of these that brought a young Alfred Wainwright to Windermere for the first time in 1930.

Having saved £5 from his wages in the council offices, the young man who had grown up in the poverty-stricken back-streets of Blackburn, got off the bus here and climbed Orrest Head, the hill above the town. He called it 'a moment of magic' seeing the mountains receding into the blueness above the dark woods and green pastures and the gentle waters of Windermere. 'A glorious panorama' without the factories and chimneys and terraces of industrial Lancashire of his early years. He was inspired, and went on being inspired all his life.

"We'd better head down," I said. "Finish in Bowness. By the steamers."

We turned around, following the one-way system through the town. Once back on the long gentle hill, there was no need to pedal, just a light pressure on the brakes so as not to zoom into Bowness. Which was a good job, because as we rounded a bend a young man stepped into the road immediately in front of us. There was another 'whites of their eyes' moment, and we were round and gone.

We crossed the roundabout in the centre of town, the Beatrix Potter Attraction off to our right, where I was certain the little girl from the ferry would be having a perfect time. The pavements were busy, and it only got busier as we arrived on the lakeshore.

A wide promenade led along to a green-and-white-painted building with a mossy slate roof - the ticket office and shop leading on to the jetty for the steamers. One of the steamers was just arriving, bright white against the dark of the woodland on the far bank. The funnel towards the stern billowed steam, which drifted away above a red flag hanging straight down over the waters of Windermere.

Rowing boats of varnished wood lined the little beach, and ducks padded around them, while gulls swooped overhead. On the promenade visitors edged their way around two swans whose orange beaks were circling for food.

There were families with ice creams, two ladies with a poodle, an Indian family, a young couple arm in arm, a group of young men with lager cans, and an elderly couple sitting quietly on a bench looking out across the lake to Belle Isle. I heard French and German, Japanese and Hindi, and it was a Japanese tourist who - inadvisably I thought - was now feeding bread to an increasingly belligerent swan.

We leaned our bikes on a railing next to hanging baskets and an advert for a steamer ride, and I thought back to some of the wild places we had cycled through. Just a bike ride away, the world was a different place, but Bowness brought in the multitudes, and the Lake District would not be the same without both sides of the coin.

We found a bench free, and as the water lapped up around the rowing boats on to the beach, I noted:

Distance for the day: 23 miles / 36 Km
Height gained: 3,175 feet / 968 metres
Hardest hill: Hardknott Pass 978 feet / 298 metres
Average speed: 8.6 mph / 13.8 Kmph
Fastest speed: 34.0 mph / 55.4 Kmph

It had been a slow day. First the two great passes, and then a slow amble past Hawkshead in no great rush, and a ride up through the town of Windermere. Yes, a slow day, but then I don't think either of us really wanted the ride to finish.

I carried on writing.

From Brockhole Lake District National Park
Visitor Centre to Bowness-on-Windermere:

The direct route:
3.5 miles / 5.6 Km
and fairly flat

By our route:
392 miles / 631 Km
39,144 feet / 11,933 metres of hills
A Grand Tour

AFTERTHOUGHTS

Yan, tan, tethera, methera, pimp, sethera, lethera, hovera, dovera.

Nine days.

I was never going to beat records. That was not what the ride was about. Richard had got his training in for bigger rides to come, and had done what he wanted to do. And nine days cycling had given me enough miles in my legs to get me over the biggest of the mountain passes on two wheels, sort of, and that had been enough of a challenge.

What else? There had been the fells, passes, lakes and rivers of Lakeland, beautiful in sun and rain. There had been Hawkshead and Borrowdale, Buttermere and Coniston, Wastwater and Windermere, and all the towns and villages of the Lake District. We had seen pele towers and priories, stately homes and slate mines, packhorse bridges and stone circles, and bumped into Celts, Romans, Norse, Normans, yeoman farmers, the mill owners of Manchester, and the National Trust, though not necessarily in that order.

Then there had been the people we had met - the chance meetings with strangers and our chat with Eddie about Lakeland farming. And the great figures of Lakeland we had come across along the way, like William Wordsworth and Beatrix Potter, Alfred Wainwright and Norman Nicholson, the Yellow Earl and Arthur Ransome.

I had to admit that my wildlife-spotting had been a bit of a failure. True, we had seen ravens, buzzards and red squirrels. I wasn't sure that Herdwicks counted. Or bears. They had been a bit easy, and there had been a marked absence of red deer and red kites, ospreys and golden eagles, and in particular, ring ouzels. I guess we were just cycling too fast.

Of course, I'd been a bit more successful spotting Cumberland Sausage and Cumberland Ale, Tatie Pot and Harter Gold Ale, and possibly rather too frequently Cappuccino and Scones.

I reached out to put a hand on my son's shoulder. "Good trip?" I asked.

"Good trip," he said.

THE LAKES AND PASSES

The lakes in the Lake District
(from the 'Visit Cumbria' website)

Windermere
Esthwaite Water
Coniston Water
Haweswater
Ullswater
Elterwater
Grasmere
Rydal Water
Thirlmere
Bassenthwaite Lake
Derwentwater
Crummock Water
Buttermere
Loweswater
Ennerdale Water
Wastwater

The big passes of the Lake District,
(from '100 Greatest Cycling Climbs')

Kirkstone Pass
Whinlatter Pass
Honister Pass
Newlands Pass
Hardknott Pass
Wrynose Pass

THANKS

First of all, thank you to Richard
for putting up with me on our cycle ride.

Thank you to Dave Freeborn at Viscom Studios
for his wonderfully drawn maps and the front cover.

Thank you to those who have read what I have written
and told me if they think I have something wrong:
Katie and Peter, Barbara, Andy, Hugh, Ian and Claire.
Though if there is anything wrong, and there probably is,
it's all my fault.

And finally a dedication. Really, more than one.

To Mary
who loved it here.

To my Mum
for whom this is her second home.

And to, well,
The Lake District.

BIBLIOGRAPHY

Books

100 Greatest Cycling Climbs: A Road Cyclist's Guide to Britain's Hills, Simon Warren, 2010, Frances Lincoln Ltd

A History of Cumberland & Westmorland, William Rollinson, 1996, Phillimore & Co Ltd

A Pictorial Guide to the Lakeland Fells: Books One to Seven, by A. Wainwright. Copyright The Estate of A. Wainwright. Reproduced by permission of Frances Lincoln Ltd.

A President's Love Affair with the Lake District, Andrew Wilson, 1996, Lakeland Press Agency

A Tour Through The Whole Island Of Great Britain, Daniel Defoe, 1724

A Walk Around the Lakes, Hunter Davies, 1979, Weidenfeld and Nicolson

Castles in Cumbria, Jean M Cope, 1991, Cicerone Press

Collected Poems, Norman Nicholson, 1994, Faber and Faber Ltd

Cumbrian Folk Tales, Taffy Thomas, 2012, The History Press

Cumbrian Rock, Trevor Jones & Geoff Milburn, 1988, Pic Publications

Cycling Touring Guides: Northern England, Harold Briercliffe, first published 1947, revised edition 2012, Batsford

Exploring Cumbrian History, Philip Nixon, 2009, The Breedon Books Publishing Company Ltd

Feet in the Clouds: A Tale of Fell-Running and Obsession, Richard Askwith, 2004, Aurum Press

Foot and Mouth - Heart and Soul, edited by Caz Graham, 2001, Small Sister for BBC Radio Cumbria

Hound Trailing, John Coughlin, 1998

I Never Knew That About The Lake District, Christopher Winn, 2010, Random House

Lakeland Villages, Jim Watson, 1998, Cicerone Press

Lakeland's Greatest Pioneers: 100 Years of Rock Climbing, Bill Birkett, 1983, Robert Hale

Memoirs of a Fellwanderer, by A. Wainwright. Copyright The Estate of A. Wainwright. Reproduced by permission of Frances Lincoln Ltd.

Tales of Old Cumbria, William Amos, 1996, Countryside Books

The English Lakes: A History, by Ian Thompson, 2010, Bloomsbury

The Lake Counties, W G Collingwood, 1902, revised by William Rollinson 1988, JM Dent and Sons

The Place Names of Cumbria, Joan Lee, 2012, Kindle

The Secret Valley: The Real Romance of Lakeland, Nicholas Size, 1930, Frederick Warne and Co Ltd

Pamphlets and guides

The Church of St Andrew, Dacre

The Vikings in Gosforth, St Mary's Church, Gosforth

The Vikings, Wasdale Head and Their Church, Bill Bailey, 2002

Maps

Ordnance Survey Outdoor Leisure Series, The English Lakes, 1:25,000

Ordnance Survey Tour Series, The Lake District and Cumbria

Sea to Sea, Sustrans

Walney to Wear, Sustrans

Websites

There are too many websites to list here, and of course website addresses change, so you can see a fuller list, plus maps of the route, photos of the places visited, and other information on the Lake District on the website:

www.lakedistrictgrandtour.co.uk

The Full English

"Mike's relaxed and chatty style is never less than entertaining, making The Full English the sort of book that can put a smile on your face even when it is cold, grey Winter outside."
Dorset County Magazine

"England's answer to Round Ireland with a Fridge – but without the fridge."
Ludlow Advertiser

"A great read. A lightening guide to the country with simple un-heroic endeavour and humour."
Velo Vision cycling magazine

"Full of self-deprecating humour."
Cumbria Life

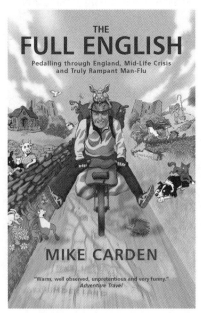

THE
FULL ENGLISH
Pedalling through England, Mid-Life Crisis and Truly Rampant Man-Flu

MIKE CARDEN

"Warm, well observed, unpretentious and very funny."
Adventure Travel

"9/10. A delightfully individual account of tripping the length of England by bike."
Cycling Plus

"An easily read book, humorous, well written and full of the eccentricities of the English."
Arrivée cycling magazine

"Articulate and witty account of one forty-something man's quest to ride from one end of England to the other."
London Cyclist

A Bit Scott-ish

"Loaded with laughs, yes, but also pathos and a certain infectious wonderment at the sheer diversity of mankind."
The Stirling Observer

"This is an easy to read, charming and very funny book taking in some of the most breath-taking sights in Scotland."
The Local History Magazine

"With Mike's engaging and witty style you are soon travelling along with him as he takes on mountains, copes with the elements of a Scottish summer and being directionally challenged."
www.cycltourer.co.uk

"Mike Carden's second cycle touring book, this time he takes a 15-day ride starting on the Orkney islands, south to the border at Berwick-on-Tweed. Mike's humorous narrative keeps rolling

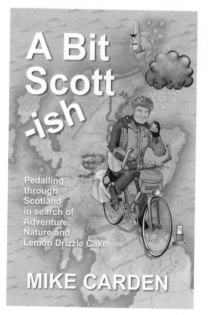

along, over the hills, through the rain and into headwinds. The variety of landladies, hostel wardens and other travellers he meets on route keep the interest and humour level high. An excellent follow-up to The Full English."
Arrivée cycling magazine

"Witty. A light touch."
Cycle magazine
(The CTC)

"A comical take on a serious challenge."
The Orcadian

"There's a café back there."
"With scones?"
"Seems likely."

For more information on

Bike Ride Books,

please find us at

www.bikeridebooks.co.uk
On Facebook at bike-ride-books
And on Twitter at @LakesGrandTour

"Hello. Um, two scones please."